white nation

To Caroline, Dominique and Aliya

radical writing

white nation
fantasies of white supremacy
in a multicultural society

Ghassan Hage

Published in 2000 by Routledge
in association with Pluto Press Australia – first reprint

Routledge
29 West 35th Street, New York, NY 10001 USA
www.routledge-ny.com

Pluto Press Australia
Locked Bag 199, Annandale NSW 2038 Australia
www.plutoaustralia.com

First published in 1998 by Pluto Press Australia and Comerford & Miller

Comerford & Miller
36 Grosvenor Rd, West Wickham, Kent BR4 9PY UK

Cover design by Wendy Farley

Cover image reproduced with permission of Australian Consolidated Press

Index by Neale Towart

Typeset by Chapter 8 Pty Ltd

Printed by McPherson's Printing Group

US Cataloguing-in-Publication Data

US ISBN 0 415 92923 7
Cataloguing-in-Publication Data is available from the Library of Congress.

Australian Cataloguing-in-Publication Data

Hage, Ghassan
White Nation
Fantasies of White supremacy in a multicultural society

Bibliography.
Includes index.
ISBN 1 86403 056 9

1. Multiculturalism – Australia. 2. Multiculturalism – Australia – History. I. Title

306.4460 994

contents

(a conjunctural)
preface

My Granny Is Seizing Power!

This work deals with the highly topical issue of multiculturalism and, as such, a warning is necessary. It is written for those who are, or aspire to be, members of the intellectual elite. These are the people who believe that knowledge is the product of hard labour; the people who believe that you need to do a great deal of time-consuming research, read a lot of books and reflect on many difficult philosophical, empirical and theoretical issues to produce intelligent knowledge.

In John Howard's Australia, there seem to be many individuals who feel 'relaxed and comfortable' in talking about issues about which they haven't bothered to read a single researched article, let alone a book. Apparently, 'life taught them'. In fact, such people are so 'relaxed and comfortable' that they believe that the more someone works at trying to learn about an issue, the more they become part of an ignorant and arrogant lot: the intellectual elite. The role of this elite is apparently simply to put down naturally intelligent people and find ways to stop them from expressing the truth they capture so effortlessly by merely living.

When I used to visit my grandmother in Bathurst in the late 1970s, she would often make comments such as 'You've been reading too much' or, even more explicitly, 'People who go to university become mad.' Although such comments helped me reflect on how and why university knowledge

clashed with everyday knowledge, I resented pronouncements such as 'You have read books, but life has taught me.'
I used to say, 'But Granny, I have a life as well you know, and
it teaches me, too. Can't you see that books and research provide me with *extra* knowledge.' I was naive even to try.

The so-called 'intelligentsia' always looks down with a really
limitless condescension on anyone who has not been
dragged through the obligatory schools and had the necessary knowledge pumped into him. The question has never
been: What are the man's abilities? but what has he
learned?' To these 'educated' people the biggest empty-
head, if he is wrapped in enough diplomas, is worth more
than the brightest boy who happens to lack these costly
envelopes.[1]

This is neither my granny, nor any of Australia's anti-intellectual populists speaking, but Adolf Hitler. And I cannot
help thinking of him when people start abusing intellectuals.
Hitler was the classic anti-intellectual: a man who had enough
intellect to be a mediocre intellectual and enough also to
realise that he wasn't a member of the intellectual elite. Like
many mediocre intellectuals, he thought he had a natural tal-
ent for knowledge, rather than realising how much hard work
is put into whatever knowledge people end up gathering.

Hitler was not, however, the sort of person who would just
sit there and take it. He was too motivated by dreams of social,
political and intellectual mobility to allow himself to just sulk
and do nothing. So, he found the time-honoured way to
'beat' the intellectual elite. This is the road often chosen by
people who want to be recognised as intellectuals, but who
are either not socially equipped to be so or feel they have better things to do than putting in the hard labour necessary to
achieve such a status. These people compensate for their lack
of knowledge by speaking in the name of 'the people'. 'The
people' becomes such a formula of success for mediocre
intellectuals that they make themselves — and some others,
too — believe that they actually *are* 'the people'.

The mechanism is very simple: 1) 'The people' already
know everything there is to know: 'life taught them'. 2)
Consequently, anything that the 'intellectual elite' says which
is not known by the people is superfluous knowledge, if not

actively against the people. 3) Therefore, any attack on the knowledge of the intellectual elite is a defence of the knowledge of the people. And who else is better at defending the instinctive knowledge of the people if not the instinctively intelligent, mediocre intellectual? In reality, 'the people' are too busy living. In addition, one can be certain that anyone who uses the concept of 'the people' is already someone who distinguishes himself or herself from them.

Driving back to Sydney from Bathurst, I used to feel safe that my grandmother and her ideas would not travel too far away from her, wherever she was … there … in her house …up in Bathurst … away from the institutions of knowledge and the institutions of power that feed them and from them.

This, however, was the 1970s. Today, and ever since John Howard made Australia for all of us, everywhere I look, whether it be in the morning paper or on the Internet, my Granny is there voicing her criticisms: 'Life has taught me', 'I am worried about the size of the immigrant intake', 'Farming has taught me', 'Ghettoes are worrying', 'Fish and chips have taught me', 'The state is *too* biased towards Aboriginal people'! It's a nightmare: my Granny is seizing power!

It is in this atmosphere that authors of the sort my Granny likes can write political bestsellers. Some can do so by elevating Sydney and Beijing's competition for the Olympics 2000 into a competition between simplistically stereotyped national moral characters and by celebrating Sydney's win with an infantile triumphalism (Beijing is polluted. Sydney is clean. 'China lost, nah-nah-nanah-nah.'). These are authors who believe that reading four or five books — as opposed to those who don't read any and those who read 'too many' — and using the word 'scholar' to describe every person who agrees with them (even when those 'scholars' haven't published a single academic work on their supposed subject of expertise) give them definite answers about the world. They write confidently, and without blinking, about how Australia can become an 'eco-superpower' with its 'green corps': a kind of politically correct, postmodern version of the 'one day my nation will be great' story, and which, of course, cannot happen until we deal with the internal enemies (Asian crime, Asian ghettoes and anything to the left of the Liberal Party wets)[2]. Some also write of the international conspiracy represented by the Human Rights and Equal Opportunity Commission.

Luckily, the Olympic committee was not on the look out for moral pollution when 'China lost'.

If there is a single important, subjective feeling behind this book, it is that I, and many people like me, am sick of 'worried' White Australians — White Australians who think that they have a monopoly over 'worrying' about the shape and the future of Australia. They are constantly finding a source of concern: look at how many migrants there are, look at crime, look at ghettoes, look at tourists. Such pathological worry is that of people who use worrying to try to construct themselves as the most worthy Australians in the land: 'Nobody cares but us real Australians. That's why we are worried and others aren't.'

Why aren't migrants worried about ghettoes and about immigration and about crime? The answer is, of course, because they are not really committed to Australia. Paul Sheehan (1998) gleefully publishes in the first pages of his book *Among the Barbarians* a list of people who criticised him — some of whom ended up receiving hate mail — and excerpts of what they have said. But far be it from him to allow this to make him think that maybe he shouldn't be so confident about the truth of what he has written. In fact, the published criticisms simply work to confirm Sheehan's view that multiculturalists are only worried about multiculturalism. Only 'real' Australians, fine, 'aggressive', and 'fire-loving Eucalypts' like him are worried about Australia.

Paul Sheehan's discourse and many others from Geoffrey Blainey to Pauline Hanson provide clear examples of the prevasive national fantasy analysed in this book; a fantasy centered around a 'White-and-very-worried-about-the-nation-subject.' It should be remembered, however, that worrying can be the last resort of the weak. There are many people for whom worrying is the last available strategy for staying in control of social processes over which they have no longer much control.

My grandmother, funnily enough, was also a great worrier. She spent a lot of time worrying about everything: she worried about Australia, she worried about the Catholics in Lebanon, she worried about my marriage and she worried

about me driving on the highway to Bathurst. It was her worrying which taught me that this is what people who are losing control over their social life (overly represented among
the elderly) do to compensate for their loss. They worry
themselves back into the processes from which they feel they-
have become alienated. (This is probably a factor in explaining the inordinate number of elderly people who feel alienated from national processes in the ranks of the White-and-
worried-about-the-nation Hansonites.)

In a book which advocates the ethical importance of the
intellectual art of listening and understanding even to the
most unsavoury views, I want to think of the anti-intellectual
elite people who have recently invaded the Australian public
sphere as a family problem. This is also how I will be treating
all those who express Hansonite views in this book — even if
some of them may not like to think of me, with my very
woggy name (if only they could hear my accent!), as a family member. And after all, like most people, I loved my
Granny.

* * *

This book synthesises ten years of work on Australian multiculturalism.[3] I have many people to thank besides my
grandmother. The first group of people I want to thank are
the many friends and colleagues who along the way have
read, discussed with me, criticised and debated, or shown a
sustained interest in some part of my work. They have either
directly or indirectly helped me persevere in sometimes difficult conditions: Claudio Alcorso, Benedict Anderson, Ien
Ang, John Bechara, Gill Bottomley, Pierre Bourdieu,
Stephen Castles, Kuan-hsing Chen, Gillian Collishaw, John
Docker, Larry Grossberg, Michael Jackson, Lesley Johnson,
Marie de Lepervanche, Meaghan Morris, George Morgan,
Francesca Merlan, Stephen Muecke, Ellie Vasta and Michael
Symonds. A big thanks to Scott Poynting for generously
offering me his proofreading skills and his general comments on a near final draft. Clive Morgan helped me edit the
references and put together the bibliography. Needless to
say, all mistakes found in the book (as well as all elements of
absolute truth, of course) are my responsibility.

The second group of people I want to thank are those who have provided me with invaluable structural support while working on the manuscript: my mother, May, and my sisters, Nada and Amale. Thanks also to my mother-in-law, Lesley, who gave me a writing refuge in Tasmania on a number of occasions. And I cannot possibly leave unacknowledged Rose Clara and the other staff at Newtown's Cafe Cinquecento where I regularly unfolded my laptop and had the best coffee in Sydney (which shows that I am an incurable member of the cosmopolitan intellectual elite).

Some of the interview material, used mainly in the last two chapters, is the product of research funded by the University of Western Sydney, Nepean, on the spatiality of ethnic relations. This allowed me to carry out a series of twenty-three intensive interviews conducted with 'White' Australians, selected on the basis of class, age and gender, in Sydney's inner west. Six of these interviews were conducted in Newtown, Enmore and Annandale, and the rest in Marrickville. The only fixed criterion was that the interviewees must have been resident for more than ten years in the suburbs in which they now lived. All the interviewees were asked to reflect upon what have been the important changes to their neighbourhood over the past ten years. As the interviews involved 'White' subjects and were likely to address issues of migration and migrant cultures, it was clear from the beginning that I, except on two memorable occasions, could not be involved in the interviewing process without inhibiting the interviewees concerned. So, I want to take the opportunity to thank the 'White' researchers who were involved in this project, in particular, Justine Lloyd and Ian Shapter, for the excellent interviews they managed to record. Kim Bailey recorded two interviews for me in Marrickville and the late Pam Benton also recorded three wonderful interviews with elderly people from Annandale. Other interview material was collected in the course of an ARC research project on ethnic relations in Western Sydney.

During both the research and the writing processes, I have benefited from a period of six-month study leave from the University of Sydney. I have also benefited from a visiting professorship at the École des Hautes Études en Sciences Sociales, courtesy of the French government and Pierre Bourdieu.

Finally, I want to offer my very special thanks to my family. My partner, Caroline Alcorso, has argued, read and edited the many bits and pieces which have ended up making this book more times than I can remember. She has been exceptionally supportive in every possible way despite her own very demanding work. I cannot thank her enough. My daughters Dominique and Aliya have helped me in various ways throughout the writing of this book: from providing massages to asking with a touch of irritation 'Will you *ever* finish this book?'.

I dedicate this book to Caroline and to them.

introduction

In the early 1990s, on one of the walls of the Nepean campus of the University of Western Sydney favoured by graffitists, there developed an exchange which was an extension of a number of 'immigration debates' that were taking place in Australia at the time. More recently, with the rise of Hansonism, these debates have been made a permanent feature of the Australian political landscape.

I have been witnessing such debates on a regular basis since I first migrated here in 1976 and, in addition to being personally implicated in them as a migrant, I gradually became interested in them as a researcher. My analytical focus, influenced by the early critiques of multiculturalism developed by the Centre of Multicultural Studies in Wollongong and others, was the way certain cultural forms of White–ethnic power relations remained omnipresent in a multicultural society, and were reproduced by the very ideologies of cultural pluralism and tolerance that were supposed to transcend them.[1] At university, graffiti were one popular form in which these ideologies were often expressed and debated.

The above-mentioned graffiti were allowed to develop on the wall for a good year or so, and I had ample time to reflect on them. They represented, in embryonic form, the social phenomenon with which I had become increasingly concerned: the structural affinity (and sometimes complicity) between what is categorised as 'racist' and the discourse of the dominant culture.

'Macedonia for the Macedonians' was the first line to grace the upper part of the wall on the right. Soon, underneath it, another line asserted that 'The glory of Greece ruled over the land.' Later, a bit further down, someone wrote a paragraph six lines long. It was a brief 'history of Macedonians' which demonstrated beyond reasonable doubt that those who were claiming to be Macedonians were slaves and sons of slaves.

At this point, an outsider to the conflict entered the debate. He had judged it important to intervene and remind the others of what seemed like an incontrovertible fact: 'May I remind you that you are here in Australia,' he urged politely. 'You are welcome to bring yourself, your family and your culture to this country,' it continued, 'but please leave your bigotry and your racism behind.' About a month later, someone crossed out the word 'culture' with a red pen. The next day, a blue pen was used to cross out 'family' and another blue pen crossed out 'yourself'.

The wall remained untouched for two weeks. Then, to the right of the initial 'Macedonian' debate, someone wrote in thick, black ink: 'Where do you think you are, you bloody wogs? Go back to your own country!'

Almost immediately someone replied in thin, red ink, 'This is their country, too! We are a multicultural society in case you have forgotten.'

'Fuck multiculturalism!' was the reply, a week or so later. 'Fuck you, you racist turd!', the multiculturalist replied on the same day.

Here was a discussion/argument begun by a number of 'ethnics', as I came to think at the time, but which had become a brawl between people who, from what I could guess, were clearly from the dominant culture: the 'Anglos'. As they fought, the writing of the 'ethnics' was eclipsed and the whole exchange became dominated by people who felt to be unquestionably in *their* own country: none of their writings allowed for the retort 'Go back to your own country, you bloody wog.'

Those who wanted the 'ethnics' to stay and those who wanted them to leave were divided as to who and what should be allowed into the national space. They were also divided in their support for or opposition to multiculturalism. They were united, however, around two things which seemed to me far more fundamental. The first was their belief in their centrality as enactors of the Law in Australia or, to put it differently, as 'governors' of the nation. The second was their conception of ethnics as people one can make decisions *about*: objects to be governed.

The way the voice of the 'ethnic other' is made passive not only by those who want to eradicate it, but also by those who are happy to welcome it under some conditions they feel entitled to set is one of the main features of these ritualistic 'immigration debates' that White Australians enjoy having so much. As we shall later see, in those debates, the 'migrants' and the 'ethnics' are welcomed, abused, defended, made accountable, analysed and measured. Ultimately, the debates work to silence them and construct them into passive objects to be governed by those who have given themselves the national governmental right to 'worry' about the nation.

The current debate dividing the population between the 'bad' Hansonites and the 'good' anti-Hansonites, most of them White and trying to outdo each other in their 'worrying', is a good example of this. Ultimately, it is the debate itself, rather than Hanson, which marginalises the Aboriginal people and the migrants most directly concerned and whose voices, as usual, are only very rarely heard in the mainstream media. This reduction of the other into a passive object of government is one of the main theses of Edward Said's *Orientalism*. In this sense, my object of study is a national reality delineated by a discourse of *internal* orientalism.

In the graffiti previously described, the person politely inviting people to leave their racism and their bigotry behind can hardly be faulted. The person who, less politely, called them wogs and asked them to go back to their own country can easily be seen as a racist. Yet, beyond and despite their differences, what is most evident is the naturalness with which they both assumed that it was up to them to direct the traffic, as it were. Both the 'racists' and the 'multiculturalists' shared in the conviction that they were, in one way or another, masters of national space, and that it was up to them to decide who stayed in and who ought to be kept out of that space.

In this book, I fuse essay-like reflections with social scientific investigations to show that these shared convictions and sentiments about oneself, about 'ethnics', about national space and about one's relation to this space far outweigh the

differences. I argue that both White racists and White multiculturalists share in a conception of themselves as nationalists and of the nation as a space structured around a White
culture, where Aboriginal people and non-White 'ethnics'
are merely national objects to be moved or removed according to a White national will. This White belief in one's mas-
tery over the nation, whether in the form of a White multiculturalism or in the form of a White racism, is what I have
called the 'White nation' fantasy. It is a fantasy of a nation
governed by White people, a fantasy of White supremacy.

As the above already makes it clear, unlike the many books
on multiculturalism which have migrants from non-
English–speaking backgrounds as their object of analysis, I
am mainly concerned with experiences of multiculturalism
within the dominant 'White' culture. It is important to
emphasise that an entity such as 'White multiculturalism' is
a *subjective* formation. By saying that it is a White fantasy, I am
interested in making claims about how *some* White
Australians experience multiculturalism rather than grand
statements about what multiculturalism is or is not.

What multiculturalism is and how it is experienced are
clearly related realities, but there are different ways of experiencing multiculturalism. For instance, migrants may experience more the social equity side of multiculturalism and
the way it affects service delivery in state institutions. White
Australians, on the other hand, are likely to be more exposed
to its cultural, identity politics aspect. At the same time, some
White Australians may experience it as 'more Asian faces in
the street', while others can experience it as 'more diversity
in the restaurants of the neighbourhood'. This is why the
White experiences I will be analysing here are specific, discursive takes on the multifaceted totality that constitutes
Australian multiculturalism today.

The above is crucial in understanding the status of categories such as 'Third World-looking people' (TWLP as
opposed to the standard NESB migrants) that I deploy in the
text. By using them, I am not making a claim that they are
generally 'more appropriate' than others. I am claiming that
they are the categories present in the White discourse I am
analysing. I am saying that when the White people who
embrace the White nation fantasy look at a migrant, what

they differentiate between are not those who are NESB and those who are not, or those who are European and those who are not, but those who are Third World-looking and those who are not.

Of course, this does not necessarily mean that the migrants who are categorised as such identify themselves in this way. In much the same way, to say that migrants and Aboriginal people are constructed within White multiculturalism and White racism as non-White objects to be governed does not mean that they perceive themselves as, or act as if they are, objects. Indeed, one of my main arguments in this work is that it is precisely because White multiculturalism and White racism, each in their own way, work at *containing* the increasingly active role of non-White Australians in the process of governing Australia that they both qualify as fantasies.

White multiculturalism works to mystify, and to keep out of public discourse, other multicultural realities in which White people are not the overwhelming occupiers of the centre of national space. It is the containment of this reality which produces what Ien Ang has described as the *ambivalence* that is at the heart of White multiculturalism.[2] As I will also argue, however, a fantasy has to be well grounded and, if it manages to sustain itself for a long period of time, it is because it constantly finds empirical validations of its main components in everyday life. So, while insisting on the fact that White fantasies are subjective realities, they do not only reveal to us the creative capacities of the human brain. Because they are enduring fantasies, they also reveal to us many important aspects of the way in which social reality is structured in Australia.

The notion of 'White' clearly raises many problems. I have come to use it because I ultimately found it more satisfactory than the oft-used concept of 'Anglo' I was initially deploying. Being interested in White subjectivity, it is clear that 'Anglo' and 'Anglo-Celtic' are far from being a dominant mode of self-categorisation by White people whether at a conscious or unconscious level. I will argue that 'White' is a far more dominant mode of self-perception, although largely an unconscious one. Furthermore, the category 'Anglo' could not account for the many non-Anglos who relate to, and define themselves through, the 'White nation' fantasy. I will be dealing with the complexity involved in the usage of the term in chapter 2. Suffice to say here that I consider 'Whiteness' to be itself a fantasy position of cultural dominance born out of the history of European expansion.

It is not an essence that one has or does not have, even if some Whites think of it and experience it this way. Whiteness is an aspiration. One of my key arguments in the text is that Whiteness and Australianness — of which Whiteness remains a crucial component — are not governed by an either/or logic, even if some people experience them this way. Rather, I argue Whiteness and Australianness can be accumulated (up to a certain point) and people can be said to be more or less White and Australian. How White they can be depends on the social attributes they possess. In chapter 2, I try to examine what some of these social attributes are.

With the recent turn towards conservative forms of White cultural politics in Australia and the media focus on extreme-right forms of this cultural politics (particularly on the rise of Pauline Hanson's One Nation Party), and despite my wish not to become a commentator on a clearly media-fed 'look-at-the-racists freak show', the importance of a social scientific interest in a White perspective on multiculturalism has become increasingly clear. This is also important because, while the study of Whiteness is becoming an important field of investigation in the United States, it remains highly underdeveloped in Australia.[3]

My interest in Whiteness developed in the early 1990s when I began examining what I have initially termed 'the discourse of Anglo-decline': a discourse which bemoans what it sees as the attack on the core British values of traditional White Australia and where the figure of the ordinary 'mainstream' Australian, the 'traditional Aussie battler', is perceived as a victim of a conspiracy to change the very nature of the country. My reflections were largely based on reading letters to the editor in the daily newspapers expressing fear that multiculturalism is leading to the decline of Australia's dominant 'Anglo' culture. I wondered why, while many academics, including myself, see multiculturalism as merely a different way of reinforcing White power, some people experience it as if it actually does lead to undermining such a power. This is what led me to begin investigating this sense of decline more seriously. As such, I was researching 'Hansonites' well before Pauline Hanson emerged on the scene and my first work, presented at a conference I organised in 1994, 'An inquiry into the state of Anglo-Saxonness within the nation', dealt with many of the themes that were to be articulated by Pauline Hanson three years later.[4]

Right from the start, my analysis of such feelings of decline was anchored in a Spinozan ethic of intellectual inquiry I acquired via Pierre Bourdieu.[5] Spinoza invites the intellectual 'not to deplore, not to laugh, not to detest, but to understand'.[6] When analysing human beings, whatever their political persuasion, I became guided by a simple yet, to me, exceptionally far-reaching question: how do humans struggle to make their lives viable? As such, I was never inclined to use *analytically* words such as 'racist' which belong to a political register and to which I clearly am not immune. That is, even when the political person in me is crying 'racist', I have attempted to maintain a stance aimed at understanding people from the point of view of their own attempts at making their life viable. I am sure that such a tension appears in the text. I am, of course, much more successful at applying such a Spinozan ethic when analysing someone who is merely expressing concern about the disappearance of a White Australia in which they felt more comfortable than I am in applying it to a professional neo-fascist such as David Oldfield. I must admit to a profound ambivalence when analysing Pauline Hanson herself, as I find myself often oscillating between deep sympathy and absolute detestation. Part of the difficulty, I think, is that one never knows with her where the ordinary concerned Australian ends and the neo-fascist party machine begins, which probably explains her political success.

Such a Spinozan–Bourdieuian stance does not make intellectual inquiry uncritical; it provides different ethical standards of critique. For instance, someone's struggle to be viable can be criticised when it is seen to impinge *too much* on other people's struggles to make their lives viable. Let me also make it clear that I do not believe that such an intellectual stance is a substitute to the anti-racist struggles carried out by political activists. I do think, however, that it is the best contribution that an *academic* can make in conflictual situations such as the ones we are witnessing in Australia today.

One question which kept surfacing as I was analysing the interviews conducted around the sense of White decline was to what extent the feeling of national loss expressed in this discourse was bound to be articulated to the strategic political goals of neo-fascist politicians. That is, had this loss been better acknowledged and dealt with, would it have found a less ugly way of expressing itself?

Answering this question takes us back to the analysis of White multiculturalism. While the politicians and academics who have given their support to multiculturalism have often concentrated on the 'gains' of multiculturalism, this 'gain' discourse has not been accompanied by an equal interest in losses. Indeed, as I have already pointed out and as I will argue throughout this book, White multiculturalism cannot admit to itself that migrants and Aboriginal people are actually eroding the centrality of White people in Australia. This is because the very viability of White multiculturalism as a governmental ideology resides precisely in its capacity to suppress such a reality. As a result of this suppression, however, White multiculturalism leaves those White people who experience the loss with no mainstream political language with which to express it. This is why, like a 'return of the repressed', the discourse of White decline was bound to express itself in the pathological political language of a home-grown Australian neo-fascism.

The book can be best seen as implicitly divided into three parts. The first part shows how the moralising division between 'racists' and 'multiculturalists' that structures the cultural political scene in Australia blurs the important similarities that exist between the two positions and indirectly inhibits the emergence of a politics capable of countering extreme-right racism. I develop the concept of the 'White nation' fantasy and show how it allows us to transcend these divisions. I begin by analysing the practices of 'racism' often conceived as examples of 'evil nationalism', and show how understanding them as 'nationalist practices' allows a far richer analysis of their nature (chapter 1).

I then proceed to examine the primary status accorded to a socially and historically constructed image of Whiteness in the national imaginary of these practices, and analyse the way they end up enacting a White fantasy of national space (chapter 2). Having developed the notion of the White nation fantasy out of an examination of 'evil nationalism', I move to look at the practices of 'tolerance' popularly perceived as examples of 'good nationalism'. I show how tolerance also delineates national practices grounded and guided by a White nation fantasy. This allows me to analyse the way the very polarity between good and evil nationalism, tolerance and racism, works to mystify the White fantasy underlying the practices of tolerance (chapter 3).

The second part of the work examines the multicultural discourse of cultural enrichment concerned with the valorisation of ethnic cultures (chapter 4), the republican attempts at highlighting the role of multiculturalism in directing Australians towards Asia (chapter 5) and the ecological concern with controlled immigration (chapter 6). I show how the dominant mode of experiencing and articulating these political discourses reveals a White-centred conception of the nation grounded in the White nation fantasy. If I spend more time examining how this sentiment emerges within 'multicultural' and generally anti- or non-racist national discourses, it is, firstly, because such outwardly 'nice' and/or benign modes of behaviour are far more dominant in Australian culture than the media's fascination with 'racists' can lead one to believe. Secondly, it is because people take it for granted that 'racist' or monocultural discourses naturally embody this conviction of White centrality, while multiculturalism is supposed to bring it to an end. In Australia, as in France, England, Germany and the United States, it is common enough today to see in the resurgent anti-immigration politics a racist politics and to view its proponents as nothing more than latter-day White supremacists. My aim, however, is to show that many of those who position themselves as 'multicultural' and 'anti-racists' are merely deploying a more sophisticated fantasy of White supremacy.

In the final part of the book, I enter the world of those who lack the capacity to 'update' their fantasy and end up articulating an experience of multiculturalism as a loss of national reality. Their White fantasy, I argue, is experienced in a permanent state of crisis and the gap between fantasy and social reality widens. This part examines the sense of trauma resulting from a fear of losing one's fantasy, and one's anchorage in the nation and the crisis of Whiteness that ensues. I also examine the way this feeling of loss becomes articulated as neo-fascist politics in the absence of other mainstream political modes of expressing itself (chapters 7 and 8).

In the conclusion, I examine the way the White nation fantasy operates to contain a different multicultural reality where the relations of dependency characterising White multiculturalism are far less dominant. I argue that White multiculturalism has a vested interest in the promotion of Hansonism and uses it as a political technology aimed at containing non-White (both migrant and Aboriginal) political demands for a more central political role in Australian politics.

Despite my occasional reference to Aboriginal people, I have become very aware, but only belatedly, that this book fails really to incorporate the problematic representation of Aboriginality within White fantasies. As such, this work is the uncritical product of an institutionalised division of labour between academics interested in 'multiculturalism' and academics interested in 'Aboriginality'. I believe such an academic division of labour is the product of a White governmental tendency to treat 'White–Aboriginal' relations and 'Anglo–Ethnic' relations as two separate spheres of life.[7] In this process, the Whites relating to Aboriginal people appear as totally unaffected by multiculturalism, while the 'Anglos' relating to the 'ethnics' appear as if they have no Aboriginal question about which to worry. Finally, this has left the question of Aboriginal–ethnic relations highly unexplored.[8] Unfortunately, I can only begin by reflecting on this tendency here and hope that future research, including my own, will correct it.[9]

I finished writing this book at the École des Hautes Études en Sciences Sociales in Paris. When I decided to continue writing this book there, I felt ambivalent. How could I finish a book about nationalism, racism and multiculturalism in Australia from Paris? As it turned out, it was much easier than I thought. I was offering French students a series of lectures on Australian multiculturalism, and this helped. There before me, moreover, were Le Pen and the French National Front. I could clearly see in their political statements a French discourse of White decline.

This French experience was very enlightening. Here we had an exceptionally strong culture of opposition to racism,

Le Pen and the National Front. There is no major newspaper that can be said to be sympathetic to their politics. Furthermore, there was a wide spectrum of oppositional politics to the Front. At one end, there were the attempts by the mainstream political elite to try to 'steal their people away from them' by flirting with some of their xenophobic utterances. At the other end, there were organisations such as Ras-le-Front who think that the only way to deal with them is by physically beating the hell out of them! Despite all this, Le Pen and the National Front continue to gain in popularity. This sense of the inability of the dominant culture to deal with the Le Pen minority and what the French call *la lepenisation des esprits* (literally the 'lepenisation' of the souls, the way in which Le Pen modes of thinking have started circulating and invading social and political culture) have clearly prefigured the development we have witnessed in Australia.

Although the current ruling Liberal Party and particularly the Prime Minister, John Howard, appear more sympathetic to Pauline Hanson's politics of anti-migrant and anti-Aboriginal populism, the oppositional culture and the range of oppositional politics that are deployed against it in Australia are not very different from those deployed in France. They are also proving just as unable to stop the phenomenon from leaving an enduring imprint on the political scene. We are clearly witnessing among ourselves *la Hansonisation de nos esprits* — the Hansonisation of our souls and our national culture. This is not a threat which can be taken lightly. It has the potential to poison the very texture of our daily lives. Indeed, it has begun to do so.

To someone of Lebanese background who has gone through part of the Lebanese civil war, like me, the day Pauline Hanson uttered the words 'civil war' in Parliament was of truly nightmarish quality, more so than anyone born in Australia can understand. If only the lady *knew* what she was talking about she would have realised how disgusting the very sound of those words is. Her video 'If you see me now, it means I have been assassinated …' was also an infantile fantasy of violence. Such embryonic flirtations with political violence are nevertheless truly sickening. There is a definite need here to squash the serpent's egg. This is why I feel that Hanson has already poisoned the texture of our daily lives.

Neo-fascist ethno-nationalism often feeds on self-fulfilling prophecies. Many neo-fascist groupings in multicultural societies have began their careers arguing that multicultural societies do not work because they lead to civil war. It is also an historical fact, however, that most civil wars in multicultural societies have been started by those very neo-fascist groupings arguing that it was multiculturalism that would lead to civil war, and who, unrealistically and with destructive effects, pushed for mono-culturalism.

Clearly, there is a need for rethinking a new cultural politics capable of recognising and dealing realistically with the sense of cultural loss from which neo-fascism is being fed. The main thesis of this book is that the dominant White culture which prevails in Australia today, as in all societies dominated by a European cultural tradition and imbued with the tradition of 'tolerance' and 'cultural pluralism', unless it opens up to the decentralising effect migration and globalisation have had on the status of Whiteness, is unable to provide such a new politics because it is itself built on the negation of this loss. To put it differently, I am proposing that the answer lies in the direction of a deeper commitment to a more far-reaching multiculturalism. This clearly runs against the dominant trend among the main political parties in Australia today. Their instinctive reaction to Hansonism has been to shy away in different ways from multiculturalism. My argument is that such a reaction is a continuation of White multiculturalism's historically weak-kneed commitment to a deeper cultural diversity in Australia, which is what has provided the opening for the emergence of Hansonite neo-fascism in the first place.

Social research is neither capable nor ought it to attempt to define ready-made political paths. It can, however, through its capacity to listen with and through people to the echoes of social suffering, furnish tools for rethinking political efficacy in a world as traumatising as ever for those who lack the social means to cope with its rapid changes.

chapter 1

Evil White Nationalists 1:
The Function of the Hand in the
Execution of Nationalist Practices

'I just saw her hand, she pulled my hair and my scarf violently, pushed me and started shouting abuse ...' This is how Siham recalled experiencing her scarf being ripped off her head by an 'Anglo' woman in a Sydney supermarket during the Gulf War. Incidents such as the tearing off of the scarf, along with many other acts of harassment directed at Arab and Muslim Australians, were widely reported as examples of 'racism' or 'racist violence' in the Australian press and in government reports at the time. The tearing off of scarfs was the most common incident registered in a report, *Racist Violence*, which followed from the government-financed National Inquiry into Racist Violence in Australia (NIRVA). According to NIRVA:

> There have been widespread reports of Muslim women having their *hijab* pulled off in the street; such attacks are more significant for their symbolic impact on the victim than for any physical harm they may do.[1]

In one case, in Melbourne, it is reported that an 'Anglo' woman 'deliberately drove into the vehicle driven by the Muslim woman wearing traditional Islamic dress, and then verbally abused her, accusing her of being an Iraqi terrorist'.[2] In another case reported in the Australian *Bulletin* magazine:

Two women, one with her children, are sitting in their car in a supermarket in a Sydney suburb. Both are wearing the hijab (Muslim headscarf). A man unknown to them drives up, rams their car, gets out, drags one of the women out and beats her to the ground before speeding off.[3]

There were many other incidents reported by the press and various anti-racist bodies, such as the burning of mosques and the throwing of rocks through Muslim shop windows.[4] The NIRVA report also lists other incidents such as 'Arabs and Muslims being spat on in shopping centres, and being taunted while walking or driving' (p. 146); all of these are classified as 'racist violence'.

While such practices and their like are clear acts of racist violence for all practical political purposes, in this chapter, I want to question the extent to which they are *best* characterised this way for *analytical* purposes. I will analyse their structure and their constituent elements: What do they aim to achieve? How do the people who execute them experience themselves? How do they classify Muslims while performing them? I will argue that there is a dimension of territorial and, more generally, spatial power inherent in racist violence that the categories deriving from the concept of 'race' cannot by themselves encompass. While such practices are 'informed' by racist modes of classification, I will maintain that they are better conceived as nationalist practices: practices which assume, first, an image of a national space; secondly, an image of the nationalist himself or herself as master of this national space and, thirdly, an image of the 'ethnic/racial other' as a mere object within this space.

In making this claim, I am not only concerned with raising a technical analytical issue. The importance of highlighting the nationalist dimension of such 'racism' is that it will allow us to demystify the exaggerated way in which the dominant culture tries to distance itself from it by obscuring the fundamental features they both share with a moralistic divide between 'evil racism' and 'good tolerance'.

Racism and the Question of Practice

The sociological tradition has a long history of perceiving 'racism' as a mental phenomenon in abstraction from the possible practices through which it can be articulated. It is generally considered as a system of beliefs, a mode of classification or a way of thinking. Furthermore, it is invariably considered as an 'evil way of thinking' about the 'self' and particularly about the 'other'. It is perceived as 'evil' both logically and politically. Ruth Benedict was one of the first to conceptualise it in this way, defining racism as a 'dogma' that maintains the 'congenital inferiority' or superiority of certain groups.[5]

From this perspective, one is confronted today with a multitude of definitions of the concept. There are disagreements over whether the term 'racism' should be reserved for traditional 'biological' forms of racism[6] or be extended to recent culturalist conceptions used to exclude people.[7] There are also tensions between the perception of racism as a 'political ideology' in the sense of a system of thought with its established 'theorists' such as 'scientific racism' and its conception as a mode of thinking present in commonsense, undertheorised forms within everyday life interactions.[8] There is general agreement, however, that racism involves a simplification of the determinants of collectively shared behaviour.

The work of the French sociologist Pierre-André Taguieff (1987), which is by far the most extensive and systematic attempt to review the many definitions of the term, gives a clear idea of the magnitude of the field of definition: racism as attitude, racism as ideology, as prejudice, as xenophobia, as naturalisation, biological racism, ethnic racism, essentialist racism, assimilationist racism, competitive racism, auto-referential racism, altero-referential racism, differential racism, inegalitarian racism and more either compete or coexist with each other in a variety of combinations vying to give a proper description of the 'essence' of the phenomenon.[9]

Despite the important insights it has allowed, this general and dominant tendency to define racism as a mental phenomenon has continually led to an undertheorisation of the relationship between the mental classification involved and the practices in which they are inserted, between what racists are thinking and what they are doing. We find a good example of the problems raised by such an approach in a much-used definition by Bob Miles, where he argues:

The concept of racism refers to those negative beliefs held by one group which identify and set apart another by attributing significance to some biological or other 'inherent' characteristic(s) which it is said to possess, and which deterministically associate that characteristic(s) with some other (negatively evaluated) feature(s) or action(s). The possession of these supposed characteristics may be used to justify the denial of the group equal access to material and other resources and/or political rights.[10]

Miles's main concern here is to clarify the conceptual field. He devotes most of his attention to a 'tight' description of the internal logic of a dominant form of racist thought. He wants to disallow a sloppy usage of the category 'racism', or what he later called 'conceptual inflation'.[11] Despite the tightness of the definition in most of the paragraph, however, as soon as we arrive at the relationship between racism and practices, the text becomes considerably vague: 'these supposed characteristics *may* be used'. Are racist categories sets of classification that are simply hanging 'out there' to be used or not used? To what extent can one posit classifications that remain unchanged by their usage?

In *The Logic of Practice*, Pierre Bourdieu criticises what he sees as the intellectualist reduction of 'the [practical] logic of things' into 'things of logic', and the treating of practical knowledge as if it has no other reason to exist than an intellectual one.[12] What Bourdieu means is that academic sociologists, by virtue of their profession, have a specific interest in, or a specific 'take' on, the beliefs and statements made about the social world. They often want to know whether such statements are true or false, whether they provide a good description or explanation of whatever it is to which they are referring. This is the logic that governs the statements sociologists themselves produce about the social world, and many of them end up assessing all statements about the social world using such criteria: are they true or false, are they good descriptions or are they not, are they good explanations or are they not? In so doing, Bourdieu argues, such sociologists assume that all knowledge about the social world has a sociological purpose. They forget that knowledge for most people who produce it has a practical purpose. It helps people do things. This practical function of knowledge — does it help me do what I want or does it not? — is a far more important criterion of truth and falsity in the practical world than the sociological mode of 'explanation for explanation's sake'.

I think Bourdieu's critique is of immense importance for the sociology of racism. When one examines the categories sociologists used to qualify racist beliefs — essentialisation, simplification, false, ideological, etc. — one can clearly see that what is assessed is whether racist statements are good sociological explanations. These categories fully exhibit the sociological failure to integrate the fact that popular racist categorisations are not out to explain 'others' for the sake of explaining them. They are not motivated by some kind of academic yearning for knowledge. They are categories of everyday practice, produced to make practical sense of, and to interact with, the world. Using them, people worry (in a specific, racist way) about their neighbourhood, about walking the streets at night, about where they can do their shopping and what kind of shops are available to them and so on.

What is the relation between the practices in which racist classifications are used and the classifications themselves? Do racist classifications define the nature of the practices to which they become articulated or are they merely a support towards achieving different ends? That is, do people use racism to achieve various practical goals, or is the main aim the assertion of the superiority of the race every time there is a racist classification in usage? Such questions related to practices and everyday deployment of racist categories are not systematically discussed in the literature on racism.

In a sense, for a more dynamic, practice-grounded, conception of racism, Gordon Allport's social psychological approach is more pertinent for our purposes. It leads him to differentiate between a variety of racist behaviours: verbal rejection, avoidance, discrimination, physical attack, extermination. From this, one gets a better sense of how racism is put into practice.[13] This raises an even greater difficulty, however, and one which is of more direct concern to us. In what way are such practices as rejection, discrimination or physical attacks 'racist practices'? We can all agree, for instance, that tearing a Muslim women's veil off her head is a physical attack. We can also agree that this attack is informed by a negative racist conception of a Muslim woman, even if this is not explicitly formulated by the person doing the tearing. Does this, however, make the attack *primarily* racist or racially *motivated?*

Of course, to a certain extent, any usage of racist classifications can be said to be racially motivated. The question, however, is how does this motivation relate to other motivations? If a White footballer, while tackling a Black opponent, emits a racist slur in the heat of the action, does the tackle stop being a football tackle and turn into 'racist violence'? Is the footballer's action 'racially motivated' or 'football motivated'? The fact that he used the racist slur may make him a racist, but does it mean that he is now playing a game called racism and that he is more concerned with asserting the superiority of the 'White race' than with playing football?

The trouble with the concept of 'racist practices' or with 'racially motivated' practices is that the belief in races or ethnicities, even the belief that there is a hierarchy of races or cultures, is not in itself a motivating ideology.[14] Racism on its own (like sexism in this regard) does not carry within it an imperative for action. One can believe that there is a White race or a Black or a Yellow race. One can even believe that the White race is superior to the Black and Yellow races. There is nothing in this belief, however, that requires one to act against members of the supposed Black or Yellow race. I can believe that Blacks and Asians are radically different or inferior without caring about where they live, whether they sit next to me on the train or whether there are 'too many of them'. As soon as I begin to worry about where 'they' are located, or about the existence of 'too many', I am beginning to worry not just about my 'race', 'ethnicity', 'culture' or 'people', but also about what I consider a privileged relationship between my race, ethnicity and so on, and a territory. My motivation becomes far more national than racial, even if I have a racial conception of the territory. This is why I want to suggest that, from this analytical perspective, and in so far as they embody an imagined special relation between a self and a territory, such practices are better conceived as nationalist practices than as racist practices, even if racist modes of thinking are deployed within them.

Racism and Power

One approach which appears closer to coming to grips with the question of practice is often formulated by intellectuals from racialised minorities. The dissatisfaction with conceptions of racism as a 'floating' mode of classification detached from practices and relations of power has been often expressed by such intellectuals.

One reason for this dissatisfaction is that an understanding of racism as essentialisation or stereotyping has frequently lead to counterclaims, often by those accused of racism, that 'Everybody's racist.' This is meant to emphasise that it is not only the majority that engages in racial stereotyping and essentialisation or even inferiorisation. To this, minority intellectuals have responded by emphasising that power is a far more distinctive dimension of racism than particular ideologies. So, to the claim that 'Everybody's racist', the answer of these intellectuals has been that, while everyone may be capable of stereotyping and essentialising others, not everyone is capable of using their racism to discriminate and subjugate others. Only the latter really qualifies as racism.

Thus, in England, Sivanandan stresses that 'racism is about power not about prejudice'.[15] Likewise, in the United States, black militants such as Carmichael and Hamilton see racism as 'the predication of decisions and policies on consideration of race for the purpose of subordinating a racial group and maintaining control over that racial group'.[16] In pointing to such questions of power in relation to racist modes of classification, these pronouncements help us to acknowledge their presence. This is already an important achievement. This power dimension is not, however, really treated satisfactorily.

Part of the problem is that the intent of such pronouncements is far more political than sociological. Anti-racist interests in an anti-racist politics and the sociological interest in explanation do not necessarily go together, as so many anti-racist sociologists like to believe. I will be treating the relation between the two more extensively in the conclusion. At this point, it is important to recognise that for intellectuals such as Sivanandan, Carmichael and Hamilton, the category 'racism' is an indicator of an existing racially defined and experienced social problem of inequity and domination in society. As such, their concern is to centre our attention on this problem and not allow a watered-down conception of racism to efface it. In this sense, they are totally correct in their emphasis.

In highlighting the question of power, they emphasise that if everyone can entertain prejudiced fantasies about a variety of 'others', it is the power to subject these 'others' to your fantasies that constitutes the social problem and, according to them, that is to what 'racism' ought to refer. They are right as to where the more important social problem lies, but it is not sociologically clear why this social problem has to be referred to as 'racism' except for the political reason that there are negative connotations historically associated with the word.

Indeed, in the course of the interviews I have been conducting since the Gulf War, it has become quite clear that the way a number of Arab migrants think about Anglo-Celtic Australians is far from being free of stereotyping and essentialisations — and is not particularly flattering. Views that 'Australians' are too inclined to drunkenness and uncommitted to their families, and statements that 'They walk barefooted like beggars', 'They don't clean their houses properly, they are always dirty and dusty', 'Their houses smell because they never open their windows', as well as a whole array of views concerning the lax moral standards of 'Australians', especially when it comes to raising children and questions of sexuality, were not uncommon. In this sense, those Arab Australians were just as racist as the Australians from the dominant White culture who were classifying them in a similar fashion.

Here one faces the importance of highlighting the dimension of power for, if I was to treat these racist essentialisations — and they *are* racist — along with the anti-Arab racism of White Australians as the main social problem facing Australian society during the Gulf War, I would have clearly missed some very important happenings. During these events, the Arab Australians did not simply suffer from being *represented* stereotypically, or from being *essentialised* or *thought of* as locked in their ethnic identity, they suffered from being subjugated. The racist pronouncements and the acts of harassment and intimidation led to a generalised fear amongst Arab people. It drove many of them to literally hide in their homes or to flee their neighbourhood. Many public outings, ferry cruises and tourist bus trips were cancelled. Even yearly occurrences such as Arab multicultural festivals were either cancelled or were drastically reduced in size. What was more important than any ideology of essentialisation was the more general process whereby one group of 'White' Australians felt *empowered*, and were in a position, to subject another (Arab–Muslim) group of Australians to such harassment.

It is to stress the importance of phenomena such as these compared to the mere expression of prejudices that Sivanandan, Carmichael and Hamilton want to reserve the term 'racism' to describe these phenomena and give them the negative stigma they deserve. Stressing this dimension of power by itself is not, however, really satisfactory, for this does not answer the question: the power to do what? In Carmichael and Hamilton's definition, for example, it appears as if the subordination of a racial group is an end in itself. The fact that these practices of subordination have a spatial–national dimension is not captured by the categories 'subordination', 'subjugation' and 'power'.

Here, however, we face another weakness in the 'racism as power' argument. By emphasising an opposition between ways of thinking and practices of domination, or, as Sivanandan does, between prejudice and power, such theorising ends up itself positing a power-free mode of classification shared by both the dominant and the dominated. The implication of Sivanandan's argument is that prejudice is the same whether expressed by the dominant or the dominated, and the only difference is that the dominant can act out their prejudice while the dominated cannot. If racist modes of classification are not the preserve of the dominant, and if dominated groups are also capable of racist classifications, the difference between them cannot simply be that the racism of the dominant is articulated to practices of domination while the racism of the minorities is not. This still assumes that the two racist modes of classification are the same regardless of what practices are carried out and from what position of power they emanate. Such a positing of a mode of perception and classification, which does not carry the traces of the position in the relation of power from which it emanates, is highly untenable.

This highlights once again that sociological analysis has to do more than examine racist classifications by themselves or substitute for this an analysis of power relation and practices of subordination. It has to capture the way these racist classifications, as classifications, bear the traces of the position of power from which they emanate and the practices in which they are located (what the practitioner wants to do with them). That is, it is not about examining in what way 'racism', when emanating from positions of power, is more about power than about prejudice; rather, it is about establishing the way in which the racist classifications of the powerful distinguish themselves from other racist classifications and reveal themselves to be forms of *empowered practical prejudice.*

On Nationalist Practices

Let us examine a bit more carefully the movement of the hand that tears the scarf off a Muslim woman's head and some of the statements that accompanied it. Clearly, when examining these acts in their totality as a social phenomenon, we cannot tell just from the movement itself whether the various persons tearing the scarf believe that it is an inferior cultural item or that Muslims themselves are inferior, or indeed anything of the sort. Not many people tear down scarfs and at the same time make grand statements about the inferiority of this or that race. In any case, as we noted above, the feeling that Muslim women are inferior, or that they are exceptionally different, on its own, does not propel action against Muslim women. We can safely deduce, however, logically as well as from the data we have acquired, that the scarf as a cultural item and as a symbol of certain aspects of Islamic culture is considered *undesirable.*

I have only managed to interview one person (interviewee A), in Sydney, who has torn the veil off a Muslim woman.[17] A researcher working with me interviewed another person (interviewee B) who expressed the 'desire' to do so.[18] Both interviewees A and B clearly deployed racial stereotyping: 'Muslims are dirty', 'Arabs are savages' (Interviewee A),

'They smell' (Interviewee B), 'There's no point reasoning with them; they're too dumb to understand' (Interviewee A). They also clearly deployed ethnic/cultural stereotyping: 'They have too many kids' (Interviewee B), 'They don't know how to look after their kids' (Interviewee A). There were also straightforward expressions of hate: 'I hate them' (Interviewee A). Most of all, however, their discourse was a discourse of undesirability, not of inferiority: 'I don't see why we have to have them here' (Interviewee A); 'They're really not the sort of people I would like to see coming to this country' (Interviewee B); 'Everywhere they go they're a problem, look at what's happening in Lebanon ... in Bosnia, even in France' (Interviewee A); 'There's already too many of them here' (Interviewee A).

Unlike notions of inferiority, undesirability certainly implies, and propels, action. The subject acts because he or she sees in the scarf, through whatever it may symbolise to him or her, a harmful presence that affects their own well-being.[19] When interviewee A was pushed to explain why she couldn't simply let the Muslim woman wearing the scarf be, she said: 'This is a Christian country. I don't see why such backward forms of putting down women ought to be allowed. Soon there'll be too many of them ... How would you like it if we end up having to put a veil on, too?'

Here we face already the limitation (but not the irrelevance) of the notion of 'racism' to explain this mode of categorisation. Concepts such as 'too many' are meaningless unless they assume the existence of a specific territorial space against which the evaluation 'too many' is arrived at. Generally speaking, the classification of an object as 'undesirable' always assumes a space where the undesirable is defined as such. Most things are 'undesirable' somewhere, and desirable (or one 'cannot care less about them') somewhere else. There is no such thing as 'undesirable' or 'too many' in the abstract.

Most humans perceive ants as a different species, and certainly as an inferior species. Yet, just on the basis of this belief, they do not perceive them as 'undesirable' or as 'too many'. They do so only when these ants are seen to have invaded spaces where humans find their presence harmful such as in their houses or on their plates. And it is only in such situations that practices of violence are directed against them. Consequently, categories such as 'too many', while embodying some form of 'racist' belief, are primarily *categories of spatial management*.[20] And in light of Bourdieu's comments mentioned earlier, they are so because they are integrated primarily in practices of managing space. In the above interview, as it was regularly the case in the interviews we have conducted, this space is always defined in national terms ('our country'). Indeed, 'ant-like' discourses such as 'I don't care what they do in their own country, but I don't want them here' are precisely the most common refrain deployed by racists today. As this refrain explicitly states, however, the issue is one of national space.

Clearly, what motivates the production of categories such as 'too many' in this context is the wish to construct or preserve not just a 'race', an 'ethnicity' or a 'culture', but also an imagined privileged relation between the imagined 'race', 'ethnicity' or 'culture' and the national space conceived as its own. As Michael Billig argues in *Banal Nationalism*, many of our words embody a national deixis which ensures that images of the nation are always 'near the surface of contemporary life'.[21] Even when people are speaking about specific localities, they often end up articulating these to the space of the nation. They may experience what they consider as 'too many Muslims' or 'too many Asians' in their street or in their neighbourhood, but they will conceive of the 'problem' in national terms.[22] It is because of the dominance of this spatial–national problem that the practice of tearing a scarf from someone's head is better defined as a nationalist practice, a practice of nationalist violence or of nationalist exclusion, rather than as racist violence. It is in this sense that racist classifications such as 'too many' and 'go home', articulated as they are to nationalist practices of exclusion, are subordinate to the practical function dictated by such nationalist practices.

The Homely Imaginary of Nationalist Practices

If, as argued above, classifications emphasising 'undesirability' cannot be conceived independently of a national spatial background against which they acquire their meaning, it is equally true that they cannot be conceived without an idealised image of what this national spatial background *ought to be like*. That is, nationalist practices cannot be conceived without an ideal nation being imagined by the nationalist. 'Too many' cannot be conceived outside of a definite national space against which it obtains its significance, yet neither can it be conceived except against a desired national space where there aren't 'too many'. As it is well known to be the case, often this desired national space is formulated as a wish to return to a former state of affairs, a return to what the nation 'used to be'. A garbage collector in Marrickville, who described himself as an 'Aussie with a vengeance', gave us his specific version of this:

> I'd say like, like I know a fair bit of people in Marrickville, you know like, ah … I'd say like, like people, like, well … the Vietnamese, I … They're sort of, ah … overpopulating the place, you know. There's still a fair bit of Aussies around, like, but …it's not the same. I'd be lucky to get a can of beer at Christmas. The Vietnamese … well … mate, they don't even know how to put their garbage in a garbage bin. And … and … well … you know … I don't want nothing from nobody … but picking up garbage is not how it used to be, you know … people, like, they leave all sort of things without putting them in plastic bags … I tell you, it doesn't smell like Australia anymore around here … you know what I mean, mate?

It is this desired how-it-used-to-be nation, here imagined on the basis of certain practices as well as on the basis of smell, which helps this nationalist categorise what is desirable and what isn't. What is classified as undesirable is precisely that which is perceived as stopping the nation from being what it ought to be like for the nationalist doing the classifying. Such images of the ideal nation are most clearly articulated around the theme of 'home'.

The discourse of 'home' is one of the most pervasive and well-known elements of nationalist practices. Strangely enough, however, it has become part of an anti-racist common sense to consider 'go home' statements as mere 'racism'. Yet, surely, the expressed wish to send undesirable others to their 'home' is as clear a nationalist desire as can be, even if it involves a racial categorisation of those one wishes to see 'go home'.[23] In the desire to send the other 'home', subjects express implicitly their own desire to *be* at home. In every 'go home', there is an 'I want to and am entitled to feel at home in my nation'. Such an imaginary nation is never formulated in its totality. Attempts at offering systematic accounts of what the nation ought to be like are only carried out by 'professional' nationalist ideologues. Furthermore, because 'home' refers more to a structure of feelings than a physical, house-like construct, it is fragmentary images, rather than explicit formulations, of what the homely nation ought to be like that we obtain by listening to people's comments. Together, however, these fragments show the national home to be structured, like many other images of homely life, around the key themes of familiarity, security and community.[24] As in the interview above, however, these themes only figure in nationalist speech as something lost and in need of being recovered. In the racist discourses articulated to the practices of nationalist exclusion we have been examining, it is always a migrant behind this loss.

Familiarity is particularly associated with practical spatial and linguistic knowledge. When the nationalist feels that he or she can no longer operate in, communicate in or recognise the national space in which he or she operates, the nation appears to be losing its homely character. Familiarity is essential for a sense of community, but the latter also requires a sense of shared symbolic forms and the existence of support networks of friends and relatives. Security is impossible without familiarity and community, but it also involves the possibility of satisfying one's basic needs and an absence of threatening otherness. In this interview with Ian, an unemployed man from Marrickville, we have an excellent example of how the themes of familiarity, community and security combine and appear interrelated:

Ian: When we came down here, as you probably know, Marrickville then was known as little Athens. It was predominantly Greeks and, ah, it was great because most of them were pretty good anyway, they mixed more ... you felt that they liked the place, you know, and they were happy to be here and quite grateful to be in Australia. Then we went through a Yugoslav stage, and a Lebanese stage, but, you know, the place was still recognisably … Australian … Even when Marrickville Road was full of Greeks, it didn't worry us. It didn't make us feel we were no longer living in Australia. People still recognised each other in the streets and you could have a quiet beer with your mates in the pub. But now, as you can tell … it's all gone …

Interviewer: Hmm, hmm.

Ian: I, I'd say Marrickville's the next biggest Vietnamese city outside Cabramatta and it's just happened like overnight. Zoom, they've bought out along Marrickville Road. You should just see up there, come straight down here and along Illawarra Road and, you know, it's just unbelievable … You can't hear a fucking word of English. Sometimes I have to ask myself, Am I on Marrickville Road? When you no longer recognise the street where you spent your childhood … That's bad mate … That's bad. And then … You want me to tell you more?

Interviewer: Sure.

Ian: Well, there's the Legends [an 'ethnic gang'] … you know people are even … a lot of people won't go out here at night, a lot of them. One time they overtook Marrickville station, and to show how they were, what's that, um, you've heard of the New York Guardian Angels?

Interviewer: Yeah.

Ian: Yeah, well, they came out here one time just trying to go and show, you know what to do around … sort of safe-guard the city trains. Marrickville was the one that broke them here. The leader got bashed and they've gone back to the States.

Interviewer: You're kidding!

Ian: Yep. This is Australia for you, mate, and they keep telling us how bad New York is. Why don't they come and bring the cameras here? … I tell you what, a lot of work needs to be done if this place is to get back to what it was like.

We can see here how the imaginary homely nation does not only operate as the background against which the unde-sirable is classified, but it also operates as a general goal. The nation as 'back to what it was like' is a spatial–affective *aspiration*. It helps to orientate the nationalist's practices and shape them into practices aiming to construct and to help make true the imaginary nation.

The Imaginary of the Nationalist Manager and the Other as Object

In the previous section, I have stressed that an image of national space is a prerequisite for the nationalist's capacity to classify others as undesirable. Just as much as an image of the nation, however, what is also implicit in this mode of classification is an image of the nationalist as someone with a managerial capacity over this national space. One cannot define and act on others as undesirable in just any national space. Such a space has to be perceived as one's own national space. The discourse of home, because it conveys a relation to the nation rather than some kind of objectivist definition of it, clearly implies not only an image of a nation that is one's own, but also of a self that occupies a privileged position vis-à-vis the nation, a privileged mode of inhabiting it. This is evident in the very categories used by the nationalist which treat the 'other' as an object to be managed (in the cases we are examining, an object to be removed from the space of the nation), while treating the self as spatially empowered to position/remove this other.

The garbage collector interviewed above is not only a 'manager of garbage', he casts an equally managerial gaze on the totality of his surrounding, registering and worrying about, for example, what he considers as processes of 'over-population'. The other interviewee, Ian, although unemployed, is even more directly managerial: he does not shy away from recommending that: 'A lot of work needs to be done if this place is to get back to what it was like.'

The difference between the imagined national–spatial manager and the managed national object emerged most clearly and dramatically during an interview conducted with a Lebanese Australian youth who was telling me the story of how he had been picked up and mistreated by two 'Anglo' policemen. One of them called him, the boy said, 'an Arab piece of shit'. He got agitated during the interview and exclaimed:

> These bloody Australians, you know ... they think they're so fucking clever, you know ... I know his [one of the police-men's] son ... he's in my school, he's a dickhead who mas-turbates in the toilet at least twice a day ... Fucking Australian shit, they're the shit. They're all shit ...

What was particularly interesting in this exclamation was that, at a formal level, the boy was using the same classifica-tion as that used by the policeman. Both involve the gener-alisation and essentialisation of 'negative' traits. Here we have an example of how 'Everybody's racist'. It would clear-ly be disingenuous, however, to see nothing but the similari-ty of the categorisation in all of this for, despite the usage of the same word and despite each of them being racist in its own way, these categorisations were not the same. And the difference between them was not just in the fact that one emanated from a defensive posture while the other was artic-ulated to a powerful policing practice. The difference in the positions of power from which the categorisations emanated, and the practical intent of the classifiers, inscribed itself on the very categories individually. This is where the recogni-tion of the spatiality of the whole phenomenon yields better analytical results than the mere category of 'racism'. This is best revealed in the *imaginary spatiality* embodied in the term used to qualify the notion of 'shit'. It is above all translated into differences in what we can call the 'bodily sense of scale' that is part of the classification.

To put it as neatly as possible, the 'Anglo' policeman's use of the word 'piece' reveals a different relation and a different conception of the *size* of the 'shit' from that of the Lebanese boy's 'they're *all* shit'. For the empowered national manager — in this case, the racist policeman — the imagined referent of the classification is a small, manageable 'piece' that can be removed. For the contextually disempowered Lebanese youth, however, this imagined referent is overwhelming; it is as if he is inundated by 'it' and unable to control it.

The very idea of an object being imagined as big or small, like 'too many' or 'too few', implies that it is imagined against a wider space which defines its size. Here we can also see that it is imagined in relation to the imaginary size of the classifier's national body. It is in this sense that, within nationalist practices, the mode of classification used always implies an imaginary relation to the nation. The relation between the sizes of imagined bodies implies an embodiment of a relation of power in which the physical bodies are situated. It is a truly bodily mode of classification. Within the empowered racist classification of the 'Anglo' policeman, *as classification*, is both the construction of the object as a small-sized, manageable object, as well as the construction of the self as a spatially empowered subject capable of managing 'small-sized objects' within a definite imagined (national) space.

The fact that the example above involves a policeman can lead one to believe that it is too specific an example from which to generalise. In fact, the spatiality of this mode of categorisation is far from being specific to this particular case. It was, for instance, a common feature of many of the categorisations of Arabs during the Gulf War. The fact that it emerges within a practice of policing helps us understand the extent to which such racist categorisations and the nationalist practices they delineate embody an image of spatial management often manifested in policing fantasies: 'You can go here', 'You are not allowed there.'

As I have already pointed out, the nationalist violence that marked the whole episode was spatially manifested in the dominance of a wish and a will on the part of the nationalists/racists to remove a variety of ethnicised (Arab and Muslim) individuals and objects from spaces considered as the racists' 'own'. The majority of the written and oral racist statements made during the Gulf War were centred on a wish to send the 'Arabs' 'back' to where they were perceived really to belong. Simultaneously, all those who engaged in physical or verbal nationalist violence implicitly conceived of themselves as spatial managers, seeing in the Arab other a mere object to be removed from national space.

Talkback radio and the 'letters to the editor' pages of newspapers were literally full of calls for the 'Arabs' to prove their loyalty to the nation or 'go home'. These calls were sometimes supplemented, sometimes fuelled, by journalists, politicians and other media 'personalities'. On radio, for example, there were common pronouncements ranging from: 'If you don't like it, rack off',[25] to the more flowery: '… our economic survival in the hands of a lunatic [Saddam Hussein]. If you want that, you, too, are lunatics and you should go back and be there with the other lunatic.'[26] It was clear that this imagined 'Arab' object that the nationalist felt empowered to manage spatially and even to remove totally from space was 'little'. Arabs were in fact so 'tiny' that, as one radio commentator fantasised, one could 'wrap them up in newspapers and send them home'.[27]

It is because the tearing off of a Muslim woman's scarf exemplifies the imaginary bodily spatiality of these nationalist practices that I chose to focus my analysis in this chapter on it. The movement of the hand in the act of tearing off the scarf can be seen metonymically and metaphorically as representing the nature of nationalist practices in general. One cannot emphasise enough the bodily spatial engagement with the social that is presupposed by this act. Nationalism, before being an explicit practice or a mode of classification, is a state of the body. It is a way of imagining one's position within the nation and what one can aspire to as a national. The hand that is deployed on the Muslim scarf is a hand whose 'owner' has a sense of its *size and power*.

While such an imaginary bodily size reflects, as I have argued, the relation of power between the nationalist managers and the national 'ethnic object' they feel empowered to manage, it also reflects an imagined mode of *inhabiting* the nation. Just as much as the nation is imagined as a homely construct, the nationalist body is also imagined to inhabit it in a specific way such as it can cast its managerial gaze on the home.

As the two formulations 'I belong to the nation' and 'This is my nation' (i.e. 'The nation belongs to me') imply, there is at least a dual mode of belonging to the national home that we need to understand. The nationalist who believes him or herself to 'belong to a nation' in the sense of being part of it, means that he or she she expects to have the right to benefit from the nation's resources, to 'fit into it' or 'feel at home' within it. This mode of belonging can be called *pas-*

sive belonging. The other mode of national belonging, the belief that one has a right over the nation, involves the belief in one's possession of the right to contribute (even if only by having a *legitimate* opinion with regard to the internal and external politics of the nation) to its management such that it remains 'one's home'. This is what I call *governmental belonging*.

It is important to stress, to avoid any confusion, that the power to govern which derives from governmental belonging is not equivalent to formal state or 'government' power. While the holding of state power can be an efficient mode of governmental power, the latter can merely be the feeling that one is legitimately entitled in the course of everyday life to make a governmental/managerial statement about the nation — to have a view about its foreign policy, for example, or to have a governmental/managerial attitude towards others, especially those who are perceived to be lesser nationals or non-nationals, to have a view about who they can be and where they can go. This is what makes the relationship between governmental and homely belonging a complex one. On the one hand, any recognition of the legitimacy of homely belonging is a recognition of some governmental belonging. On the other, governmental power, in being the power to have a legitimate view concerning the positioning of others in the nation, is the power to have a legitimate view regarding who should 'feel at home' in the nation and how, and who should be in and who should be out, as well as what constitutes 'too many'.

It is clearly this governmental belonging which is claimed by those who are in a dominant position. To inhabit the nation in this way is to inhabit what is often referred to as the *national will*. It is to perceive oneself as the enactor or the agent of this will, to the extent that one identifies with it precisely as one's own will. It is what makes the nationalist a subject whose will can be exercised within national space. It is also by inhabiting this will that the imaginary body of the nationalist assumes its gigantic size, for the latter is the size of omnipresence, the size of those whose gaze has to be constantly policing and governing the nation. It is also, by the same token, the inability to represent and inhabit such a will which makes the other a national object.

Conclusion

Let us pause here and summarise what we have defined as a nationalist practice of exclusion so far. A nationalist practice of exclusion is a practice emanating from agents imagining themselves to occupy a privileged position within national space such as they perceive themselves to be the enactors of the national will within the nation. It is a practice orientated by the nationalists' attempt at building what they imagine to be a homely nation. In this process, the nationalists perceive themselves as spatial managers and that which is standing between them and their imaginary nation is constructed as an undesirable national object to be removed from national space.

The hand that tears off the scarf is a hand that is orientated by an image of the kind of national space it wants to construct with the removal of this scarf. In the negative 'I don't want this scarf in my nation' communicated by the act of tearing, there is a positive statement: 'I want my nation to be "like this".' Such a 'like this' can be a very vague image of the nation, but without it nothing can be qualified as desirable or undesirable, and, in this particular case, we can be certain that this idealised image of the nation as a goal does not include Muslim scarfs.

Many people in Australia, however, have more or less strong views about what Australia ought to be like. Most have more or less clear ideas about what and who they consider as desirable or undesirable. Clearly, not all go about removing what they consider undesirable in the nation when they encounter it. Not all of them feel *nationally empowered* to do so. As we have argued above, the person who deploys his or her hand on the scarf is clearly someone who believes that they have a right to manage the space of the nation in this way. But what does it take to do so? How does one feel entitled to assume such a managerial role?

chapter 2

Evil White Nationalists 2:
The 'White Nation' Fantasy

The previous chapter stressed the spatial dimensions of nationalist practices. Whether at a macro level such as the race-based segregational spatiality of apartheid or the homogenising spatiality pursued by genocidal racism, or at a micro level in practices such as forbidding an Aboriginal person to enter a pub, stopping a Greek woman from being promoted to a managerial post or shouting at a Muslim Australian to 'go home', the spatiality of nationalist phenomena appears, to a certain extent, to be obvious. In all such examples, nationalist practices seem to be necessarily grounded in an image in which the nationalists construct themselves as spatially dominant, as masters of a territory in which they have managerial rights over racialised/ethnicised groups or persons which are consequently constructed as manageable objects.

Their specificity does not lie in their inferiorisation or essentialisation of the other, but in the construction of the other as an object of spatial exclusion. This will to exclude is not explained primarily either by race or ethnicity, but by the specific image of the racialised *nation* that the nationalist is aiming to construct. To look at these practices this way is not to exclude issues of race from helping us to explain them. It is, however, to put it in the back seat, to allow us a fresh perspective on what propels and shapes such practices.

Having analysed the various components of nationalist

practices, I would like to move now to an equally important issue unexplored so far. How do some people inhabiting the nation manage to take up such a managerial position within it and not others? Clearly, not all those within national space feel the nation to be their own to an equal degree. Newly arrived migrants who may dislike an 'Anglo', for example, are not likely to feel nationally empowered to act violently against them.[1] Even not so newly arrived migrants, who might feel quite at home in Australia, will not necessarily feel empowered to do the above. In the sense that this notion was developed in the previous chapter, they may experience passive homely belonging, but not governmental belonging.

They are unlikely to worry about 'numbers' and 'overpopulation', and they will rarely feel capable of legitimately telling anyone, let alone an 'Anglo', to go home. While, as we shall now see, such modes of national belonging are not as clearly structured around an Anglo–ethnic divide as the popular common usage of this categorisation implies, the above is enough to make it clear that the extent of one's governmental belonging within national space is a question of cultural entitlement. It is to this question that we now need to turn in order to understand in what sense we can call these practices White nationalist practices.

From Citizenship to Practical Nationality

To begin with, I would like to clarify what is meant by *national belonging* as the term has been used above, and to differentiate it from the concept of 'citizenship', which is often taken as its equivalent.

As in most nations, citizenship in Australia is the main *formal* indicator of national belonging. As Jean Leca has pointed out: 'The majority of modern states establish a link between citizenship and nationality.'[2] The act of taking on citizenship has also been termed 'naturalisation', implying a process of acculturation, of belonging to a national cultural community. For the Australian government, the acquisition of citizenship by non-Australian–born people is assumed to be an acquisition of nationality. This is also taken to be the case by some Australian academics. Thus, Laksiri Jayasuriya claims that: 'In a pluralistic society, social cohesion prevails when there is a sense of belonging to a nation. This sense of belonging arises from a common citizenship.'[3]

There are a number of reasons, however, why a sociological conception of national belonging, one that necessarily aims at examining the *practical* deployment and significance of nationality in the social — how people experience and deploy their claims to national belonging in the everyday life — cannot be satisfactorily equated with formal citizenship.

Formal citizenship can reflect a practical mode of national belonging only in the ideal situation where the formal decision to include a person as a citizen reflects a general communal will. In fact, this is only imaginable in the popularly idealised fantasies of the Greek republic, where the decisions to include citizens are conceived as having been truly communal (made by all citizens). In a representative democracy, where the power to grant citizenship is delegated to the state, there is an important, and historically growing, incompatibility between the state's formal acceptance of new citizens and the dominant community's everyday acceptance of such people. This is especially so when there is a clearly dominant, culturally defined community within the nation. In such cases, the acquisition of formal citizenship does not give any indication of the level of practical national belonging granted by the dominant cultural community. This is largely because the basis of communal acceptance remains determined by questions of cultural descent far more than by state acceptance. How much more differs according to the history and the political tradition of specific nations.

In Australia, the rift between the granting of citizenship by the state and the acceptance of those citizens by those who consider themselves from the dominant culture has grown considerably in the post-World War II era. To be asked for your Australian citizenship papers, and to produce them, *institutionally* legitimises the holder of the citizenship to do whatever they set out, and is within their rights as citizens, to do. At the same time, however, the very possession of these citizenship papers is stigmatising at a practical, non-official level since their possession and production is only required from those who have not acquired their citizenship by birth. Thus, what is the proof of national belonging to the state (citizenship) can, in a practical sense, operate as proof of national non-belonging to the dominant culture.

This does not mean that official state policy is totally immune to such discriminatory 'culturalist logic'. A dramatic example of this was the state's internment of Australian citizens of Italian and German origin during World War II. Oswald Bonutto wrote that, for the internees, 'naturalisation certificates were not worth the paper on which they were written, and their cherished rights as Australian citizens disappeared overnight'.[4] My argument is that the dominance of this cultural–national belonging over formal belonging is a reaction to specific historical events only when it is applied to the state. Within the everyday logic of the way individuals and groups from the dominant culture interact with minorities in social life, it constitutes the norm.

To avoid any analytical confusion, I will use the derivatives of 'nation' — 'nationality' or 'practical nationality', 'national belonging', etc. — to refer mainly to issues of *practical–cultural* national acceptance at a communal, everyday level, and will take citizenship to refer to *institutional–political* acceptance. Barry Hindess, although he is speaking of citizenship, perceives it in terms that makes it closer to what we will be referring to as nationality when he points out that:

> Notions of descent (and the apparently more respectable surrogate notion of a distinctive national culture that cannot readily be acquired by persons who are not born into it) have always played an important part in the way citizenship has been understood within particular communities.[5]

Another important weakness of the notion of citizenship for our analytical purposes is that it is unable to help us in our quest for what allows certain people to assume a managerial position within the nation. Clearly, citizenship may at best be a prerequisite for taking up such a governmental position, but it is certainly not a sufficient condition for it. One of the most sociologically unhelpful aspects of the usage of the formal conception of citizenship to refer to national belonging is that the either (a national)/or (not) logic it embodies, and which is uncritically taken on board by many analysts, does not allow us to capture all the subtleties of the *differential modalities of national belonging* as they are experienced within society.

While practical nationality does erect a boundary between nationals and non-nationals, it is more important to recognise that it has a cumulative nature and is unequally distributed within the nation. In the daily life of the nation, there are nationals who, on the basis of their class or gender or ethnicity, for example, practically feel and are made to feel to be *more* or *less* nationals than others, without having to be denied, or feel they are denied, the right to be nationals as such. The either/or, inclusion or exclusion conception of national belonging is paradoxically less present in everyday popular conceptions of the nation than it is among social analysts. People strive to accumulate nationality. They recognise themselves as more national than some people and less national than others. They are also recognised by others in a similar fashion.

This is made quite clear when examining the everyday language referring to national belonging in Australia and which constantly negates an either/or conception of Australianness. People talk of others as being 'almost Australians'. One migrant can refer to another migrant saying: 'He is more of an Aussie than I am.' Such a 'more or less' qualification is also used between non-migrant Australians. Just as importantly, people interested in 'enhancing their national profile' are constantly converting some cultural achievements they have acquired or a personal characteristic they possess to make claims of being more of a national than, or at least as national as, others. They can make nationality claims by converting their length of stay in Australia: 'I've been here since the late 1950s. I've been an Aussie before he could say, "G'day mate."' They can convert their capacity to speak the national language into more nationality and consider those who don't as lesser nationals: 'You only have to listen to him; he's really more of an Englishman.' Furthermore, people struggle to put more value on the capacity of certain cultural possessions to be converted to Australian nationality than others. When researching in Annandale, one of the researchers reported part of a street still divided by a struggle between its elderly Catholics and Protestants, with claims by individuals in both groups along the line of 'we are the real Australians'.

It is because of the above that practical nationality is best conceived as a form of national 'cultural capital'. Cultural capital, according to Bourdieu — whose work I will be using extensively here — represents the sum of valued knowledge, styles, social and physical (bodily) characteristics and practical behavioural dispositions within a given field. In short, they are material and symbolic goods constructed as valuable within the field and specific to it.[6] Bourdieu-ian analysis involves, as a first step, the positioning of the social object of research within a field. The field represents an analytical construct (a potentially existing relational social reality) with which the researcher constructs and makes sense of the research object. It is a market-like structure in which individual and collective subjects are involved in various competitive and conflictual struggles over the accumulation and the deployment of modalities of 'capital'.

In much the same way, practical nationality can be understood analytically as the sum of accumulated nationally sanctified and valued social and physical cultural styles and dispositions (national culture) adopted by individuals and groups, as well as valued characteristics (national types and national character) within a national field: looks, accent, demeanour, taste, nationally valued social and cultural preferences and behaviour, etc. For Bourdieu, the accumulated cultural capital within a given field is ultimately converted into symbolic capital, which is the recognition and legitimacy given to a person or group for the cultural capital they have accumulated. Within the nation, it is national belonging that constitutes the symbolic capital of the field. That is, the aim of accumulating national capital is precisely to convert it into national belonging; to have your accumulated national capital recognised as legitimately national by the dominant cultural grouping within the field.

Consequently, at the most basic level of its mode of operation, national belonging *tends* to be proportional to accumulated national capital. That is, there is a tendency for a national subject to be perceived as just as much of a national as the amount of national capital he or she has accumulated. Thus, a national subject born to the dominant culture who has accumulated national capital in the form of the dominant linguistic, physical and cultural dispositions will yield more national belonging than a male migrant who has managed to acquire the dominant national accent and certain national cultural practices, but lacks the physical characteristics and dispositions of the dominant national 'type'. This male migrant in turn can yield more national belonging than another female migrant or than a more recently arrived migrant who has not even mastered the basic national language or any of the dominant cultural practices.

Such an approach, although in need of further refinement, allows us already to make significant gains on the either/or model of belonging. It also allows a far more subtle understanding of the dynamic of cultural dominance within the nation than that yielded by the 'Anglo–Ethnic or White–Aboriginal equals Dominant–Dominated' model often used in the analysis of national cultural dominance. With a cumulative conception of nationality, we can capture analytically, for example, the way the differences between 'Anglos' and 'ethnics' vary depending on what 'Anglos' and what 'ethnics' we are talking about. As importantly, we can better capture the crucial differences in the claims of national belonging that exists among 'ethnics' and 'Anglos' themselves.

Migrants arriving in a new nation can accumulate nationality by acquiring the language, the accent, duration of residence, mastering of national-specific cultural practices, etc. — in other words, by assimilating. The extent to which they can actually accumulate national capital is linked to the cultural possessions and dispositions (what Bourdieu calls 'habitus' — one's historically acquired structure of the personality) they bring with them. It obviously makes a difference whether one already possesses a certain amount of cultural capital by being born to a cultural group or a class (in the socioeconomic sense) that makes one already in possession of important elements of the dominant national capital. Elements such as language, looks, cultural practices, a class-derived capacity to intermix with others from different cultures (cosmopolitanism), all of these give the person either some already contextually validated national symbolic capital or the advantages of proximity with the dominant national culture which can quicken the process of cultivating and accumulating national capital.

While all of this does secure the accumulator elements of national belonging, it does not necessarily translate into the position of national dominance we are seeking to understand. In line with the distinction we have made between passive belonging and governmental belonging, it can be argued that the accumulation of national capital does not only lead to quantitative differences in belonging, but also to qualitative ones. Clearly those who aspire to dominate the field are those who accumulate governmental belonging. Some migrants, for example, through sporting success, manage to accumulate a high degree of what we have called in the previous chapter 'passive homely belonging', but this does not necessarily translate into a position of national dominance. It is governmental belonging which gives one not only the position of cultural dominance within the field, but also, as we have seen, the power to position others within it. This tends to make governmental belonging a field in itself which shares the characteristics of what Bourdieu has called the 'field of power'. It is in examining the dynamics of the field of national governmental belonging as a field of power that we can begin to understand the specificities of the latter.

Guardians of the National Order: The Field of Whiteness and the White National Aristocracy

Bourdieu introduced the concept of 'field of power' in his work *The State Nobility*, in an attempt to refine his analysis of the ruling classes. He argues that the concept of a ruling class gives a too homogeneous idea of this social force. Instead, he aims to analyse this ruling class as itself constituted by a field in which various people hold various capitals which give them power vis-à-vis the rest of society, but which are not of equal value in the field of power itself. In this sense, members of a ruling group are unequally endowed with capital and power, and are competing amongst themselves for domination within the field of power. How can this be of help in the analysis of the dominant national culture?

There is a considerable lack of a systematic approach in

sociological literature to multiculturalism when it comes to the categories used to refer to the dominant cultural group in colonial and post-colonial Australia. Categories such as 'White Anglo-Saxon Protestants', 'Whites', 'Anglos', 'Anglo-Celtic', 'European', while usually communicating the specific feature of the dominant that their user wishes to emphasise, also manage to mystify either the logic behind, or the mode of conceiving different periods in Australian history that corresponds to, the specific usage of each. It is here that Bourdieu's notion of the field of power can be of great help.

From such a perspective, we can consider all of the above categories as referring to cultural possessions which allow their holders to stake certain claims of governmental belonging relative to the weight of the capital in his or her possession. Being 'male', 'European', 'of British descent', 'of Irish descent', 'Protestant', 'Catholic', 'rich in economic capital', or 'a good sportsperson', or having 'a white skin', 'an Aussie accent' or 'blond hair', all of these operate as national capitals in the sense that their possession allows the person who owns them to claim certain forms of dominant national belonging. Clearly, however, not all of these capitals are of equal value. Having blond hair is valuable, but if one has blond hair and an 'East European accent', this does not make one more national than having brown hair and an Australian accent. Thus we can say that the Australian accent is more valuable than the blond hair as a national capital. This can be further refined, depending on the sociological investigation, to analyse how a broad accent may be more valued in some national spheres, while devalued in others. In this Letter to the Editor, the writer relates his experience of the valorisation of his 'looks' over length of stay:

> The thing about the current immigration debate is that it is irrefutably based on skin colour and racial appearance. I know this because, ironically, I am looked at and judged an Australian because of my blond hair and blue eyes.
>
> I look like one. I sound like one, but I have only lived here for six of my seventeen years. My family migrated from England; I have no Australian roots or heritage, and I am not a citizen here. A person who has lived here for twenty years, or was born here, may not be perceived as an Australian, if they do not have 'the look', but as an immigrant.

This is so sad but very common, illustrating perfectly the agenda of those decrying multiculturalism and a pluralist Australia, and the confused and hurtful nature of the debate.[7]

One also has to remember, however, that the value of each capital is constantly fluctuating, depending on various historical conjunctures as well as the internal struggle within the field of national power. Thus, the category 'Anglo-Celtic', while telling us something about the dominant culture, mystifies the struggles of valorisation between Englishness and Irishness which characterises Australian history. The totality of such struggles to determine and accumulate what is 'really' Australian, or what is 'more' Australian, gives the Australian field of national power its particular historical characteristics. It is this field that I propose to call the field of Whiteness, and those who aspire to occupy it and assume a governmental position within it, and consequently within the nation, I will call White Australians.

It is important to stress that what I am interested in here is the field of national power and governmental belonging, not any national belonging. This is important because, clearly, in Australia, Aboriginal Blackness is also constructed as a national capital which allows national belonging. It is a capital, however, which only allows functional and passive belonging. We are still a long way from having Blackness valorised in the Australian national field of power. Blackness, however, is present in the field of power as a marker. It allows various non-Blacks an access to Whiteness. All the cappuccinos, macchiatos and caffe lattes of the world that are neither black nor white, skin-colour wise, can use the Blackness of the Aboriginal people to emphasise their non-Blackness and their capacity to enter the field of Whiteness. Other people also have a strategic interest in promoting a categorical Black–White divide which gives Whiteness a solidity it does not really have.

Whiteness as I will be using it here does not, however, refer only to skin colour. White skin colour is certainly a valuable capital in claiming one's belonging to the nation as a governmental White Australian, but it should be remembered that even white skin colour is cumulative and falls under a more or less, rather than an either/or logic, even if some have an interest in making it fall under such a logic. Whiteness, like all identities, needs, as Judith Butler has argued, 'to establish the illusion of its own uniformity and identity'.[8] In an article concerned with the definition of Whiteness in the United States, Jonathan Warren and France Twine demonstrate very well that Whiteness is far from being the essentialised, fixed racial category it is often posited to be. They give the example of a New Yorker who, on visiting New Zealand, notices that: 'The people were very white. Not New York White (i.e., ethnic, blended, beige), but naked, pasty, underdone: white, white.'[9] Furthermore, they show how, in the United States, the 'White' racial category has expanded to include people previously constructed as non-White.

In Australia, there are many examples of struggles over defining people's Whiteness. Some Lebanese, for example, as J. McKay and T. Batrouney relate, had to struggle to establish their Whiteness to be allowed entry to Australia under the White Australia Policy. One Lebanese leader argued that 'Syrians were Caucasians, and they are as white a race as the English. Their looks, habits, customs, religion, blood etc. are those of Europeans, but they are more intelligent.'[10]

'Whiteness' is an everchanging, composite cultural historical construct. It has its roots in the history of European colonisation which universalised a cultural form of White identity as a position of cultural power at the same time as the colonised were in the process of being racialised.[11] Whiteness, in opposition to Blackness and Brownness, was born the same time as the binary oppositions coloniser/colonised, being developed/ being underdeveloped, and later First World/Third World was emerging. In this sense, White has become the ideal of being the bearer of 'Western' civilisation. As such, no one can be fully White, but people yearn to be so. It is in this sense that Whiteness is itself a fantasy position and a field of accumulating Whiteness. It is by feeling qualified to yearn for such a position that people can become identified as White. At the same time, to be White does not mean to yearn to be European in a geographical sense.

To yearn to be White Australian is clearly to belong to a specifically Australian variant of the dominant North European tradition of domination over 'Third World-looking people' — the term which sums up best the way the dominant Whites classify those 'ethnics' with very low national capital and who are invariably constructed as a 'problem' of some sort within all White-dominated societies.

I refer to the field of governmental power in Australia as the field of Whiteness because such a White Australian persona, the cultural descendant of the North European tradition of domination, constitutes the ultimate ideal of the field: what all processes of cultural accumulation yearn to be, with more or less success, in order to dominate the field. Such a White ideal, like all capital, is not only something to be accumulated, but it is also an historical construct and an object of struggle over its content. What is not yet historically challenged, however, is precisely its most general characteristic as an off-shoot of the dominant persona of the White European coloniser type. Thus, there may be a struggle as to whether this ideal type has to remain male as it has always been, or whether it is more Protestant or Catholic, or whether it is specifically Australian or a variant of the British, but there can be no struggle in the foreseeable future that would try to challenge this European Whiteness with a Chinese or an Arab ideal of what an Australian is. Only Aboriginal people can offer a *morally* credible form of alternative governmental capital, but such a capital is also impossible to valorise in power terms.

To a certain extent, the choice of the term 'Whiteness' to refer to this field of accumulation and its ideal is arbitrary. It is better, however, than 'Britishness' and 'Europeanness', which leave out many of those who are eligible and who do accumulate governmental belonging in Australia today. Whiteness is also better than Europeanness for our purposes because certain Europeans, particularly dark-skinned Europeans, have to struggle to valorise their Europeanness in Australia. To say that nationalist practices are White nationalist practices is to say that they are necessarily enacted by those who claim some form of governmental belonging to Australia and that these people do so on the basis of claiming in some way to belong to such a field of Whiteness, to lay claim to being, in some shape or form, legitimate White Australians. Again, only Aboriginal people can make such claims outside the field of Whiteness.

Whiteness, then, as I am using it here, is an aspiration that one accumulates various capitals to try to be. Analytically speaking, it is not an essence. This, however, does not mean that some of those aiming for dominance within the national field do not themselves claim it as an essence. It is here that one can locate the major difference that structures the field of national governmental belonging.

In Chapter 1, in the analysis of the tearing off of the Muslim scarf, I referred to an 'interviewee A', the only person I have interviewed who has actually pulled down a Muslim woman's scarf. I can now reveal with greater analytical gains that she was, in fact, a Lebanese Christian Australian. Now, one can think of a 'reason' why a Lebanese Christian would want to act in this way against Muslims. Such a person could still be motivated by the effect of the Lebanese civil war and the animosity it has left behind. As we have argued in the previous chapter, however, there is a big difference between determining such reasons for acting and establishing what has empowered such a person to act. The fact that during the interview the Lebanese Christian woman invoked a definition of Australia as a 'Christian country' can allow us to analyse her action as proceeding from a belief that her own Christianity was convertible into more governmental Australianness than the Islam of the other Australian whose religion has no value whatsoever as far as governmental belonging is concerned. Her Christianity made her more White.

We can see, in the above example, how people can accumulate certain forms of Whiteness and in so doing claim more governmental belonging over less capital-endowed others. It is clear, however, that the claim for dominant belonging made by this Australian Lebanese woman is very contextually limited. It cannot go much further than the encounter with Muslims and a few others. Indeed, in the interview she claimed to be the victim of racism herself, but blamed it nevertheless on the Muslim Lebanese who 'have ruined our reputation in this country':

> Last year, I went for a job interview. Everything was going really well and we were telling each other jokes. Then, the director said to me, 'Lillianne, that's French, isn't it?' and I said, 'No, that's actually Lebanese.' If I tell you that the look

on his face changed immediately ... It's becoming impossible in this country ... When you say 'I am Lebanese' to a French person, they know that there are Lebanese and Lebanese. But here you'd think it's the lowest nationality on earth. You show someone your university degree from Boston and you say you're Lebanese and they immediately think that it's a forgery ... And who's fault is it? It's clearly not the Australians' fault. After all, their views have developed because of a certain experience ...

The above does not only give us some clues concerning this person's motivation in attacking the Muslim woman, but it also allows us a significant insight into the very nature of national capital. For in the very tearing off of the scarf, the woman has not only valorised her Christianity, but is also struggling for a valorisation of 'the Lebanese' within the Australian national field. This is because she clearly perceives that her Lebaneseness operates as a kind of negative capital in the field. She struggles to retrieve its value by using her Christianity and clearing 'bad' Lebanese from the field so that the quality 'Lebanese' can be recognised again in all it's goodness and value in the national field. This general usage of Christianity among some Lebanese migrants (and others) is most noticeable in the often too visible crosses worn by some. While there are many other reasons why such crosses are worn, it is clear that, for some, it is a deployment of Christianity aimed at offsetting other negatively valued traits in the field of national belonging. This is why such deployment is most noticeable among people who are perceived, and perceive themselves, as too 'Third Worldish' to be appreciated by the dominant culture.

The field of national power is, then, a field where people's position of power is related to the amount of national capital they accumulate. This dynamic of accumulation reaches its limitations, however, when it comes face to face with those whose richness in national capital does not come from a struggle to accumulate and 'be like' White Australians, but who appear 'naturally' White Australians. It is here that the 'democratic' logic of accumulation we have examined so far reaches its limits and faces what Bourdieu calls the 'aristocracy of the field'.

Aristocracies emerge because, just as the dominant aim to naturalise the value of their capital, so they also attempt to *naturalise their hold on it*. The holders of a national capital, such as, for example, Europeanness, not only struggle to make Europeanness a very valuable possession that would make those who 'have it' clearly Australian. They also struggle to appear naturally European so as to make 'being European' not a matter of acquisition, but something with which one is born. While the naturalisation of the dominant capital works to undermine the legitimacy of any other aspiring capital, the naturalisation of the privileged hold the dominant group has on the dominant capital aims at creating symbolic barriers to its accumulation by the less capital-endowed groups. Thus, the dominant always aim to naturalise the field itself by naturalising the positions of all those who are located in the field. It is in doing so that the dominant tend to construct themselves into an aristocracy vis-à-vis other subjects: into subjects whose rich possession and deployment of the dominant capital appears as an intrinsic natural disposition rather than something socially and historically acquired.[12]

The aristocratic logic ensures that, regardless of how much national capital one accumulates, *how* one accumulates it will make an important difference to its capacity to be converted into national recognition and legitimacy. No matter how much national capital a 'Third World-looking' migrant accumulates, the fact that he or she has acquired it, rather than being born with it, devalues what he or she possesses compared to the 'essence' possessed by the national aristocracy. The latter are those who, in Bourdieu's parlance, only have to be what they are as opposed to those who are what they do. They are nationals and behave nationally because they are born nationals, as opposed to the other groups who have to behave nationally to prove that they are nationals.[13]

It is those national aristocrats that assume that it is their very natural right to take up the position of governmentality within the nation and become the national managers they are 'destined' to be: subjects whose rich possession and deployment of the dominant national capital appears as an intrinsic natural disposition rather than as something socially and historically acquired.[14] Bourdieu's introduction to the concept of aristocracy in the context of his research on education is worth quoting at length:

> Whereas the holders of educationally uncertified cultural capital can always be required to prove themselves, because they are only what they do, merely a by-product of their own cultural production, the holders of titles of cultural nobility — like the titular members of an aristocracy, whose 'being', defined by their fidelity to a lineage, an estate, a race, a past, a fatherland or a tradition, is irreducible to any 'doing', to any know-how or function — only have to be what they are, because all their practices derive their value from their authors, being the affirmation and the perpetuation of the essence by virtue of which they are performed. Defined by the titles which predispose and legitimate them in being what they are, which make what they do the manifestation of an essence earlier and greater than its manifestations, as in the Platonic dream of a division of functions based on a hierarchy of beings, they are separated by a difference in kind from the commoners of culture, who are consigned to the doubly devalued status of auto-dictat and 'stand-in'.
>
> Aristocracies are essentialist. Regarding existence as an emanation of essence, they set no intrinsic value on the deeds and misdeeds enrolled in the records and registries of bureaucratic memory. They prize them only in so far as they clearly manifest, in the nuances of their manner, that their one inspiration is the perpetuating and celebrating of the essence by virtue of which they are accomplished. The same essentialism requires them to impose on themselves what their essence imposes on them — noblesse oblige — to ask themselves what no one else could ask, to 'live up' to their own essence.[15]

This is why the aristocratic tendency contradicts and limits the dynamic of accumulation that is constitutive of the national field. On the one hand, the fact that national capital can be accumulated operates like a 'democratic incentive' which provides aspiring nationals with the impetus to 'play the game'. It is the belief that capital is 'up for grabs' for whomever can grab it and accumulate it, that it will lead anyone who succeeds in accumulating it to gain more recognition and power (symbolic capital), which provides the national field with its dynamic. On the other hand, however, the aristocratic ideal aims at stunting this dynamic of accumulation and at entrenching a static order. It fosters the belief that no matter how much capital one acquires through active accumulation, the very fact of this acquired capital being an *accumulation* leads to its devaluing relative to those who posit themselves to have inherited it or to possess it innately without having to accumulate it.

The aristocratic logic ultimately aims to establish that only those who have the innate capacity to dominate can really be said to possess enough capital to dominate the field. It sets essences into the highest order of capital that one can possess. Paradoxically, however, it sets them as a capital that is not freely available on the market for accumulation.

In this interview with an Australian-born Lebanese girl, we have a clear example of how this aristocratic logic works to differentiate between national aristocrats and those who appear as non-natural Australians:

> No matter how much you try to fit in, they find a way to remind you that you're not really one of them. And it's always at a really bad time. It takes you by surprise … and … it's really painful. Like one night I was out with my school friends. I've known them forever you know. We've been together for ages … Well, anyway, we went to this dancing spot in George Street and we were all having a fantastic time … not a worry in the world. The waiter came and we were ordering drinks and it took me a while to order and, out of the blue, one of my friends said to him, 'She doesn't drink any alcohol, she's Lebanese.'
>
>   They all laughed thinking it was a great joke or something … I mean … It's silly, of course … They all knew I was Christian for a start … But what really irks you is that … here you are, having a good time, and suddenly you realise. You're having fun with your friends and you see in them just that, your friends, and suddenly you realise that they look at you and what they see is a Lebanese. Look, it's not that I am not proud to be Lebanese, it's just that sometimes it is used to make you feel on the outside. You know… well… that's how I felt anyway.

It is in the accumulation of such 'insignificant' moments that the national aristocracy distinguishes itself from other nationals in everyday life.

Deploying the category of national aristocracy can help refine, or at least make more systematic, the analysis of cultural dominance within the nation. What the above entails is that the national capital one needs to accumulate in order to maximise homely belonging to the nation is not the same as what one needs to accumulate in order to maximise governmental belonging. The identity traits and characteristics that need to be accumulated in order to feel at home in Australia are not enough to constitute their holders into a national aristocracy. To maximise one's governmental belonging, there are further specific elements that need to be accumulated; it is those elements that constitute what I have called Whiteness, and it is only by naturalising its hold on this Whiteness that a group can achieve aristocratic status. In so doing, a group succeeds in imposing its symbolic violence on the national field by naturalising its aspirations and ideals into national aspirations and ideals.

As governmental belonging emerges within the power to position others within the nation, national aristocracies also consolidate their power by naturalising their own topography of the nation: the positions that constitute the national field and the capital needed to occupy them. Aristocratic national groupings do not only struggle to impose on others specific national 'values' and a specific national identity. Intrinsic to their struggle is also an attempt to impose a specific *national order* in which they have the dominant position. It is through such a process that they manage to become the enactors/representatives/inhabitants of the national will analysed in chapter 1.

In a variation on the inclusion/exclusion understanding of national belonging, it is often claimed in certain critical analyses of nationalism stressing the biased nature of national types or national ideals that they are exclusionary. For example, a common critique of the traditional dominant post — World War II Australian national character is that it is sexist and racist, and that it excludes women and non-Whites.[16] In fact, such a critique conflates the exclusion from the ideal of the dominant with the exclusion from the dominant national ideal.

A national ideal does not only idealise the position of the dominant within the nation, but also a whole series of positions and the relations between them. It consists of a map of what for the dominant are idealised positions and idealised types occupying those positions. That is, the dominant in the national field do not only have an ideal of themselves in the field, but also an ideal of all the positions in it, that is, an ideal of the field itself which they struggle to impose. As Wacquant has pointed out:

> In the course of these struggles, the very shape and divisions of the field become a central stake, because to alter the distribution and relative weight of forms of capital is tantamount to modifying the structure of the field.[17]

This is why aristocracies aim to naturalise the positions that define the structure of the field in which their dominance is grounded. Consequently, part of the struggle within the national field is to actualise the groups' vision and division of the field. National subjects not only struggle to accumulate and position themselves in a dominant position within the field, but also to position others where they deem them to belong.[18] In so doing, they are also engaging in the already examined construction of their nation as 'homely', as a place 'where everything is where it is supposed to be'. It is ludicrous, for example, to say that the 1950s White Australian national ideal of mateship and muscular surfers was sexist because 'it excluded women from the nation'. It is certainly sexist because it excluded them from the idealised dominant position where subjects maximise their dominance over the nation, but this is not the same as excluding them from the nation. The dominant ideal of the nation, by being an ideal of a national field, consists not only of an ideal of the dominant male, but also, among many others, of the ideal female — as well as of the position of this female in relation to the dominant male. Indeed, the White Australian woman who felt comfortable in the position allotted to her, as a struggling mother in the bush or as a 'sheila on the beach' felt to belong fully, in the sense of being part of the nation, and was perceived to belong fully, to the nation, even if it was recognised that such a position gave her less *governmental* belonging than the dominant White Australian males.

Consequently, to constitute a national aristocracy, a group needs more than just a sense of dominant homely belonging to the nation by birth. It also needs to have a dominant and essentialised sense of governmental belonging, for it is precisely the maximisation of governmental belonging that constitutes the logical end of aristocratic domination in the field. In the struggle to naturalise their dominance over the nation, the national aristocracy has to do more than naturalise the dominance of their own 'national values' and their hold on those values; they have to naturalise their own national order and their dominance within this order. It is the establishing of this order that is behind the nationalist practices we have been examining so far. In achieving such a dominance, the national aristocracy aims to transform itself from an *interested* party in a struggle, with its own specific order to impose, to the natural *disinterested* protector and guardian of an equally natural national order. That is, it transforms itself from mere competitor in the field to the natural governor of the field: born to rule the nation. It is through this 'magical' artifice that it manages to pronounce itself as the will of the nation and the protector of its order.

The 'White Nation' Fantasy

We have now reached another stage in our analysis of nationalist practices. In the first chapter, we stressed the homely spatiality of these practices and the position of the dominant as a spatial manager. In this chapter, we have established the different processes through which such a spatial manager becomes entitled to take up such a managerial position and become the expression of a homely national order whose will it appears to be expressing. In the specific case of Australian nationalist practices, we have characterised this entitlement as a process of accumulating Whiteness. It is a process of establishing a White national order that reciprocally valorises the very Whiteness that operates as its principle of organisation, the White national will that is behind it and of which it is the expression.

Throughout this analysis, however, we have stressed that the position of Whiteness is more an aspiration for the White subject that yearns to occupy it. In fact, many aspects of nationalist practices operate as aspirations. In the previous chapter, I argued that the homely nation is itself an aspira-

tion that guides the national subject's practices. Indeed, if
nationalist practices were not motivated by such an aspiration, if the nation was totally homely and there was no need
for it to become more homely, there would be no need for
nationalist practices in the first place. There would be no
need for a nationalist! In this sense, one can say that White
nationalist practices provide a kind of framework to allow the
very existence of the White nationalist. It is because of features such as these that the nature of the whole national construct assumed by nationalist practices has the consistency of
a fantasy in the psychoanalytic sense of the term.

In the previous chapter, I stressed that nationalist practices
are necessarily moved by an ideal imaginary nation.
Statements such as 'Wogs go home' are implicitly those of
the sort 'I like my nation without migrants': they are discourses which reveal images of an ideal, to-be-achieved
nation or, more exactly, an ideal, to-be-achieved national
order. Such an ideal national order can already be defined as
a 'fantasy'. Here fantasy would be used in the commonsense
understanding of the term: something one yearns for, but
which is considered somewhat unrealistic to achieve. In this
sense, we may want to call this national ideal a fantasy in that
it is far-fetched to expect that one's nation can be exactly like
one dreams of it being. In what follows, however, I will be
using fantasy in a different sense, one borrowed largely, but
not exclusively, from psychoanalysis. This conception does
not negate, but rather incorporates the above meaning of
fantasy.

Let us examine more closely the White nationalist practices
of exclusion on which we have centred our analysis so far. The
imaginary nation is by no means the only ideal that moves
and shapes these practices. In fact, we can say that nationalist
practices are largely constituted by a series of ideals and
yearnings (of 'as ifs') which mark the difference between
what is and what the nationalist believes ought to be.

To begin with, White nationalists operate 'as if' they are
securely the masters of national space. As we have seen, however, Whiteness is itself an ideal that the nationalists have
constantly to struggle to achieve. If some nationalists achieve
recognition as essentially White, this is only because they
have succeeded in dominating the national field. Their dom-

ination operates as a mode of symbolic violence whereby the very idea of questioning the naturalness of their Whiteness is censored from the field. That is, it is as an effect of an ongoing process of struggle to dominate that these nationalists appear 'as if' they are essentially White. As such, they are destined to go on struggling to maintain such symbolic violence for the fear of losing such a dominant position is inherent. This position of dominance is even more tenuous in the case of those who engage in acts of racist/nationalist violence.

I have argued, for example, that the hand that moves to pull down a scarf is the hand of a subject who feels empowered to make his or her desired nation come true. At the same time, however — and here is the paradox that makes the whole construct a *fantasy* of dominance — the deployment of such a personal violence by the person tearing off the scarf must emanate from a position of disempowerment.

As is well known, nation-states are built around nationals disinvesting themselves of the capacity to deploy personal violence and investing this capacity in the state.[19] Nationals with a high degree of governmental belonging don't need to deploy personal violence for national purposes. They are secure in the knowledge that the state is acting out their violence for them. In this sense, those who engage in such personal violent acts feel that they have lost this special relation to state power. They feel that the state is no longer doing their violence for them. They feel that their governmental national belonging is threatened or in decline. Nevertheless, they think they have a legitimate claim to represent the national will embodied in the state.

This is why they feel that they should take matters back into their 'own hands', as it were. The hand that tears off the scarf is a literal example of this. This is why such nationalist practices appear to emanate from both empowered and disempowered people at the same time. The violent nationalist act is not merely the act of any disempowered person, but also the movement of someone who in addition feels they *ought* to be more empowered. It is in this sense that this type of nationalist practice operates as a fantasy of empowerment.

Furthermore, we have argued that the nationalist treats the other as an object. Yet, if the other was already such a malleable object, why is there such a need to act on 'it'. Clearly, the nationalist practice of exclusion is guided by the desire to make an other that is not quite an object into an object. That is, part of the work of the nationalist practice is to construct the other into as much of an object as possible. It is precisely that other which exhibits too much will, independently of the will of the ruling nationalist, who becomes in danger of being excluded and removed from national space, for it is the existence and rule of the dominant nationalists' will and only this will which makes the nation homely for them. What were the Muslim Arabs in Australia during the Gulf War? Primarily the agents of a will foreign to the nation: an Iraqi will or a Muslim will — a will which was imagined to be unwilling to submit to the national will represented and enacted by the nationalist.

We can see that, everywhere we turn, what we are faced with is not an actual, essentially White, governmental nationalist, ruling over an already established national order where others are securely considered as objects. Instead, all of these are *yearnings* that nationalists try to bring about in the very process of engaging in the nationalist practice. Most of all, however, it is a yearning to reconstitute themselves as true to the fantasy of the all-powerful nationalist in the homely nation and so on. Looking at it this way, nationalist practices embody a fantasy of the self as a fulfilled nationalist, more so than a fantasy of the nation, for in this yearning nationalists establish their very *raison d'être*.

In psychoanalysis, particularly Lacanian psychoanalysis, fantasy does not only refer to an imagined 'land of the good life' pursued as a goal by the subject. Fantasy also includes an ideal image of the self as a 'meaningful' subject. That is, fantasy gives meaning and purpose to the subject's life, and the meaning and purpose which makes life worth living is itself part of the fantasy. People don't *have* fantasies. They *inhabit* fantasy spaces of which they are a part. We can see that this is precisely how the nationalist appears to be located within nationalist practices.

'I want my nation to be homely' is part of a fantasy which includes an imaginary ideal, a to-be-achieved homely nation (as it is imagined by the subject yearning for it). This fantasy also includes, however, the implicit belief: 'I am a nationalist capable of pursuing the task of building a homely nation.'

This belief in the self as a nationalist, as a subject who considers that life is meaningful — since he or she believes he or she has a purpose for living it (building the idealised nation) — is just as much a part of the fantasy construct as the ideal nation itself. It is in this sense that fantasy is not outside the subject, but is the very world the subject inhabits. A national fantasy is the very way nationalists inhabit, experience and conceive of their nation and themselves as nationalists. The nationalist in this construct is always a nation-builder, a person whose national life has a meaning derived from the task of having to build his or her ideal homely nation, a national domesticator. This is why the most vocal nationalists are often people who feel unfulfilled in other fields of social life. Nationalism becomes the means of giving one's life a purpose, a sense of possibility (usually the possibility of social, economic or political status mobility), when no other areas of social life provide it with this purpose.

In *Suicide*, Durkheim argues that:

> All man's pleasure in acting, moving and exerting himself implies the sense that his efforts are not in vain and that by walking he advances. However, one does not advance when one proceeds toward no goal, or — which is the same thing — when the goal is in infinity. Since the distance between us and it is always the same, it is just as if we have not moved. Even our feeling of pride looking back at the distance covered can only give a deceptive satisfaction, since the remaining distance is not proportionately reduced. To pursue a goal which is by definition unattainable is to condemn oneself to a state of perpetual unhappiness.[20]

While Durkheim's argument is clearly a valid one at the level of consciousness, Lacan makes another one which, although it appears opposite, merely operates at a different level of reality: If a man reaches his goal than he will become goalless and loses his *raison d'être*, or, as a Chinese proverb has it, if a man finishes building his house, he dies. The very fact that the nation is a yearning is what makes the nationalist exist as a meaningful person. At the same time, however, Durkheim's point remains valid in that such a yearning has to be perceived to be grounded in existing possibilities, otherwise it cannot constitute something worthwhile pursuing.

Such a conception of the imaginary nation as fantasy has been most consistently developed in Zizek's important work on the rise of ethnic and national chauvinism in Eastern Europe.[21] Zizek's analysis attempts to make sense of the affective relationship between the ethnic/nationalist chauvinists and their national home — what Zizek refers to as the 'Nation-Thing'. The Nation is a Thing, in Lacanian terms, because it is 'something more' than the 'features composing a "specific way of life"'.[22] This 'more' of the national home constitutes itself as 'what gives plenitude and vivacity to our life', which is the Lacanian definition of a Thing.[23] Consequently, Zizek argues, 'what is ... at stake in ethnic tensions is always the possession of the national Thing'.[24] Nationalists are constantly worried that the other is going to steal their Thing (their fulfilling nation) away from them. It is by taking this argument to its logical end and imputing on the national home the ontological consistency of the Thing as posited by Lacan/Zizek that a radical change in the conception of both the national home and the other within it is introduced.

For Lacan, the Thing has the status of the object-cause of desire. It is that which is desired — an object of desire, the goal — and, at the same time, that which causes desire — i.e. causes the subject to exist as a desiring subject. If I do not posit a desired nation, I cannot exist as a nationalist. This is so because desire emerges in the subjects' attempt at overcoming what psychoanalysis postulates as a constitutive lack that can never be overcome. The subjects come to exist as desiring by relating to a Thing constructed as that which will satisfy their desire. On the one hand, the Thing cannot be fully satisfying since its attainment cannot overcome the original lack. On the other, for the subject to continue to exist, it has to continue trying to attain the Thing as if it were attainable. Thus, the Thing, for it to be a Thing, has both to cause the subject to try to attain it and yet it has to be unattainable.[25] It is in that sense that the Thing stages *a fantasy space*, since 'in Lacanian theory, fantasy designates the subject's impossible relation to *a*, the object-cause of its desire'.[26] As Zizek explains:

> What the fantasy stages is not a scene in which our desire is fulfilled, fully satisfied, but on the contrary, a scene that realizes, stages, the desire as such. The fundamental point of psychoanalysis is that desire is not something given in

advance, but something that has to be constructed — and it is precisely the role of fantasy to give the coordinates of the subject's desire, to specify its object, to locate the position the subject assumes in it. It is only through fantasy that the subject is constituted as desiring.[27]

It is from such a perspective that the nation can be understood as an object-cause of desire, as the staging of the fantasy space the nationalists are after in their practices of pursuing/constructing the ultimate homely 'space of fullness' into which they can melt.

This linking of the nationalists' struggle to control their social environment to their very struggle to 'be' — to have a fulfilled life — points to the *affective dimension of nationalism*. It seems to me that this dimension has been far too often neglected by analysts and that theories of nationalism that do not take on board psychoanalytic theory will always be less than complete. This is all the more so since nationalist practices distinguish themselves in the political field by the high degree of affectivity loaded onto them. As we shall see, for example, one cannot possibly hope to understand the nationalist politics of Hansonism by abstracting from the fact that it constitutes, at its very core, a mode of affective politics.

To begin with, the ideal domesticated 'home' of the nationalists — whether it is their nation, their neighbourhood, their street or, as is often the case, all of these combined — in so far as it is their Thing, is not something that has the status of a 'concrete' existence or even something that can ever actually exist. That is, just like any Thing, the imagined national home is a fantasy space in which the nationalists' very being as desiring subjects is staged. It is something nationalists believe in and feverishly pursue as a goal, while at the same time being unattainable since, in attaining that goal, the nationalist subjects would simply cease to exist as homely/national subjects, as domesticators. This explains why nationalists never believe their goal of a 'national home' ever to be achieved. There is always something or someone standing in the way requiring further action by the nationalists in the pursuit of their goal.

Finally, there is a need to recognise that such a perspective adds a very important dimension to our analysis of the nationalists' conception of the other within the ever pursued/never attained homely national space. While we, as social analysts, may recognise that this fully domesticated national home is a fantasy space, unattainable by its very nature, nationalists never perceive it as such. It is precisely the belief that this homely domesticated space *can* be achieved that drives them to pursue it. If this was the case, however, how do nationalists reconcile the belief in the possibility of this homely domesticated space which 'keeps them going' with the practical fact that they never reach their goal (which subconsciously they don't want to reach as it would mean their 'death')?

It is in this context that an important function of the 'other' emerges. If this fantasy space is to be perceived as possible, it requires something to explain its failure to come about. Here lies the crucial function of otherness within the spatial imaginary constructed by the nationalist's fantasy. Rather than disturbing a domesticated space which does not and cannot actually exist, the other is what allows nationalists to believe in the possibility of such a space eventuating. It helps them avoid having to face the impossible nature of what they are pursuing, the traumatic kernel of the *real*, by constructing the other as that which stands in the way of its attainment. It is in this sense that the other is *necessary* for the construction and maintenance of the fantasy.

This crucial dimension of national otherness, well developed by Zizek, remains unrecognised in the sociological analysis which takes literally the nationalists' belief that the other is someone that disturbs their homely space. These sociological analyses, often accompanied by pleas of tolerance and understanding, or by policy recommendations to manage the 'effects of difference', can reproduce the nationalists' own belief in the perturbing function of the otherness they are inviting the nationalists to tolerate — i.e. the belief that there was an initial homely space that could be perturbed in the first place. As Zizek put it:

> What we conceal by imputing to the other the theft of enjoyment is the traumatic fact that we never possessed what was allegedly stolen from us; the lack ("castration") is originary, enjoyment constitutes itself as "stolen," or, to quote Hegel's precise formulation from his Science of Logic, it "only comes to be by being left behind".[28]

In summary, the conception of nationalism as a fantasy of homely domesticated spaces has some important descriptive and analytical advantages. First, it helps us understand that the world of nationalist practices, while grounded in existing practical reality, is not a world where this reality is represented 'as it is', but rather as it should be for the nationalist. In it, the nationalist fantasises not only about how the nation should be, but also about how his or her own position in the nation ought to be. Secondly, by linking nationalist practices to the very yearning to 'be', it contains within it an explanation of the affective nature of the nationalists' relationship to their fantasy and to otherness within it. It helps us understand why nationalists get 'so heated up'. Finally, such a conception of fantasy incorporates within it the dynamic principle behind nationalist practices: rather than just telling us how nationalists conceive their other (essentialising etc.), it *also* tells us why they are always pursuing/aiming to control and objectify their other.

Conclusion

Having relied on the work of Zizek in the preceding section, I will conclude in a 'Zizekian' way by using a popular Hollywood film to summarise the nature of the argument I have developed so far. In *Falling down*, Michael Douglas plays the role of a man whose world is disintegrating. His primary experience of disintegration is the breakdown of his family. As the film follows his desperate attempt at 'rebuilding his family', however, we can see that to him the experience of breakdown extends also to the breakdown of the 'neighbourhood', the breakdown of the nation and the American way of life.

The film begins with Douglas's character, D-Fens, in a car, stuck in a traffic jam, when a fly enters the vehicle. D-Fens 'snaps' as he unsuccessfully attempts to get rid of the fly. This provides a powerful metaphor of what follows: D-Fens's attempt at regaining control of his 'home space'.

Throughout the movie, the main character moves within and across overlapping spaces — his car space, his family space, his neighbourhood space, his national space — as he encounters one fly after another: feminists, fascists, bureaucratic mentalities, as well as a variety of racial and ethnic others, all appear as uncontrollable flies in the 'hero's' space of being, his *home*, as he attempts to regain control of this space so that he can travel again 'on the freeway of life'. 'Where are you going?' he is asked, at one stage of the movie. 'I am going home,' he replies.

It is within this process that, when he enters an ethnic neighbourhood, he exhibits his 'racism'. This racism is not primarily about essentialising the other or believing them to be inferior. It is primarily about considering them as 'racial/ethnic flies': as an other modality of life that either constitutes an intrusion into D-Fen's space of being or that has transgressed on the locality allotted to it within that space so as to disturb its familiarity or, more fundamentally, its ability to provide the D-Fens with a sense of satisfaction.

We have in this film a good illustration of the mechanics of the nationalist practices of exclusion and the mode of categorisation that goes with it, as I have described them above. The 'racist' categorisation of otherness occurs within a practice of domesticating the social environment in pursuit of a homely space. The film, however, points to yet another dimension of this pursuit. Because of the emotionally charged portrayal of the 'hero', the film reminds us that the space of the home that the nationalist is trying to recover by chasing the 'fly' is not just a functional space, but also an affective one, a space where he is staging the very meaning of his life.

As I began by arguing in chapter one, where we started the analysis of these nationalist practices of exclusion, there is more than an analytical issue at stake in the understanding of these practices as primarily nationalist rather than racist. There is also a political dimension to which, in conclusion, I would like to return. The classification of these practices as 'racist' has often helped to construct them as if they belonged to a minority mode of thinking totally alien from that held by the majority. A clear example of this can be found in the NIRVA report we analysed in the previous chapter.

The inquiry into 'racist violence' on which that report was based was held following what is referred to as 'an apparent increase in the incidence of racially motivated violence in Australia'.[29] The report rigorously details hundreds of cases of 'racist violence' selected from submissions made to it during its three months sitting. Yet in the preface we find:

> The evidence presented to the Inquiry indicates that multiculturalism is working well in Australia. In spite of our racial, ethnic and cultural diversity, our society's experience of racist violence, intimidation and harassment is nowhere near the level experienced in many other countries.[30]

The point here is not to claim that multiculturalism is not working well. Indeed, in so far as it means an interaction between people from different cultures benefiting all parties involved, there is plenty of empirical evidence that it is. What is interesting in this introductory paragraph is how the very claim of a multiculturalism working well becomes dependent on the creation of an ontological gap between it and 'racist violence'. Multiculturalism is working well and belongs to one (mainstream) reality, and racist violence is occurring in another (marginal) reality. Multiculturalism is in one valley and racist violence another, as the Lebanese metaphorically put it. And the two are not supposed to be related in any way.

It is this kind of differentiation which helps to demonise one group as 'racist', while constructing another as angelically 'multicultural' that I want to deconstruct. Showing that violent practices such as ripping a scarf off a Muslim woman's head is better conceived as 'nationalist' than 'racist' is the first step towards this deconstruction, for it opens the way to enable us to perceive the fundamental similarities between such evil nationalists and their good 'tolerant' national counterparts.

chapter **3**

Good White Nationalists: The Tolerant Society as a White Fantasy

Waves of discrimination and harassment against sections of Australia's population, such as the ones examined in chapter 1, are a regular occurrence in Australian society. Since the anti-Arab wave of nationalist violence of the early 1990s, there has been a number of waves of anti-Asian violence, most recently following the election of the Liberal government and the re-emergence of extreme-right forms of nationalist politics. Subjection to this nationalist violence, fed by racist modes of classification, is a constant feature of Aboriginal daily lives. Yet, and despite this, there is constant characterisation of these practices as an oddity in the Australian landscape.

As I have argued, the characterisation of these practices as 'racist violence' has played an active role in encouraging a perception of them as marginal, and unrelated to, the mainstream of Australian culture. This mainstream culture, on the other hand, is depicted as the very example of the liberal 'tolerant' society.

Indeed, it is often by reissuing calls for 'tolerance' that politicians think it best to counter this 'racist violence'. This in turn helps further to construct 'tolerance' and mainstream culture as if constituting a radical polarity with the 'racism' they are supposed to combat.

At a time when the nationalist persecution of Arab Australians was at its most intense during the Gulf War, and after several months of silence, this is what the Australian Prime Minister of the time, Bob Hawke, had to say following the visit of an Arab-Australian delegation appealing for his intervention: 'I appeal to all my fellow Australians to be understanding, to be charitable and to appreciate that these are loyal Australians entitled to differences of view, but they must be protected.'[1] This statement is a quintessential example of the 'anti-racism' deployed routinely by the Australian State and which has its basis in the widespread belief that what one needs to do in the face of racism is to reassert the fact that Australian society is built on 'tolerance'. Thus, an ideal-type newspaper headline reads: 'Claims of racism in Australia are exaggerated, even hysterical, and overlook an abundance of tolerance.'[2]

One can open the paper and read that a number of school kids 'attacked Ms. Rafida Ali, [while] still wearing their school clothes'. Furthermore, 'the victim was threatened with a gun, subjected to the most degrading abuse, and physically attacked.'[3] And while the reporter asks: 'Why did they do it? With what wickedness are they possessed that they are able to set upon a defenceless woman with such absence of conscience, with such callousness?', we can read another reporter telling us about a school where '35 per cent of the students are from non-English–speaking backgrounds and [the school] is fine tuning a program called "Talking tolerance to teenagers" ...'[4] There is abundant empirical evidence of the dominance of this discourse of tolerance and its variants, both in the interviews conducted as part of this research and in the many public political statements made available by the media.

In this chapter, I want to examine more closely what it means *to practise* tolerance. I will develop the argument that these practices, like those dubbed 'racist violence', are nationalist practices. I will further argue that, although they are perceived as morally 'good' practices, they are structurally similar to the 'evil' nationalist practices of exclusion that they are supposedly negating. Those who execute them, 'good' as they are, share and inhabit along with White 'evil' nationalists the same imaginary position of power within a nation imagined as 'theirs'. In fact, they enact the same White nation fantasy analysed in the previous chapter.

The Paradoxical History of Tolerance

Tolerance is hardly, of course, a theme specific to Australia. It is a dominant liberal value throughout the world and is becoming even more pervasive. As forms of fundamentalism, ethnic particularism and intercommunal conflict appear to be increasing, notions such as the 'tolerant society' and variants such as 'cultural pluralism' become particularly attractive. They are used both as descriptive categories of societies that maintain a semblance of social cohesion despite being 'ethnically' and 'racially' diverse and as prescriptive categories for the many, not so lucky, conflict ridden post-colonial formations. Thus, in a paper presented at the 1992 British Sociological Association conference, the Ukrainian sociologist Tanya Koshechnika argued:

> There are several reasons for the importance of studying and promoting political tolerance in post-Soviet republics. One of them is the deepening of the inter-ethnic conflicts; the increasing national and religious prejudice creates a situation in which tolerance could be seen, if not as a solution, at least as a possibility to alleviate the communication between the ex-Soviet republics and different ethnic groups.[5]

Despite its current dominance in the West, the theme of tolerance makes its initial appearance as a political/practical state policy in the Muslim empires that followed the Islamic expansionary wars. It is only much later that it makes an emergence in the Europe of the Enlightenment. In both cases, however, tolerance or toleration emerged as a state policy with an anti-discriminatory intent, aimed at regulating relations between various religious communities.

Given the religious foundations of the Islamic state, the policy of tolerance was a result of an automatic translation of the Islamic *Shari'a* law towards religious minorities. Under the *Shari'a*, Christians and Jews, being 'people of the book', were to be tolerated. They were the *dhumma* or those to be protected, albeit for an extra tax which no doubt provided the rulers with another incentive for their toleration.

In Christian Europe, laws advocating tolerance such as the English *Toleration Act* of 1689 appeared after centuries of religious intolerance epitomised by the Inquisitions. There, the calls for tolerance came both from inside and outside the Church. While some commentators argued for tolerance by appealing to 'reason' (e.g. Bayle 1786), the more influential, such as Locke in his *A Letter Concerning Toleration* (1689) and, later, Voltaire in *Traité sur la Tolerance* (1763), base most of their argument on a return to Christian religious texts.

What is striking about the early periods of state-advocated tolerance is how often they remain, very much like today, marked by *intolerance*. In England, the *Toleration Act* introduced in 1689, while easing some of the penalties imposed on dissenting clergy by the 'Clarendon Code' of the 1660s,[6] coexisted with a whole series of discriminatory practices against Nonconformists who continued to be shut out of public offices, both civil and military.[7] At the same time, discrimination against Roman Catholics remained in full force, including restrictions on their freedom of movement.[8] Some of these restrictions remained till much later, even after the *Roman Catholic Emancipation Act* was introduced in the early nineteenth century (1829). The latter contained 'provisions against Catholics exercising certain rights of patronage, enjoying named offices, and even a clause — never carried into effect — for the suppression of religious orders of men.'[9]

This coexistence of tolerance and intolerance is well exemplified by the politics of tolerance under Islamic law. Under Muslim rule, the *dhumma* status of Christians and Jews legitimised a whole range of discriminatory measures aimed at establishing the superiority of Islam and its protection. The 'tolerated ones' were to wear special clothing; they were forbidden to ride horses or to carry guns; they could not build new churches or synagogues, or practise their religion publicly in front of Muslims. These laws aimed at the marginalisation of the non-Islamic communities, although not always strictly implemented, meant that the latter had to suffer in certain circumstances from what Maxime Rodinson describes as 'outbreaks of intolerance on the part of the Muslim mob.'[10] The same kind of 'outbreaks of intolerance' have also been a permanent feature of Australia's multicultural society.

Australian Tolerance and Multiculturalism

The dominant discourse of tolerance in Australia for the past twenty years has been the one associated with the state-sponsored multiculturalism that emerged in the early 1970s.[11] The equation of multiculturalism with tolerance is widespread throughout the political spectrum in Australia. For the liberal historian Robert Hughes, 'multiculturalism means tolerance'.[12] For more conservative commentators such as John Hirst:

> I am ambivalent about the multicultural terminology. I used to oppose it, then I decided that since many Australians had interpreted multiculturalism to mean simply tolerance, there was a case for accepting it.[13]

Since its emergence, multiculturalism has been portrayed as marking a radical break with a previously racist Australian past characterised by the promotion of the White Australia policy, which barred non-Whites from entering the country, and by the more recent policies of assimilation and integration.

There is a well-known history that multiculturalism holds about its own historical emergence that is well worth recounting as it shows how the state-upholders of the policy go about distinguishing it from its predecessors. According to this history, the policy of assimilation, embraced by successive Australian governments from the end of World War II until the late 1960s, was an extension of the White Australia policy in its dealings with the wave of post-colonial (non-English–speaking background)[14] migration that arrived in Australia to meet the country's post-war reconstruction needs.[15] Assimilationist Australia could not tolerate cultural differences and promoted instead the primacy of its Anglo-Celtic heritage. It explicitly required non-British migrants to adopt the language, the culture and the values that are part of this heritage and to relinquish the distinct cultural practices and attitudes of their home countries.

The policy of integration, which followed that of assimilation, is seen as characterising a transitional period. It was briefly pursued by Billy Snedden, the then Liberal Minister for Immigration in the late 1960s and entailed a recognition that recently arrived migrants could not possibly assimilate in the way it was previously assumed. Migrants would be allowed to maintain their cultural identity for some time after their arrival and, although eventually they would become integrated in mainstream Anglo culture, transitional, culturally specific services would be necessary to ensure that this integration, along with the complete 'Australianisation' of the second generation, was a smooth process.

If, in its recognition of the existence of needs specific to the migrant population, integration foreshadowed multiculturalism, its upholding of the ultimate primacy of Anglo culture showed it still to be a product of an assimilationist mentality. It was the emergence of multiculturalism in the midpseventies, or so the story goes, that ushered in the truly pluralist 'cultural egalitarian' era where migrants were not only allowed, but were also positively encouraged to keep the cultural traditions of their home country alive. Australia was a nation where various cultural groups coexisted in one big 'family', as the first state ideologue of multiculturalism, the then Labor Minister for Immigration Al Grassby, put it. Australians were from different cultural backgrounds and no culture or cultural group could claim to be 'better' than the others. As an ideology, multiculturalism, everyone was told, was both the description of a reality (the existence of cultural diversity in Australia was a fact) and an attitude that needed to be promoted (Australians should accept this diversity and see it as something positive). Australia had moved from being an intolerant to being a tolerant society. In *The Tyranny of Prejudice*, Al Grassby, seen by many as the father of the policy, recalls how he aimed, when he was Minister, to 'turn the classrooms of the nation into crucibles of tolerance.'[16]

Despite its fairy tale-like progression and 'happy ending', this (hi)story does account for an important aspect of the social reality reflected and promoted by multiculturalism. Even though it cannot operate with a 'soft' notion of culture which excludes, for instance, political and legal traditions, multiculturalism has opened up a space which permits the articulation of diverse cultural forms, as well as facilitating the interaction between them. At the level of social policy, the services provided to migrants have increased in quantity and quality. Furthermore, a redistribution of state resources in favour of migrant non-White Australians allows the latter to create various structures that help them in their continuing struggle for equality within Australian capitalism. Undoubtedly, as far as these non-White Australians are concerned, multicultural tolerant Australia is a better place to be than its historical predecessors.

As in all tolerant societies before it, however, multiculturalism has remained marked by continuing intolerance, prejudice and racism. As Jock Collins has argued in a comparison of Australian and Canadian multiculturalism revealing similar problems with the latter: 'The Australian and Canadian experience suggests that prejudice co-exists with tolerance, as does racism with social harmony and multiculturalism with ethnic inequality.' [17]

While petty prejudices and racism coexist continually in everyday life with non-prejudiced forms of interaction, sometimes these petty prejudices become reflected at the level of the multicultural state itself, or take on a generalised mass character. Thus, the 1970s saw incidents such as police raids on the houses of hundreds of Greek migrant workers, aiming to uncover a mythical Greek social security conspiracy constructed out of stereotypes of the migrant proneness to dishonesty.[18] The early 1980s saw a particularly powerful resurgence of exclusionary nationalism similar to that examined in the previous chapter in relation to the Gulf War, but which both preceded that conflict and continued well after it. As with all tolerant societies, the transition from tolerance to intolerance can be quick and does not require any shake-up of Australian institutions. It simply happens as if it were a normal occurrence within a tolerant society and despite the efforts of the advocates of tolerance to portray intolerance as an exceptional state of affairs. Thus, in the outbreak of exclusionary nationalism following the election of the Liberal Party to government in 1996 and the emergence of Hansonite ultra-right nationalist politics, a letter to the editor states:

> ... Due solely to the Hanson–Howard nexus in the course of a few months, Australians have descended from the prospect of becoming the tolerant, fair-minded nation we had deluded ourselves we already were, to once more being the insular, suspicious and negative people of the 1950s.[19]

How are we to understand this coexistence of tolerance and intolerance, and the easy shift from the dominance of one to the dominance of the other, whether in the early Islamic period or in today's multicultural societies such as Australia? Attempting such an understanding requires us to move away from an examination of tolerance as a principle preached by politicians, priests and intellectuals, and to examine it in its sociological dimensions from the perspective of those who practise it.

Tolerance and Power

In his work *Toleration*, Preston King gives us an elaborate examination of the many vicissitudes of the term. He begins his analysis by pointing out that:

> There is something intolerable about the concept of 'tolerance'. For if one concedes or promotes a power to tolerate, one equally concedes a power not to tolerate ... Where we empower an agent to be tolerant, we empower him equally to be intolerant.[20]

King is pointing to something that all the preachers of tolerance find it useful to forget: when those who are intolerant are asked to be tolerant, their power to be intolerant is not taken away from them. It is, in fact, reasserted by the very request not to exercise it. This is something a number of other thinkers who have critically reflected on the term well understood, from Mirabeau to Lyotard. Mirabeau once declared:

> Je ne viens pas prêcher la tolérance; ... le mot tolérance ... me paraît, en quelque sorte, tyrannique lui-même, puisque l'autorité qui tolère pourrait ne pas tolérer.[21]

Lyotard, in *Heidegger and 'the Jews'*, argues that:

> Today, hatred comes softly as integration of 'the Jews' into a permissive collectivity in the name of the 'respect for differences'... The modern version of the church can lend itself to this show of tolerance. One has to keep in mind that ... tollere and aufheben connote, at the same time, the suppression as well as the elevation of what one tolerates.[22]

It is this 'power to suppress' dimension that has been continuously mystified by liberal writing on tolerance, beginning with Locke's and Voltaire's classical texts. In the latter, the mystification occurs as a result of an emphasis on an abstract–philosophical relationship between 'religions' rather than on actual practical relations between people belonging to religious groupings. It is from such a perspective that Voltaire can make pronouncements on 'universal tolerance', implying a kind of 'communism of tolerance' whereby the capacity and the power to tolerate is equally distributed among all those doing the tolerating.[23] Likewise, Locke is capable of beginning his *A Letter Concerning Toleration* by advocating the concept of 'mutual tolerance', presupposing a rather absurd relation between 'tolerators' without any 'tolerated'.[24] In the absence of a sociological perspective which grounds the possibility of tolerance in the existing social relations of power, this possibility is idealistically located in the prescribed adoption of a rational–ethical ('truly' religious) attitude.

Yet, the sociological dimension of the relationships of power in which the discourse of tolerance is grounded manages to escape out of the many fissures of the moral/prescriptive writings of both Locke and Voltaire. This happens, for example, when Voltaire slips into a more sociological language to talk explicitly of 'the dominant religion'.[25] More implicitly, when Locke urges toleration since 'it is only light and evidence that can work a change in men's opinions; and that light can in no manner proceed from corporal sufferings, or any other outward penalties', he reveals that those he is urging to be tolerant are necessarily those who have the power to inflict on others penalties and corporal sufferings — a power that the advocacy of tolerance does not wish to challenge.[26]

From this perspective, we can now understand that the coexistence of tolerance and intolerance in 'tolerant' societies was not due to the fact that tolerance was somehow not forcefully implemented. Rather, it is that those who were and are asked to be tolerant remain *capable* of being intolerant or, to put it differently, that the advocacy of tolerance left people *empowered* to be intolerant. When they wished and felt capable of exercising their power to be intolerant, people did, since the advocacy of tolerance never really challenged their *capacity* to exercise this power. Indeed, it merely reproduced and reasserted their belief in their capacity for intolerance. Those addressed, or to use a technically more correct word, those interpellated, by the discourse of tolerance see in the very address a confirmation of their power to be intolerant. In fact, they would not be interpellated by this discourse if they did not recognise that they are already in a position of power which allows them to be intolerant.

Multicultural tolerance, like all tolerance, is not, then, a good policy that happens to be limited in its scope. It is a strategy aimed at reproducing and disguising relationships of power in society, or being reproduced through that disguise. It is a form of symbolic violence in which a mode of domination is presented as a form of egalitarianism.[27] More formally, it is very close to what Bourdieu termed 'strategies of condescension'. These are the strategies:

> … by which agents occupying a higher position in one of the hierarchies of objective space symbolically deny the social distance which does not thereby cease to exist, thus ensuring they gain the profits of recognition accorded to a purely symbolic negation of distance ('he's unaffected', 'he's not stand-offish', etc.) which implies the recognition of a distance (the sentences I have quoted always have an implicit rider: 'he's unaffected for a duke', 'he's not stand-offish, for a university professor', etc.). In short, one can use the objective distances so as to have the advantages of proximity and the advantages of distance, that is, the distance and the recognition of distance that is ensured by the symbolic negation of distance.[28]

In much the same way, as I have argued above, to say of someone that he or she is tolerant always implies a 'rider' ('He/she is tolerant for someone who has the power not to be.'). Likewise, it gives the tolerator the advantages of proximity not given to the overt intolerant and the advantage of distance residing in the very power to be (in)tolerant.

Indeed, it seems that the ones who are concerned by the call to tolerate can only be the *same people* who feel entitled to engage in intolerance: those we have analysed as belonging to the White dominant culture. When the request

'Tolerate!' is made, only those who recognise in themselves the capacity not to tolerate are likely to raise their heads. Why would anyone bother asking someone who has no power to be intolerant to be tolerant? And why would those who are not in a position of power feel that the call for tolerance is of any concern to them? Indeed, while many people issue calls for tolerance in Australia, those who actually make direct statements concerning how tolerant they are are always and inevitably White Australians. The very idea that a newly arrived migrant is tolerant of White Australians is clearly ridiculous. One newspaper correspondent put it quite explicitly:

> Diversity is welcome; my concern is the means our society is developing to protect it.
>   Like many white middle class males, I was reared on Gladstonian liberalism ... at its best, a belief in the individual and mutual tolerance.[29]

All statements in the range of 'I don't mind if more migrants come to this country' or 'I don't mind if people speak Arabic in the streets' are emitted by people who *fantasise* that it is up to them whether people speak Arabic on the streets or not, whether more migrants come or not, and that such happenings are dependent on their capacity for tolerance. Such people are claiming a dominant form of governmental belonging and are inevitably White Australians in the sense we have described in the previous chapter. Those in a dominated position do not tolerate, they just endure.[30]

Tolerance, National Space and Power

What does one do when one tolerates? Asking this question already highlights an understanding of tolerance as an active practice emanating from a position of power as it puts it in opposition to its common theorisation as an 'attitude'. In the latter form, it is perceived as a passive suspension of action — to 'refrain in engaging in an act' of intolerance — rather than an action in itself. Thus, King argues that 'to tolerate generally means to endure, suffer or put up with a person, activity, idea or organisation of which one does not really approve.'[31] We can see here how King, despite his excellent uncovering of some of the logic of power that underlies tolerance, does not follow through the significance of this uncovering. By equating tolerance with endurance, he simply negates the specificity of tolerance as an empowered practice. Enduring is coping with something over which one has no control. Tolerance, contrary to this, always presupposes a control over what is tolerated. That is, tolerance presupposes that the object of tolerance is just that: an object of the will of the tolerator. Tolerant acceptance, then, is never a passive acceptance, a kind of 'letting be'. This is inadvertently shown by King when he argues that:

> The consequence involved in tolerance, on balance, is acceptance, and it flows from an interruption of the objection. Thus the tolerant consequence is necessarily equivocal — involving either the surrender of some negative impulse or the indulgence of some *limited* act of association. When we tolerate an *x*, we accept it in the sense either that we associate with it or do not interfere with it in some limited sphere. *[emphasis in the text]*[32]

King's passive acceptance ('interruption of an objection', 'not interfering') is contradicted by the very word he emphasises: 'limited'. For to say 'not interfere with it in some limited sphere' means necessarily, that in tolerating, one is not merely engaging in a passive act. One is actively interfering by placing limits. It is precisely this setting of limits that constitutes the active component of tolerance: there is no tolerance without a setting of limits.

Writing from the standpoint of the dominant religious groupings of their respective countries, Locke's and Voltaire's pleas for tolerance do not stop them from feeling empowered to set the *limits* of tolerance. To tolerate is not just to accept, it is to accept and position the other within specific limits or boundaries. This concern with limits and boundaries emphasises, above all, the *empowered spatiality* that is part of tolerance.

It is this discourse of limits that makes clear that those who tolerate imagine themselves to be in a position of spatial power. Likewise, the tolerated others are imagined by definition to be present within 'our sphere of influence'. They are part of 'our' nation, but only in so far as 'we' accept them.

Their belonging to the national environment in which they come to exist is always a precarious one, for they never exist, they are allowed to exist. That is, the tolerated are never just present, they are positioned.

Clearly, this power to tolerate is then the same imagined power we are now familiar with: the power to position the other as an object within a space that one considers one's own, within limits one feels legitimately capable of setting. The 'I don't mind Arabs' of tolerance, like the 'too many' of the exclusionists, assumes a space where the Arabs are 'not minded' and where one can claim governmental belonging. A banal and often encountered tolerant statement makes this clear: 'I don't mind more migrants coming here.' It is this 'here' that embodies the national spatial imaginary behind tolerance, for there is no sense in an Australian declaring his or her tolerance of the Sikhs in India. Some, however, are quite happy to see themselves as tolerating them in Queensland or Perth, even if they, themselves, live in Sydney. Thus, for this interviewee from Tempe, in Sydney:

> I think it is outrageous what is happening in Port Hedland [the detention of illegal immigrants, mainly 'boat people', in Western Australia] ... I really feel those people should be allowed in ... There's only a few of them anyway ...

The 'few of them' of the tolerant stands clearly in opposition to the 'too many' of the racist. It does, however, point to another important similarity between practices of tolerance and practices of nationalist exclusion. Both categorisations are based on the same principle of desirability/undesirability. Like the 'evil nationalist' engaging in exclusion by categorising the other as undesirable, the 'good, tolerant nationalist' engages in inclusion by categorising the other, if not as 'desirable', at least as 'not that undesirable', as in the 'there's only a few of them anyway' above. Clearly, as far as intercultural/ethnic/racial relations are concerned, to be worthy of being addressed by the discourse of tolerance, you have to be positioned within the dominant culture. It is this fact that makes all calls for tolerance in Australia mainly of concern to White Australians. If 'racist violence' is better understood as a nationalist practice of exclusion, 'tolerance', in much the same way, can be understood as a nationalist practice of inclusion. Both, however, are practices confirming an image of the White Australian as a manager of national space.

This recasting of the opposition between tolerance and racism into an opposition between nationalist practices of inclusion and nationalist practices of exclusion is not a mere renaming, for it allows us to begin to deconstruct the very opposition between the two. We can begin to see how little difference there is between the two, not just in the fact that they both are practices of spatial power, but also in the fact that they are *similar* practices of spatial power. To understand this, we need to examine another important dimension of the discourse of 'limits of tolerance'.

Tolerance and Intolerance: Beyond Good and Evil

Besides revealing the power of the dominant to set their own spatial boundaries, the discourse of limits also reveals the lines where the tolerant can legitimately become intolerant. This is explicitly present in the classical texts where the tolerant are allowed, indeed urged, to become intolerant against those who fall beyond the limits, as it were, such as towards fanatics (Voltaire and Locke) or atheists (Locke).[33]

In France, the notion of limits became officially enshrined in the 1980s by the government's promotion of the concept of *seuil de tolerance,* the threshold of tolerance, a category of governmentality aimed at the spatial control of the presence of the tolerated other, mainly people of African origin, whereby white French citizens are considered to be capable of tolerating a certain number of Africans in their neighbourhood beyond which they can become intolerant.[34] Australian discourses of tolerance often express their intolerance of those who are seen not to respect the unity of Australia or its democratic values and institutions. If that is the case, people committed to tolerance are people who are also continuously practising the exclusion of legitimised objects of intolerance.[35]

But what about the nationalist practices of exclusion examined in the previous chapters: are they executed by people committed to exclusion only? That is, does the fact that they practise intolerance make them *essentially* intolerant people? If we listen carefully to what such people say, we find that in fact they are only practising exclusion to the extent that they believe that those they want to exclude have transgressed what they believe are *their* limits of tolerance. Thus, in the previous chapter, we quoted a White Australian claiming that there are too many Vietnamese, but at the same time he claimed that he thought Greeks were fine. Although we chose to highlight his wish to exclude the Vietnamese, we could have easily concentrated on his tolerance towards Greeks, saying that the Vietnamese were beyond his limit of tolerance. Here is another example in an interview with a man from Lakemba:

> In twenty-two years I've been here. I got to know many of them [Muslims in Lakemba]. In fact, I became good friends with a guy called Ahmad and he invited me a number of times to dinner at his house. We even had a few beers together. But that was different from what is happening now. They've really taken over. It's become intolerable[!].

Here the difference between the tolerable and intolerable is a question of number. This now retired railway worker was quite happy to tolerate Muslims while there were only a few of them, but not now when they've become 'too many'. What 'too many' represents is the possibility of becoming beyond control and losing the status of being an object of the will of the nationalist manager. Here we see that tolerance, like the practices of exclusion, is primarily about the realisation of the national will as enacted by the nationalist. Those who are not tolerated are precisely those who trespass beyond the spaces allotted to them and develop a will of their own.

This leads us to an important conclusion: the difference between those who practise nationalist exclusion and those who practise nationalist inclusion is not one of people committed to exclusion versus people committed to inclusion, but rather one of people with different thresholds of tolerance. It is the discourse of the dominant that transforms this difference of threshold into a difference between tolerant and intolerant because in doing so it mystifies into an essentialist ethical choice (are you or are you not tolerant?) what is a socially determined differential capacity for tolerance. That is, those who engage in practices of intolerance do not do so because they are uncommitted to tolerance, but because they feel that someone has exceeded their own threshold of tolerance and that they are entitled to put them back where they belong, within the limits and boundaries of tolerance they have set for them. By taking the nationalist practices examined as our object in the first two chapters and calling them exclusively nationalist practices of exclusion, we were in fact succumbing to the symbolic violence of those whose threshold of tolerance is represented by the state and who do not need to deploy personal violence to maintain their vision of national space. We could have just as easily called them practices of tolerance and inclusion on the basis of what they tolerate.

If we can differentiate between practices of tolerance and practices of intolerance, it does not follow that this difference is that between tolerant and intolerant people. This is not to minimise the differences between thresholds of tolerance among the population, but to highlight the fact that it is not simply a divide between good, tolerant people and bad, intolerant people. Rather, it is a difference of capacity of tolerance between people who equally claim the capacity to manage national space. There is no tolerant nationalism and intolerant nationalism. Both are about realising a vision of national space through tolerance and intolerance, through the exclusion of some and the inclusion of others.

It could be argued, however, that while it is true that the difference between the tolerant and intolerant nationalist is only a difference between thresholds of tolerance, it is important to stress the *basis* for tolerance and intolerance; that what characterises the practices of exclusion we have examined is that they exclude on the basis of *race*; that what really differentiates practices of tolerance is precisely their non-racist mode of categorisation of otherness. This is, however, incorrect, for racism is just as often associated historically with tolerance as it is with intolerance. The constant association of racism with 'intolerance', 'exclusion' and 'extermination' is, at least partly, the product of the weight of the history of Nazi extermination camps on the Western image of what constitutes 'racism'. In Australia, there is the further weight of the White settlers' exterminatory practices towards the indigenous population. In fact, despite the tragic power of these events, tolerant racism is far more pervasive historically, from slave societies to societies structured by the exploitation of ethnic/racial industrial, domestic and cultural labour and 'value'. We are yet to hear of the slave owner who wanted Blacks to 'go home'. This, in turn, highlights the fact that often tolerance is structured around a discourse highlighting the 'value' of the other to be tolerated, in the sense of the capacity to exploit this other, a capacity closely linked to that of being able to position such an other.

Indeed, often the history of tolerance as an actual practice is to be found in the history of *exploitation* even more so than in the history of grand statements about the toleration of other 'religions'. It is slaves, domestic servants and other forms of exploited labourers — people who are seen as inferior, or in negative terms, by the dominant — who, because of their value as objects of exploitation, are accepted and included within the dominant's space, while, at the same time, the limits of their inclusion are carefully traced.

This valuing and this exploitation are not restricted to the exploitation of labour. Often the discourse of tolerance is linked to a discourse of cultural value/usage. The Black servants that accompanied White aristocratic women — and that the latter tolerated in their proximity merely because they served to emphasise their paleness — are a good example of such valuing/positioning/toleration.[36] Voltaire argued for the tolerance of the Calvinists on the basis of their cultural value. If tolerated, Voltaire asserted, they would be 'enriching'. As we shall see in the next chapter, it is this same discourse of enrichment that often accompanies the valuing and tolerance of ethnicity within White multiculturalism.

Consequently, as we have argued so far, the practices of tolerance, like the practices of intolerance and exclusion, are nationalist practices aimed at the management of national space. And, like all such practices, they involve a mode of classification specific to the shared position of power from which they emanate. It is a mode of classification based on a differentiation between manager and managed, a national subject imagining themselves capable of exercising their will within the nation and a national object perceived as an object of value, only capable of submitting to the will of the national subject. If the nationalist practices of exclusion emphasise a capacity to remove the other from national space, the nationalist practices of tolerance emphasise a capacity to position them in specific places so that they can be valued and tolerated. In a much quoted passage by Foucault, Guillaume de la Perrière states that: 'Government is the right disposition of things arranged so as to lead to a convenient end.'[37] Nothing embodies this governmental fantasy of order better than the White nation fantasy delineated in the discourse of tolerance.

We are now in a position to appreciate *one* of the reasons for the sterility of the calls for tolerance in the face of acts of intolerance. If we re-examine Bob Hawke's call for tolerance quoted earlier, we can now see more clearly its limitations and its sterility as an 'anti-racist' statement. We now know that when he says 'my fellow Australians', he can only be having a dialogue with those fellow Australians who feel capable of being intolerant, that is, White Australians. Instead of saying, 'There are some Australian citizens who are capable of terrorising other Australian citizens and getting away with it. We must not allow them to have this power,' what the Prime Minister ends up implying is, 'There are some Australian citizens who are capable of terrorising other Australian citizens and getting away with it. Be charitable and protect their victims.' Not only does this kind of statement leave the power of the racist unchallenged, but also it does not even empower the victims of exclusionary nationalist practices to resist. It reduces them to helpless objects one is encouraged to protect and to whom one should be charitable.

The essential question that the former prime minister's statement raises, but fails to confront is protect them from whom? The unconscious unwillingness to confront this issue arises directly from the fact that the people being asked to be charitable are the very uncharitable White Australians from whom the victims need to be protected! It is here that the nature of tolerant 'anti-racism' reveals itself most: it is not about making the powerful less so, it is about inviting them not to exercise their power. It invites those who have been uncharitable to be charitable, but it does not remove from them the power to be uncharitable. On the contrary, it indirectly consecrates and reproduces the White fantasy that animates this whole process.

In the wake of the press coverage given to the incidents of tearing Muslim women's scarves, a film studies colleague and a group of his students produced a video with an anti-racist intent. The video featured a Muslim girl in an Australian school being harassed by a group of boys who eventually pull down her scarf. The girl passively retreats until a White girl comes forward picks up her scarf, gives it back to her while putting her arm around her (rap music in the background).

I could not help focusing on the movement of the White girl's arm. Protective though it was, it kept reminding me of the very movement of the hand it was supposedly negating — the hand that pulled down the scarf. Like it, it was a hand that had a sense of its spatial power and, also like it, it has moved onto something/someone perceived as a passive object. The hand that pulls the veil down and the hand that picks it up and protects it replay with bodily gestures the graffiti commented on in the introduction. Some graffitists wanted the migrants in, some wanted them out, but ultimately they all shared in the making of a White national fantasy, a conception of national space where they, as White Australians, are cast in the role of governing subjects and where the non-White other is a passive object. Rewriting this story visually, with hand movements instead of words on walls, helps re-emphasise what I have highlighted in the previous chapter: the spatiality that is part of this whole drama and which makes it more a matter of 'nation' than a matter of 'race' or 'ethnicity'.

Of course, this protective movement of the hand did not actually happen, as far as it is known. Its importance is that the film-makers produced in spatialised visual form the dominant perception of what good 'non-racist' interaction with 'others' ought to be about. The film, like all discourses of tolerance, operates not as a challenge to the practices of exclusion, but as a White fantasy space reproducing the centrality of a White national governmental subject within the nation.

It could be quite rightfully argued at this point that, despite all this, it is better for the state to advocate tolerance than intolerance. This is quite true. One needs, however, to remembers that state policy is not restricted to an option between allowing intolerance to flourish and advocating tolerance. As Preston King argues, if one wishes to challenge someone's power to be intolerant, one can go further:

Although it might be desirable that one tolerate the lily of the valley, the fox in the snow, the child in the alley, the caw of the crow, it might also be equally or more desirable that one enjoy no such power to tolerate in the first place. In short, given the power to tolerate, it may be well to do so. But calling that power into question it may be better to destroy it.[38]

Having stressed so far, however, the inability of the discourse of tolerance to be an effective opposition to the nationalist practices of exclusion, in the remaining section of this chapter I want to examine how the dominant White culture, by being grounded in a White fantasy of the nation, is *unable* to foster strategies aimed at going 'beyond tolerance'.

Tolerance as White fantasy

Let us listen to Simonne talking about her move to Enmore:

Simonne: I really feel at home here ... I like the multicultural feel.

Interviewer: Hmm ...

Simonne: You know, I originally came from around Manly. I mean, I love it there ... I liked living there because of the ocean. But, ah, it's too conservative ... You miss out on what makes Australia such a nice place.

Interviewer: Is ...?

Simonne: You see a mixture of people here, you see the, the, the Indian culture or, down the south end of Newtown, it's the Fijian Indians and then you, you see the Asian people and ah, and ah, I like going to the deli and ... ah visit George's.

Interviewer: Yeah?

Simonne: Mad Greek! Don't tell him I said that [laughter]. He's great, like he runs a really good delicatessen there and then there's the, ah, the supermarket up the road which is run by a Korean family, they're always really friendly and pleasant to you when you go in there. And, ah, you've got Ivan the Butcher, he's, he's, quite a personality. So there you go, I am familiar with all these people and they're all very different. It's really great.

One notices here how a homely feeling, what makes Australia such a nice place, is generated by the presence of diversity. At the same time, we see how talk moves from specific locales to the level of the nation. Underlying this homeliness is a fantasy of a national order based on a clearly positioned otherness: Indians are here, Koreans are there ... and in the centre of it all is the White Australian bestowing her tolerance.

Slavoj Zizek explains fantasy space through the example of Penelope, a character in a short story by Patricia Highsmith, who is 'pathologically attached to her pets' such that 'in the garden behind the house, all her deceased cats and dogs are exhibited, stuffed.'[39] Penelope's fantasy aims at re-creating a world in which she is in total control of her 'love' and desire to compensate and mask the failure of her relationship to her husband. What characterises such a fantasy of control is precisely that that which is living is positioned around the subject as an object, as something 'dead'.

In much the same way, the fantasy of White tolerance is a fantasy of a national order occupied by 'dead' ethnics — ethnics as objects of the national will. This is made more explicit by this elderly man from Marrickville:

> I say hello to the neighbours and they say hello back to me and ... I just do my thing and they do their thing. The lady next door, she's Italian: I might go into the bathroom there and she's singing opera next door. She's into the opera business. And the people next door, ah, they're Vietnamese school teachers, you know, they all got young kids, you know, ah, like they're all nice people. There's a couple of Greeks, in the street, they're all nice people, you know, everyone in the street knows me, and you know, they've probably seen me stagger past some nights drunk goin' home. But ah, you know, like, like Marrickville, you get the Greeks up there near the post office with their beads you know, in the hand you know, sittin' there and, you get some Aborigines up there near the other end of the post office drinking their plonk or whatever, you know, they never cause no trouble ... The only problem are those new Vietnamese up the road. They are like ... they don't want to know ... they only talk among themselves as if they're plotting or something ...

We can see how this very tolerant discourse embodying a fantasy of a neatly positioned otherness constituting the national order ends with an 'intolerant' statement. And the object of intolerance is not an essentialised other. It is not 'the Vietnamese'. It is a special kind of Vietnamese. One that is a national threat, not a racial threat. It is that ethnic other which appears to conceal a will of its own, the other that is 'plotting or something'. This emphasises the object nature of the other who is *not* plotting and therefore can be safely tolerated.

But in just the same way as the White nation fantasy enacted by the nationalist practices of exclusion operates as a form of yearning, in what I have shown to be a series of 'as ifs', so, too, does the White nation fantasy of tolerance. If the former is one which acknowledges a certain loss of governmental power, however, the White fantasy of the tolerant society is one of denial.

In an astonishingly ideological — in the sense of advocating a specific ideology — passage, Preston King argues that:

> The promotion of toleration basically presupposes an inequality, but an inequality that has to be accepted. The promotion of democracy basically presupposes an inequality, but one that can and should be removed. It should be clear that these two types of promotion, where they obtain in different spheres, are not necessarily incompatible. But there is an important type of difference between them which it is perhaps always useful to remain aware of. Where one perceives a lack of toleration, and encourages it, what one is basically encouraging is a change in *attitude*. Where one perceives a lack of democracy, and encourages it, what one is basically encouraging is a change of *structure*. Thus a predominant feature of the commitment to toleration is the concern with psychology, while a predominant feature of the commitment to democracy is a concern with institutions.[40]

While the argument correctly sees that the advocacy of tolerance does not change structures (relations of power), it wrongly slips into arguing that it has no effect on structures and should be merely treated as a psychological (non-social/structural) phenomenon. One effect of such an approach is that the 'tolerant attitude' is conceived, in a continuation of the liberal tradition, as the product of an adherence to a belief or a principle that one values more than the action of ridding oneself, through intolerance, of an undesirable object:

> It is clear that tolerance is not merely a matter of suspending action against an item that is objected to. Crucial to it is the rationale for the suspension of such action. In the event, this rationale consists in the introduction of a competitive and incompatible objection, one that is accorded higher status, and one which accordingly prohibits the operationalisation of the objection first advanced.[41]

From such a perspective, King fails to see the importance of the *interest* of the dominant in the advocacy of tolerance. He does not ask the question: what does one gain, generally, from the relation of power one is positioned within as the dominant and, more particularly, what does one gain from reproducing this relation of power through tolerance? Thus, those who tolerate do not gain anything from their toleration except maybe some broad sense of satisfaction from adhering to their principles.

Yet, when Locke argues that 'it is only light and evidence that can work a change in men's opinions; and that light can in no manner proceed from corporal sufferings, or any other outward penalties', he is not only shown, as argued above, to be addressing himself to the dominant.[42] He is also revealing that tolerance is a strategy: its aim, 'light', is the same as that of subjecting people to corporal suffering, it is merely perceived to be more efficient in achieving such an aim. Locke is here following a long tradition of writers from Sebastien Castalion, in his *Conseil à la France désolée* (1562), onward, who saw the advocacy of tolerance in terms of the opposition between coercion and consent/hegemony, and the strategic desirability of the latter over the former.[43]

King comes face to face with this strategic intent while examining the work of Castalion and many others. He examines, for example, Michel de L'Hôpital's work *Le but de la guerre et de la paix* (1570), where the author advocates tolerance almost solely on the basis of the impossibility of winning the war against the enemy (the Huguenots). Here King acknowledges that: 'L'Hôpital's book is primarily argued on the grounds of utility, not principle.'[44] Nevertheless, King tries to 'save' his theory by arguing that: 'ultimately, the principle is always there. This essentially reduces to the notion that a man's conscience is inviolable, that one cannot meaningfully be compelled to believe what one regards as false.'[45] The weakness of King's argument does not lie in that no such principle can be found in L'Hôpital's work. It lies in his inability to perceive that the principle that 'one cannot meaningfully be compelled' itself derives from the experience of the *inability* to compel.

The above also highlights the question of the social conditions of the possibility of tolerance, and gives us a further insight into its complexity. While it remains true that the advocacy of tolerance reproduces the same relation of power that existed in the period of officially sanctioned intolerance that usually precedes it, it is nevertheless also true that it results from a reassessment by the dominant of their ability to dominate, usually due to the capacity of the dominated to resist/challenge domination. This was something clearly seen by Renan in his study of the rise of 'clerical liberalism'. Renan (1947) argues that the main reason the Church had adopted tolerance was that it found itself unable to use force against its enemies.[46] So, while tolerance reproduces the same relation of power, it is the product of a change in the balance of forces between the dominant and dominated, in the interest of the latter, within that relation. More importantly, an essential aspect of the advocacy of tolerance as a strategy of reproduction by dominant groupings is that they strive to mystify that element of coercion and to present tolerance as if it were a mere benevolent choice on their part.

The official history of multiculturalism in Australia, as presented in the beginning of this chapter, is a clear example of this. It is here that we arrive at one of the mystifications enacted by the White nation fantasy of multicultural tolerance. Multicultural tolerance is presented as the result of a mere choice of policy made by enlightened people, mystifying the important fact that it is, *as well*, the product of the increased power, the resistance and the struggle of migrant Australians. Because the White Nation fantasy is dependent on the staging of the ethnic other as an object, it cannot help but mystify this element which would put it face to face with the will of the ethnic other. We find this denial in the discourse of acceptance, which has always been present along

with the discourse of tolerance within Australian multiculturalism.

The theme of acceptance obtains its positive 'anti-racist'
value within multiculturalism through its opposition to rejection. If the White Australia policy and assimilation were
about treating Australians from a non-English–speaking
background as outsiders, multiculturalism is about fully
accepting them as Australians. Outside this opposition, however, the 'non-nationalist' claims of such a discourse become
much more ambiguous and contradictory. To begin with, the
popular language of acceptance, often encountered in the
form 'They're just as Australian as we are' or 'They're
Australian, too', reinforces the placing of the Anglo-Celtic
Australians in the position of power they acquire within the
discourse of tolerance. When Phillip Ruddock, the current
Liberal Minister for Immigration, spoke at a meeting of Arab
Australians following the election of the Liberal Government
in early 1996, he addressed the crowd with: 'I look around
me and I see Australians.' Judging from the crowd's reaction,
he was the only one who seemed unsure about it in the
room, and it only had the effect of placing him in the position of the White acceptor, decreeing the Australianness of
the ethnic other. In this way, the very act of acceptance operates as an exclusionary force on the accepted. For why is it,
one might ask, that an Australian-Lebanese person needs to
be accepted and reassured about the nature of his or her
Australian identity in an already established multicultural
society? As this Greek-born Australian who migrated to
Australia in 1928 recounts, the alienating effect of this acceptance is clearly felt by the migrant :

> Australian fella [said to me once] ... 'Don't worry, boy,' he
> says, 'You're one of us now.' He says, 'We accept you as one
> of us.' Well, that hurts, doesn't it? He says, 'Well, we accept
> you as one of us.' Well, what the hell am I? In other words,
> he still looks at me as a wog, doesn't he? Well that hurts.[47]

Seen from this perspective, the accepting enunciation
'You're Australian' becomes similar to the 'You're a grown-
up now' directed from parents to teenagers. Not only does
the identity become granted — that is, it can be withdrawn
— and a power relation is drawn between those who do the

accepting and those who are accepted, but also, as importantly, a question mark is put over the suitability of this identity and its genuineness: if *it goes without saying* that the migrant is Australian, there would be no need to say it. Acceptance translates into doubt.

This is not, however, the main fantasy constructed by tolerant acceptance. More importantly, in the assertion of this power to accept, there is a denial of the fact of its relative loss. To pursue the metaphor of the teenager addressed by his parents, it must be recognised that 'You're a grown-up now' *does* reflect the fact that the teenager is growing up. One does not say 'You're a grown-up now' to a five-year-old either. What is important, however, is that this growing up is happening independently of the will of the parents. In a sense, the growing up of the child is inevitably putting her beyond the parents' control. From this perspective, we can understand that their 'You're grown-up now' becomes an ideological means of appearing to be in control over something over which they have no control. It is this same kind of mystification that operates with the 'You're Australian now'. It allows the White Australians who engage in this form of acceptance to live in a fantasy space where the Australianness of the ethnic other appears as if it is under their control at a time when the migrant is becoming inexorably Australian independently of their will. It is in the ways described above that we can see how the White nation fantasy of tolerance is based on a denial of the loss of power resulting from the increased capacity of non-White Australians to enact something akin to an *Australian* ethnic will.

In an address to a 1992 Productive Diversity in Business conference, a kind of economically orientated multicultural festival where everyone celebrates the virtues of tolerance, the National Party leader, Tim Fischer, declared: 'The nation as a whole has much to gain from the diversity of a population who consider themselves *Australians* first.' This is a classical tolerant statement where the other is welcome, but within limits, of course. Here the limits are set by Tim Fischer: swear allegiance to Australia first. This demand may appear as eminently reasonable, but it nevertheless embodies the very nature of the White nation fantasy articulated to tolerance.

The point, of course, is not that Australia does not need a population who consider themselves Australians first. But why does Tim Fischer need to say this? Most evidence points to the fact that, in much the same way as in any process of migration, the more migrants stay in Australia, the more they consider themselves Australians first. This process happens because that is how migrants end up being comfortable defining themselves. Such a matter-of-fact happening cannot, however, be acknowledge by Tim Fischer, for he is not *really* worried about migrants becoming Australians first. He is worried about asserting his role as a White Australian who can demand such a commitment from lesser Australians. He is worried that migrants may become Australians despite him and regardless of his will, and then remove him from the national centre stage he wishes to occupy.

Appendix to Chapter 3

Ethnic caging

I have had no direct experience of the conditions in which 'boat people' and others find themselves following their 'capture' by the Australian State. Apart from having met and spoken to some refugees who have now settled in Australia, like many people, my experience is primarily through the media. Most vivid in my consciousness are intimations of caging practices: people behind fences, hands clutching wires, guards. I've seen the films and the photos, and listened to and read the reports of government officials justifying the way they 'handle' the situation. Of course, in the well-established traditional pattern of knowledge dissemination, the 'point of view' of the caged, from the budgie to the prisoner, is seldom or never heard. The government categorises as 'non-persons' those who have attempted illegally to enter Australia's internationally recognised territories.

To many, the images of these 'ethnics behind cages' — for this is how they come across — are shocking. Even if one is supportive of the practice and does not feel particular empathy towards the 'caged', the practice still stands out as *extra*-ordinary. Indeed, a nationalist register is sometimes evoked to call this 'ethnic caging' un-Australian. It strikes many Australians as so shockingly 'other' to the Australia they experience in their everyday life. It is certainly different from the 'tolerant' Australia we commonly experience in our everyday life.

The reason why the images of 'ethnic caging' can shock in a tolerant society is obvious enough. At the most basic, ethnic caging appears as a negation of the *historical direction* Australia is pictured to have taken within multicultural discourse: multiculturalism as the historical rise of an ethic of goodwill towards ethnic otherness. If nothing else, multiculturalism encompasses a present struggle by the Australian State to appear to be 'nice' to ethnic otherness in contrast to a past history constructed as a time when Australia was 'not so nice' — the White Australia Policy, assimilation, etc. The 'then we were nasty, now we are nice' polarity clearly structures the imaginary history of multiculturalism and underlies most of its conceptual apparatus. In this context, ethnic caging *appears* as a historico-ethical reversal.

There is, however, a more recent comparative multicultural paradigm within which ethnic caging stands out as an equally shocking phenomenon. Here, the comparison is international rather than historical. It has emerged in light of the atrocities associated with Eastern European nationalism, particularly the ethnic cleansing of the Bosnian wars. This comparison is structured around what is conceived as two radically different types of nationalism: a nationalism of extermination and a nationalism of tolerance. One is an 'Eastern' nationalism which always aims to eradicate ethnic otherness. The other is a 'Western' nationalism which always aims towards the appreciation and the valuing, and therefore the protection, of this ethnic otherness. Clearly, multicultural Australia is perceived here as very well entrenched in the 'Western' camp, while the 'Eastern' camp is constructed as totally other.

It is clear why ethnic caging shocks within the above dichotomy. The concentration-camp–like images it fosters make ethnic caging appear closer to ethnic cleansing than to anything remotely linked to multicultural appreciation and tolerance. The lack of respect for the humanity of the people concerned, the caging bureaucracy set up to deal with the 'non-people', accusations that institutional procedures are not being respected and that due process is not being followed in dealing with the 'caged', all of this works to position these practices further in the domain of 'Eastern otherness'. Are these remote northern outposts of Broome and Port Hedland really part of an Australia that wants itself to be so nicely tolerant? How can they be?

The government is clearly aware of this 'image problem', and many of its pronouncements on the issue aim at distancing the 'nature of Australian society' from 'what is happening at Port Hedland'. Port Hedland is 'not Australian society' in the same way the refuge seekers are 'non-persons'. At first sight, this idea of a non-social space inhabited by non-people does not seem like a credible idea, but the message the government intends to convey is implicitly quite efficient and credible: dealing with the illegal refuge seekers in this way does not reflect in any way on the values Australians hold regarding how their society should be internally structured. The fact that Australians are committed to kill, if necessary, the soldiers of an invading army does not mean that Australian society values killing. If we are willing to be nasty in protecting our nice nation, it does not mean that we have stopped being a nice nation.

So, the issues raised by the illegal arrivals are shown — convincingly, one must add — to have nothing to do with how Australians live their lives inside Australia. They have to do with a different set of issues such as: Does Australia have a territorial integrity or doesn't it? Are we a nation capable of protecting our borders or aren't we? Are we capable of enforcing the international procedures set out for entering our nation, and that are followed by thousands of migrants, or are we going to allow people to 'jump the queue'? We can see how these questions are clear governmental questions: are we or are we not in control of the national social space?

Although, the practice of ethnic caging is morally abhorrent, the government does make sense in stressing that illegal border crossings cause problems for the nation in terms of the issues raised above. What is questionable, however, is the neat separation between the internal problems of a nation (social organisation, social values) and its external problems (defence of borders, sovereignty) that is implied by this mode of argument. Can 'we' really be nice to ethnics in the internal organisation of the nation and cage them in its external organisation without there being any relation between the two?

This does not mean that the way 'we' treat illegal refuge seekers is bound to affect the way 'we' end up treating ethnic otherness within the nation. My critical intent is more analytical than prescriptive. I want to argue that the mode of categorising and dealing with national otherness in the process of defending the nation from external threats is intrinsically linked to the way national otherness is categorised and dealt with internally. Both emanate from the same structure of categorisation of national otherness, but they are different deployments of this structure in different contexts. That is, as far as ethnic caging is concerned, the mode of categorising ethnic otherness implied in the context of perceiving it as an external threat to the nation is not at all unrelated to the way ethnicity is perceived internally within multicultural-ism. In fact, I want to argue that ethnic caging is best under-stood in the same way a symptom is conceived in psycho-analysis: a phenomenon which expresses a repressed struc-ture that constitutes and underlies all of the reality of which it is a part. In this sense, the categories of ethnic caging express a structure of perceiving ethnicity which constitutes and underlies all of Australian society rather than being external to it. It reveals the whole construct on which the tol-erant society is erected.

To examine this, we need to make a detour and return to the differences between passive homely belonging and gov-ernmental belonging that were introduced in chapter 1. To a certain extent, each of these belongings involves inhabiting a different imaginary of the nation. Governmental belong-ing, as we have seen, is an inhabiting of the national will. Passive homely belonging, however, can be best seen as an inhabiting of the national body.

All nationalist practices operate on both levels in that they are always attempts at constituting the nation both as a national body and as a national will. The degree of emphasis on one or the other is contextual, but the two are necessari-ly intertwined. This relation between body-building and will-building is the hardest to conceive. One gains a hint of what it entails by examining a similar relation in the process of the human body's fight against a disease — a process which can be conceived, for our purposes, as one of 'body-building' in which a human bodily will is fighting for the control of the human body against an otherness invading it. The problem, of course, is that whatever we end up referring to as the human bodily will is not independent of the body. It refers to a capacity of the body to act, organise and defend itself. The onset of a disease is the onset of matter coming together to form a will other than that of the body, a 'counter-will' aim-ing to colonise it. The bodily will's aim is to eradicate any such counter-will, an endless job. On the other hand, the more the disease invades the body, the more it weakens the bodily will/capacity to fight it that is inherent in the body. Thus, in the process of fighting against a disease, one can move from a stage where the will of the body to fight other-ness is present, to another stage where a further quantitative bodily loss to the disease leads to a qualitative loss of a bodily will. This is the stage where, without the body actually dying, it is no longer capable of offering any resistance — where the human body's will to fight the disease has ceased to exist. The body becomes controlled by the counter-will of the disease. That is, the counter-will successfully manages to colonise the body and submit it to its own 'order'.

In some tribal societies, humans who are still physically alive are pronounced dead precisely when there is no longer a hint of a will in the body. This is when disease or 'death' takes over. Thus, for a volitional human body to exist, it is not enough for it to be 'alive'. It is very hard to understand what this minimum necessary for the living body to continue to act as a bodily will is, but it is clear that there is a need for enough of the body to 'come together' to order itself *and* to constitute itself as the ordering principle of the rest of the body for this wilful bodily existence to come into being. The exclamation 'Pull yourself together!' is a brilliant capturing by popular consciousness of this process in situations where someone appears to be 'all over the place'. The exclamation is an exhortation for the will to take control of the body and order it such that it can stop disintegrating and regain its capacity to be 'operational'.

The point of all of the above, of course, is to emphasise that nationalists also imagine their nation to be in need of 'pulling itself together' in order to exist and be recognised as a nation by the international community. As with the human body, enough of the national body has to 'come together' and order itself into a national will that can order and govern the rest of the nation. This is what being recognised at the United Nations often entails. It is this national will which ends up governing the national body. If a national counter-will has emerged, we can also see that the struggle against it by the governmental national will develop in ways similar to the struggle of the human body against disease. This is what nationalist practices, as we have already seen, are all about.

There is a point in the fight against a national otherness which has constituted itself into a national counter-will (referred to often as a national disease), where the fight is transformed from one where the national will is aiming to stay in control of the totality of the national body it used to govern, to a fight for that minimum necessary for a national will to remain existing and without which the nation is declared dead. This is why, as with the human bodily will, this governmental national will is engaged in a constant struggle to eradicate not otherness as such, but the capacity of any otherness to constitute itself into a national counter-will. In some ways, we can say that struggles over the national body are struggles over the kind of life nationals can live, while struggles over the national will are struggles over life itself. One is a battle over the quality of life; the other a battle over life and death. This is why the latter struggle, where the national will is more at stake, is often deadlier.

During the Bosnian war, when the Bosnian Serbs become nasty, it was not because they are inherently different from us or from anybody else as nationals. It was because what was at stake was the very formation of a Bosnian Serb national will. The Bosnian Serbs were not fighting over 'Who is going to live in my nation?' They were fighting over 'Will my Bosnian national will live and order the nation?' So, here we have an example of nation-building turning nasty and deadly precisely because what was at stake was not the health of the Bosnian national body, but the life or death of a Bosnian national will capable of governing this body. The quest for ethnic purity is the quest of an ethnic will that is still in formation and still aiming for dominance within the nation. The tolerance of impurity is the preserve of the already well-established ethnic will, secure in its domination of the nation. Nationalists in quest of a national will are not willing or capable of dealing and coping with other national wills. They exterminate them.

When we have a situation where the issue of the national will has been reasonably settled — where the national will has achieved an enduring, although never final, capacity to keep otherness in check, and feels secure in its capacity to stop this otherness from forming a counter-will — national wills are more easygoing with national otherness. This is when they tolerate/not tolerate, accept/not accept rather than merely exterminate. This is when we get a national managerial parlance: 'You come here, you go there.' 'I don't mind you living here.' 'We're better off if you live there.' At the same time, however, while being more pleasant when dealing with national otherness, the national will is still constantly aware of the danger of the otherness constituting itself into a national will and has to ensure that this otherness does not do so and so come to endanger the national will's existence as such. This is why national otherness, even when it is tolerated, has always to be under the threat of extermination to ensure it does not 'take over'.

If we take this brief analysis to Australia and examine the way in which national otherness is conceived within it by the White dominant culture, we find another reason why the series of differentiating criteria that Australian multiculturalism operates with in terms of 'nice'/not so nice' nation-building, extermination/tolerance, Eastern/Western nationalism are not as dramatically different as multiculturalist discourse would like them to be.

White Australia has not, of course, always been tolerant, as the multiculturalists remind us. Well before the caging of illegal refugees, there were many examples of other instances of caging in Australian history. The Australian colonising national will exterminated and caged Aboriginal people literally and metaphorically, and, in an exemplary fashion, started valuing them when they no longer constituted a communal counter-will in themselves — when they were no longer capable of endangering the British-constituted colonising national will. More recently, Australians engaged in a massive exercise during World War II of caging and detaining 'ethnics', including some who actually held Australian citizenship.

Why were Italians and Germans who were 'tolerated' in the 1930s and early 1940s detained and caged during World War II? Because wars emphasise the problematic of the national will. Many things that are perceived as harmless in peacetime become perceived by the dominating national will as dangerous for national survival in wartime. This also explains anti-Arab violence during the Gulf War. The national will cannot cope with the idea of others who may potentially subvert it by acting in the name of another national will (potential spies, the enemy within, etc.) to roam freely within the nation.

What I have argued throughout this chapter is that multicultural tolerance does not escape this logic of nation-building. The multicultural national will, like all national wills, tolerates national otherness, but only in so far as this national otherness is in no danger of constituting a counter-will. Indeed, within multiculturalism, we find many examples where, when the national multicultural will is threatened, multiculturalism starts showing a rather nasty side.

To take an example from everyday life today, it is enough to examine the way the notion of ethnic concentration is perceived and turned into a problem by the committed multiculturalists themselves. Multiculturalists are, of course, always readily emitting statements such as: 'We like diversity' or 'We like ethnicity'. Once they see a concentration of ethnicity, however, it is remarkable how they turn a bit on themselves. As we shall see in the next chapter, some even assert, in a matter-of-fact manner, that the whole point of multiculturalism is to avoid ethnic concentrations or ethnic ghettoes.

What does 'too many' mean in the expression 'too many Vietnamese' living together? Why aren't 'too many' Whites living together a problem? Why is the concentration of ethnic otherness such a problem? Because, as Elias Canetti intimates in *Crowds and Power (1973)*, concentrations can produce collective will. For instance, what differentiates the concentration camp from the mere prison at the level of its communal effect is precisely that concentration camps, by being 'prisons of concentrations', imprison and break not just individual members of a community, but also the communal will itself. So, otherness scattered around the nation is fine. Once 'they' start concentrating, however, they could become an alternative will and the national will has to go in and disperse them.

Indeed, the multicultural discourse that perceives the concentration as a problem always ends up turning national control over it into a problem. Someone else, an-other, often dark, criminal forces, disease — these are often perceived by a collective White imaginary as controlling ethnic ghettoes. So what is happening here? A typical national will perceives in the concentration a potential counter-will, and readies itself to exterminate it in order to transform it once again into a will-less ethnicity that can once more be appreciated and tolerated. This is all done lovingly from *within* multiculturalism.

We are now finally in a position to deal more meaningfully with ethnic caging. Often, in the public discussion of illegal refuge-seekers, we hear things such: 'There's only sixty boat people', 'eighty boat people', etc. Also, people like the person quoted in the beginning of this chapter rightly point out that in terms of numbers, it's nothing. Australia has taken many more. So why all the fuss?

Indeed, if the question was about these ethnic others inhabiting the national body, it wouldn't have been a problem. When we are talking about people 'jumping the queue', however, we are not talking about people who are merely taking a position allotted to them in the national home. This 'queue' is nothing other than the manifestation of the national will. Having seen what this queue looks like in an embassy located in a Third World country, it may not be as civilised as the queue in a David Jones department store, but it is a part of the national order, the order imposed by the national will for entering the national body. This is why it is not a matter of numbers: whether two people or one hundred jump the queue, what they have done is engage the nation at the level of its national will. They have literally tried to subvert the national will. They have activated something no national will can perceive without turning nasty: they are ethnic others who have exhibited a will of their own. That is why they are so dangerous.

The national will does not care about the reason why the other hasn't followed the proper channels set out by that will for entering the nation. What it cares about is that it is a national will and it must be capable of enforcing its proper channels, its queues, its order. Otherness must not be allowed, under any circumstances, to show this national will to be weak. You make it shaky and the national will will have to act accordingly. Ethnic caging is not the caging of ethnic numbers, it is the caging of ethnic wills. It is, as the government itself argues, an example for others: don't try to activate your own will. One will rules in Australia and this is how it is going to be.

As the man falling from the skyscraper in the French film *La Haine* says to himself, 'So far, so good'. So far, so good because, if Australia did not have a sizeable ethnic population, ethnic caging as a message for other *external* ethnic wills

about the wish of the Australian national will to keep on ruling the nation would be relatively without problem. It is
unproblematic, that is, in a world where the very condition
of the existence of nations has to do with the capacity to
enforce national procedures for crossing borders. Australia
is a multi-ethnic country, however, and hence this message is
not as unproblematic as it may first appear.

I do not think that these images of caged ethnics I started
by referring to have grabbed my attention just as an academic. I think they affected me, in part, because I was watching
them as an 'ethnic'. That is, because of the make-up of
Australian society, we cannot escape the fact that the message of ethnic caging, even if directed primarily at ethnic
wills external to Australia, becomes also a message directed
at the ethnic wills inside Australia itself. In this process, ethnic caging obtains an added significance which needs to be
explored.

Caging is a very interesting phenomenon. For a number of
years, I have actually been studying the domestication of
animals and its relevance for understanding the domestication of people within nations. That is why caging grabbed my
attention almost immediately as an interesting mode of
nation-building. As a result, I would like to refer here to the
work of the early French naturalist, Geoffroy de St Hilaire,
who, in 1861, wrote a book on the domestication of animals.

De St Hilaire differentiates between three states to which
humans can reduce animals in the process of subordinating
them to their needs. They can be captive, tame or domesticated. Captive animals are those who have to be caged or
physically restrained to remain subjected to humans.
Without this physical restraint, they would go back into the
wild unaffected by their experience. That is, captive animals
have not yet undergone any major transformation in their
mode of conceiving how they should live. They still conceive
of the 'good life', if one can say so, in the same way that they
did when they were first captured. Tame animals, on the
other hand, have internalised their state of captivity such
that the physical restraints are no longer needed as an instrument of subjugation. Their idea of the good life has
changed, and they are happy being around the humans who
tamed them; caging is no longer necessary to retain them.

The difference between tame and domesticated animals is even more important. For de St Hilaire, animals that are tame are always so as individuals of a species. What differentiates the domesticated from the tame is precisely that domestication involves the reproduction of the species in captivity. That is, the domesticated are subjugated as a self-reproducing community of tame animals.

De St Hilaire's differentiation of the three states is exceptionally interesting in light of what we have been discussing so far. What is the significance of the difference between captive animals and tame animals as far as our present analysis is concerned? One is tempted to say quickly that captive animals are caged, while tame and domesticated animals are not. There is an element of truth in this, but it is not the whole truth. Tame and domesticated animals are, in fact, often caged. They are not trusted to know that they are not supposed to go certain places and therefore may need to be fenced in. I think what is more important than the difference between caged and not caged is the difference in the function of caging. For captive animals, caging constitutes the main instrument of their subordination. Tame and domesticated animals have incorporated their state of subordination — cages are used to control their movement, to position them within domestic space, rather than as the main instrument of their subjugation. More importantly, however, what does it mean when we say that captive animals have not changed their conception of the good life, while tame and domesticated animals have?

In our terms, it simply means that captive animals still have a will independent of the human domesticator while, for both the tame and the domesticated animals, this will has become subjugated to the will of the domesticator. Here is my point: if we can easily recognise in the wilful caged animal the wilful refuge seeker who has not submitted to the order of the national will, are we not also invited to recognise in ourselves, those ethnics who have 'successfully settled in Australia', the tame and the domesticated animal whose will has been subjugated as the very condition of belonging to the domestic space of the Australian national will? That is, by virtue of the absence of a cage to subjugate us, are we not always post-caged? Mustn't we have undergone a real or metaphoric caging which has shaped our communal wills such that we can no longer constitute any possible counter-will for the Australian governing national will, as the very precondition of our becoming the subjects of tolerance rather than the subjects of extermination or caging?

It is in this sense that Port Hedland works as a psychoanalytic symptom: what are these pictures of ethnic caging being offered to us but images of ourselves as domesticated Third World–looking ethnics that constitute the very support for the reproduction of the White national fantasy of a multicultural Australia?

A dominant culture in which tolerance is grounded in the necessity of ethnic caging cannot possibly produce a politics which counters a racism which sees, in all Third-World–looking migrants, undesirable people who ought not be accepted into the nation. For it is a culture which is merely producing, through its enacting of the White nation fantasy, the very conception of Third World–looking migrants proposed by the 'racists'. The difference is that it argues that, *despite this*, they ought to be tolerated. When the tolerant says to the racist, 'I know how you're feeling but …', they indeed do know how they are feeling.

chapter 4

White Multiculturalism: A Manual for the Proper Usage of Ethnics

Every year, Sydney celebrates its Carnivale. For two weeks, the city projects its diverse multicultural faces to itself and the world (of actual and potential tourists). A quick glance at the Carnivale program clearly reveals the extent of this diversity. With its diversity in ethnic origins, in types of activity (from an International Food and Wine Fair where you can 'eat your way around the world' to multilingual computer games at the Powerhouse Museum), the Carnivale is a festival in which Sydneysiders and visitors are treated to some of the best that 'multiculturalism can offer'.

This emphasis on what 'multiculturalism can offer' is important. For, as well as the obvious financial and tourist motivations behind it, Carnivale is also constructed and used to legitimise 'multiculturalism' as something *valuable*. As the New South Wales Premier (and Minister for Ethnic Affairs) of the early 1990s sees it: 'No other celebration in Australia has such a powerful and distinctive theme — the value and meaning of multiculturalism in Australian society'.[1] For the managing director of Westfield Holdings Limited, the major sponsor of Carnivale: 'Carnivale offers the people of NSW the opportunity to celebrate multiculturalism and to learn from others who have joined our society from other lands.'[2]

The theme of cultural enrichment is one of the key themes of Australian multiculturalism. Its main emphasis is the recognition of the *value* of the various cultures present in

Australia and the value of the interaction between them.
This is stressed in opposition to ethnocentrism and is portrayed as transcending one of the major defects of the White
Australia/assimilation period: the unwillingness to accept
that non-White cultures have a contribution to make to the
development of a more general Australian culture.
Responding to an attack on Sydney taxi drivers' supposed
inability to speak English, New South Wales Premier, Bob
Carr, said: 'I had a good discussion with a Somali-born taxi
driver recently about his experience with meditation and
crystals. I was just struck by the comfortable cosmopolitan air
that he was able to bring to his task'.[3]

In this chapter, I want to show how the discourse of enrichment encapsulates a White nation fantasy for those White
Australians interpellated by it. As I will argue, it is only in its
opposition to ethnocentrism that the notion of enrichment
appears in such an attractive pluralist garb. Left to itself, it
reveals an important inherent opposition — the opposition
between enriched and enriching cultures. For the White
Australian articulating it, the discourse of enrichment still
positions him or her in the centre of the Australian cultural
map. Far from putting 'migrant cultures', even in their 'soft'
sense (i.e. through food, dance, etc.), on an equal footing with
the dominant culture, the theme conjures the images of a
multicultural fair where the various stalls of neatly positioned
migrant cultures are exhibited and where the real Australians,
bearers of the White nation and positioned in the central role
of the touring subjects, walk around and enrich themselves.

The multicultural fair itself has, however, changed dramatically over the years. Initially securely positioned in the role
of 'feeder', migrants have increasingly become willing to be
touring subjects wanting to be enriched themselves. Any
walk around a multicultural fair clearly shows this today. It is
this reality of the 'ethnic eater' that White multicultural fantasy tries to 'block'.

The Stew that Grew and the Anglo who Just Could Not Stop Cooking

The Stew that Grew is a children's book I used to read to my
daughters in the early 1990s.[4] Set in Victoria during the gold

rush, the story is about how miners from different ethnic backgrounds combined the various ethnic-specific ingredients in their possession and made the 'Eureka stew'. It aims to symbolise the making of the Australian nation. As often happens with children's books, I was made to read this one a number of times. It was only after several readings that I began to realise that there was something not quite right in the celebration of the *value* of cultural diversity that was at the core of the story.

The book, far from celebrating diversity — or rather, in the process of so doing, appearing as a negation of White ethnocentrism — celebrated a White nation fantasy in which White Australians (in this case, an Anglo-Celtic couple where the Anglo male had primacy) enacted their capacity to manage this diversity. As I critically examine this book, I will analyse how the structure, the themes and the images of ethnic relations contained within the White fantasy find their way into the White experience of various other areas of Australia's social life.

The book begins with a multi-ethnic rush of people seeking gold, all pictured on the first page in their various ethnic costumes.

> They came from all parts, by ship, horse or train,
> And most were still poor when they went home again,
> But many found something more valued and true
> That Christmas they brewed the Eureka Stew.

Stew cooking begins with Molly O'Drew giving four potatoes to her husband, Blue, who peels them and throws them into a cauldron. But, as Molly O'Drew remarks, 'It wasn't much of a feast.' In the meantime, 'Twenty-one diggers sat hungry and tired' until Molly 'stepped into their midst' and said:

> I know of a way we can all be fed.
> Put what you've got in that pot next to Blue
> And together we'll make our own Christmas stew.

This leads to all sorts of 'ethnic' characters arriving on the scene and adding to the stew their own ethnic-specific ingredient. O'Malley rose first with some Spuds, then it was the Rudds turn with some carrots that Blue chopped to pieces and bounced the lot in. Then came Taffy with leeks and Nell with a turnip, old Hugh with some barley and Leopold with some Brussels sprouts, Maria Mazzini with some zucchini, Heinrich and Hans with some sauerkraut, Jacques with onions, Abdul with garlic, Wong the Chinese with a bagful of peas, and many others. We even have, towards the end, a Johnny Barcoo joining in 'with Yams and the tail of a red Kangaroo'. Finally:

> Then the last thing of all was cast in by Blue
> — but just what it was, nobody knew.

The opposition that structures the work on its surface is the classical opposition that structures the discourse of multicultural enrichment and valorisation. The initial poverty of the Anglo-Celtic combination — 'not much of a feast' — is contrasted with the richness of the diversity that ends up constituting the stew. In much the same way, the multicultural valorisation of ethnic food which stresses its enriching qualities in everyday discourse is often contrasted with the supposed poverty of the Anglo-Celtic culinary tradition.[5]

The opposition which is maintained at the level of ingredients is not, however, maintained at the level of *agency*. And it is mainly at this level that the White nation fantasy that is engraved in the text begins to transpire. Crucially, while everyone throws in their ingredient, one person is allowed a monopoly over cooking from the beginning of the story until its end: the White Australian 'Blue'. Even the patriarchy which would have otherwise structured the lives of a mining Anglo-Celtic couple is forgotten for the sake of making the true Blue Aussie male the main *will* behind the whole process.

Furthermore, whatever minimal agency the ethnics who put in their ingredients have, their will is only activated following a request by Molly. Luckily, Molly thought of this, otherwise those ethnics would have kept on just sitting there feeling 'tired' and 'hungry'. Here we come to one of the crucial elements of the discourse of valorisation.

Valuing requires someone to do the valuing and something to be evaluated. The discourse of enrichment operates by establishing a break between valuing negatively and valuing positively similar to the break which the discourse of tolerance establishes between tolerance and intolerance. In much the same way, however, as the tolerance/intolerance divide mystifies the more important divide between holding the power to tolerate and not holding it, the distinction between valuing negatively/valuing positively mystifies the deeper division between holding the power to value (negatively or positively) and not holding it.

Heidegger's critique of the discourse of value perfectly brings out the less-than-egalitarian assumptions underlying it. As he put it:

> It is important finally to realize that precisely through the characterisation of something as 'a value' what is so valued is robbed of its worth. That is to say, by the assessment of something as a value what is valued is admitted only as an object of man's estimation. Every valuing, even when it values positively, is a subjectivizing. It does not let things: be. Rather, valuing lets things: be valid.[6]

In the context of Australian multiculturalism, the point being made is not simply that the discourse of enrichment places the dominant culture in a more important position than other migrant cultures. More importantly, this discourse also assigns to migrant cultures a different *mode of existence* to Anglo-Celtic culture. While the dominant White culture merely and unquestionably *exists*, migrant cultures exist *for* the latter. Their value, or the viability of their preservation as far as White Australians are concerned, lies in their function as enriching cultures. It is in this sense that the discourse of enrichment contributes to the positioning of non-White Australians within the White nation fantasy.

In *The Stew that Grew*, most of the migrants not only remain deprived of the capacity to contribute to the actual cooking process, but they are also voiceless. It is Blue who is given the task of declaring the relative value of each ingredient: 'They sure look tasty,' said Blue, '… This is sure to be different …' Blue's valorisation takes a rather perverse turn when the Aboriginal Johnny Barcoo comes with his Yam and Kangaroo tail, to Blue's exclamation:

> "Now there's the taste of Australia," said Blue,
> "That's sure to make it a fair dinkum stew!"

If it isn't bad enough that the Aboriginal people have to wait for an a posteriori declaration that they are the 'taste of Australia' by a White Australian, judging from the pictures, they do not even stay around to eat from the stew. Their value is one of an *unperturbing* enrichment, as if Blue and Molly were saying: 'Thank you for enriching us with what can make our national cultural production distinctively Australian. Now please go back to your bush so we can enjoy being enriched without you annoying us with your presence!'

A real example of this disposition surfaced in an interview with a bank manager who had recently moved to Marrickville. The interview began with him stating that the main reason behind his move to the area was 'to enjoy the cultural diversity the area has to offer. It's the part of Sydney I've missed most.' (He had moved to Adelaide for a three-year period.) Ten minutes into the interview, however, the discussion moved to architecture and migrant housing, and he had this to say: 'They [the migrants] have really ruined the place, haven't they?' For this person, there was no contradiction between migrants being enriching and them 'ruining the place', for their value derived from their services, not from them inhabiting the area.

Overall, while *The Stew that Grew* works as a valorisation of the many ethnic ingredients (valuable ethnic objects) which have helped make the stew, it also works to valorise Blue's capacity as a cook: an ode not only to the White Australian capacity of recognising the value of ethnicity, but also, above all, to the White Australian art of *mixing*.

Ultimately, it is in this art of mixing the ethnic ingredients thrown into the pot that Blue's contribution stands out. He does not contribute any ordinary ingredients to the stew; as far as his contribution is concerned, 'just what it was, nobody knew'. Blue's contribution was something akin to what Christ injected into the basket of loaves and fish to make them multiply. His contribution allowed the mix to work and expand, and it is precisely why it is the most valuable of all. Left to themselves, those ingredients would not have even mixed, let alone made this most memorable stew.

To have a multicultural society you need many cultures. Left to themselves, however, these cultures are bound not to mix or at least not to mix properly without leading to ethnic tensions and wars. For the mix to work, it has to be guided by a White essence, that most valuable of all ingredients: the democratic-tolerance-freedom-of-speech ingredient that only the White aristocracy really knows how to throw into the Australian stew. Indeed, for the journalist Paul Sheehan:

> There is an enormous difference between the self-evident diversity of Australia's multi-racial society and the big protective tent under which this diversity is thriving. Take away that big tent — Australian culture — and this diversity curdles into State-sponsored tribal animosities.[7]

Or, as Northern Territory Premier Marshall Perron less dramatically puts it:

> ... our western knowledge, education traditions and English as an international language are among the most valuable assets that we bring to our regional trading partnerships. We need these attributes, together with our liberal democratic traditions, to help bind our increasingly multiracial society together.[8]

However, the democratic spirit that the true 'Blues' of Australia can throw into the national stew is clearly not enough. It is merely the spirit that guides the mixer who still has to do the hard work of regulating the mix by controlling the measurements and diluting the concentrations. It is to this discourse of measuring and controlling the 'mix', as it is present in immigration debates, that I will now turn to show the recurrent governmental White fantasy that propels it.

Getting the Mix Right: Measurement and Numbering Pathology

In an article titled 'How to get the mix right', Professor Gavin Jones, the coordinator of the demography program at the Australian National University, wrote that 'Australia's immigration policy ... has contributed both to the substantial population growth ... and to the diversification of the population in terms of ethnic mix and geographic origins.'[9] Professor Jones, like all those who wish to talk about immigration, laments the fact that one cannot talk about it without being labelled. And while 'some racists will seek to gain a cloak of respectability by expressing concerns about social cohesion', one can express such concerns without being racist. Professor Jones himself, far from being a racist, finds the whole situation at present quite enriching:

> These days, about 30 000 Asian immigrants enter each year, and although there are potential flashpoints, the modification of Australia's population composition has proceeded with a remarkable degree of calm.
>
> The increase in the ethnic Asian proportion of the Australian population — now 6% — is, in my view, of great benefit, not only in diversifying Australia's cuisine and culture, but in building the close family and business links that will facilitate Australia's effective integration into the region.

What really makes Australia such a peaceful phenomenon — such a 'good stew' — is precisely that we have a good mix: 'We are fortunate that there is no one dominant ethnic group among the migrants.' All will not necessarily continue to go well, however, and since 'ethnic tensions at home would hardly promote' that very goal of effective integration in the region, 'there is also an ongoing need to promote and monitor community cohesion in Australia'.

We can see how the fantasy of *The Stew that Grew* is being replayed here. The whole construct operates as a fantasy space staging the professor in the role of the White governmental cook. A cook happy with the way the stew is proceeding, but worried nevertheless — worrying, as we have seen, is essential, for if the White governmental subject wasn't worried there would be no need for him to exist. Here, it is the professor's informed worry that helps him assert the necessity of the presence of his watchful governmental eye, demonstrated by the capacity to master the numbers. His worry is to ensure that the recipe is always followed: 'no one dominant ethnic group among migrants'. For, of course, one dominant (White) group among non-migrants is not a problem since that group, imbued unlike others with democracy, tolerance and the principle of freedom of speech by its very essence, is not predisposed to create ethnic tensions. It is only predisposed to solve them through numbering, measuring and mixing.

Such worries about mixing and mixtures are a constant feature of Australian media reporting about immigration and multiculturalism. Three years before Jones's article, some people had similar 'worries' in celebration of the tenth anniversary of a famous 'are we mixing well?' speech made by academic historian Geoffrey Blainey, a renowned worried mixer. In a newspaper article written by the reporter David Jenkins, with the suitable measurement-conscious title of 'Quarter-Asian Australia', Jenkins appeared very worried about the mix:

> What has happened on the Asian front in the past decade? Have we become more or less tolerant towards Asians? Do people worry about the 'Asianisation' of Australia?
> A look at the demographics suggests we have 'Asianised' faster and more thoroughly than anyone — including Professor Blainey — could have anticipated in 1984.
> ... Today, the Asian percentage of the population has not only jumped significantly, it remains on a steep curve.
> ... Can we carry it off? Can we rearrange the demographic mix without recreating the tensions one finds in much of Western Europe and North America?[10]

Although, there appears to be so many Asians in Australia, Jenkins's 'you' and 'we' is, of course, Asianless. Who else but a White 'you' and 'we' can be seen to have the impression of seeing an Asian 'stay with them'?

> If you walked down the street and saw someone who was ethnically Asian, that was the impression that stayed with you, whether the person was born here or not.

Who else can worry about 'carrying it off' despite the Asians? And, of course, who else can worry about the mix? Asians do not worry about the mix, they are the mix. Jenkins, however, is worried:

> ... there are signs that all is not well. The fact that members of the Vietnamese and Lebanese communities tend to concentrate in certain areas has given rise to a concern that we are creating 'ghettoes'. In postcode 2166 (Cabramatta), 83 per cent of the people are overseas-born or are the children of people born overseas.
> ... through good management and good luck, Australia

has faced many of the problems faced by other countries. Can we continue to do so?

Of course, nothing worries the mixer like the concentration.[11] Like a lump of flour in the stew, it is the proof of either a substance resistant to mixing or a weakening of the mixer's capacity to mix. To back his worries, Jenkins provides us with the highest concentration of professorial White regulators of the mix, all emitting views on 'how much' is good, and all 'worried', of course:

> Professor Jamie Mackie says, he's worried we might again be going 'a bit too fast' on Asian migration at a time of high unemployment.
>
> 'We only need one serious race riot and it will undo 30 years of good work. We always said in the IRG that a key consideration was the Australian community's capacity to absorb non-white immigrants without undue stress.
>
> 'In 1960, we thought the number should be about 1,500 Asians a year.
>
> 'Within 10 years we were calmly absorbing about 10,000 without any problems at all. But I became a bit uneasy later at the speed at which the number jumped from 24,000 Asians a year in about 1982 to 60,000 a year after the publication of the Fitzgerald Report [in 1988].'

Given his credentials as a master governmental cook, and a virtuoso numerologist, 'we', of course, should all understand the seriousness of the situation since Professor Mackie became 'a bit uneasy' when 'the number' jumped. The fascinating thing is to see how the White Nation fantasy can give stage to a governmental nationalist capable of believing that their 'feeling uneasy' is something that ought to worry the nation. Professor Viviani of Griffith University, on the other hand, is not 'feeling uneasy'; she is reported to be just uncomfortable. 'I thought 140,000 was way too high in a period of rapid social change in Australia,' she said. 'I'm more comfortable with something between 70, 000 and 100,000.'

Some people do not express such explicit sentiments, they simply enact their governmental role by merely enumerating. For Dr Price, the high priest of numerology:

> Assuming a long-term advantage of 140,000 a year, with the same ethnic composition as the net immigration of

1986–91, then, in the year 2020, the ethnic strength of the Asian component would be some 4.03 million in a total population of 24.66 million; that is 16.3 percent.

Like Jenkins's 'In postcode 2166 (Cabramatta), 83 per cent of the people are overseas-born or are the children of people born overseas', just what these statistics reveal other than the paranoid governmental desire that propels them is unclear. Such enumeration definitely reaches pathological dimensions at times, such as in this newspaper article by Marc Llewellyn with the title 'Nguyens are up with the Joneses':

> A Vietnamese name is among the 10 longest listings in Telecom's new Sydney White Pages for the second year running.
>
> Nguyen (pronounced N'win), is the most common name in Vietnam and eighth most common in Sydney's new telephone book. The name also recorded the biggest increase; with 218 more entries this year than in 1993.
>
> The national marketing manager of Telecom White Pages, Mr Warwick James, said Telecom expected Nguyen to overtake Taylor and jump into seventh place by next year's edition.
>
> 'Only in Sydney and Melbourne is there such a challenge to the dominant Anglo-Saxon names,' he said. 'The other names are pretty constant across the country.'[12]

Again, this news item appears as if it is naturally made to be news. It is only so, however, from within a White fantasy of governmentality. Yet again, what one is supposed to glean from all this other than that someone has their worried eye on the telephone book is unclear. Why is it news? Should the Taylors worry? Should they start breeding? These questions are only relevant from within the fantasy that generates them. Reading this, however, I could not help thinking of Keith Douglas who, as described by David Greason in *I Was a Teenage Fascist*:

> ... whiled away his ample spare time marking off Jewish-sounding names in the telephone directory. 'That way we'll know where they are when we take power,' he told me.'[13]

Here the pathological governmentality behind the innocent numerological exercises becomes less implicit.

As all of the above intimates, this White multiculturalism, by being concerned with the acceptance, positioning and numbering of otherness in order to maximise its *value,* is a practice that aims at creating and managing an 'economy of otherness' — a system of producing and regulating the value of otherness to maximise the homely feeling (the taste of the homemade stew) of the White Australians positioned at its centre. It is in this sense that White multiculturalism reveals itself as a White fantasy of national 'governmentality' in the sense defined by Foucault. For, if the nationalist practices of exclusion look like negative practices aimed only at the beheading of otherness, White multiculturalism appears as a process of 'fostering ethnic life' and ethnic value. This process reached its epitome during the period of the Keating Labor Government and the rise of 'productive diversity'.

Productive Diversity: The Production of Ethnic Surplus Value

The discourse of productive diversity emerged following the election of the Bob Hawke's Labor Government in 1983 and was part of right-wing Labor's economic rationalism discourse. The discourse aimed, among other things, at justifying various social policy interventions on the basis of economic soundness. It accompanied Hawke's inclusion of 'economic efficiency' as a principle of multiculturalism. This marrying of cultural value with economic value was perfected by the Keating government.

For Keating, multiculturalism constituted an economically exploitable resource in the form of hitherto untapped potential. The point was to create the social conditions at both a micro and macro level to allow such potential to become utilisable. It was believed that this would give Australia an 'advantage' it was much in need of in a competitive international environment: 'We have realised that our future depends on making ourselves relevant to the rest of the world.'[14]

This was the chief function of productive diversity and what made it valuable. It was constructed as a key aspect, if not *the* key aspect, of the multicultural era ushered in by Keating:

There have been three distinct phases in Australia's postwar response to its immigrants.

The first phase was characterised by an expectation that immigrants would fit into the dominant Anglo-Australian culture.

The second was characterised by the encouragement of tolerance and respect for diversity, and the effort to ensure access and equity regardless of ethnic origin. And this effort will continue.

But we now have the beginnings of a third phase.

We now must take advantage of the potentially huge national economic asset which multiculturalism represents.

That is what Productive Diversity is about.[15]

The distinctiveness of Keating's discourse of valorisation was that it went beyond the dominant valuing of ethnic cultures at the level of consumption. It was an attempt at a productive valuing. In the sphere of consumption, ethnic cultures yielded for the White valoriser the cultural value embodied in them. To consume a Thai meal was to enjoy its cultural value, its Thai-ness, so to speak. With productive diversity, it was a question of activating ethnic cultures to make them yield not cultural satisfaction, but more money capital. It is in this sense that one can see it as a cultural exploitation of ethnicity to make it yield a kind of ethnic surplus value. It was a much clearer discourse of exploitation rather than consumption. This was precisely the theme of a famed conference on productive diversity in business where the key discussion paper was prefaced by the quote: 'Ask not what you can do for them, but what they can do for you.'[16]

The conference involved incredibly original directives in the modes in which one can use one's local ethnics to make them yield their potential capacity to produce surplus. Thus:

One of the charms of international travel is to experience different landscapes, different food ... Australia needs to offer 'Australian experiences' to visitors ... In seeking to understand which qualities about our country appeal most to different nationalities, it is only necessary to ask immigrants from those countries for advice on the best way of selling aspects of the Australian identity to incoming tourists.[17]

Now at one level, and an important one, there is clearly nothing 'wrong' with this usage. It can be seen as a further integration of ethnic difference in the mainstream of Australian society and, as such, another step on the road to further empowerment. The problem, however, is that, like multiculturalism in general and the discourse of valorisation and tolerance in particular, there is no single way in which this productive diversity is conceived. Also, judging from the statements emitted by those who are concerned by it, its dominant understanding constitutes an economic extension to the space of the White nation fantasy.

The single most important indicator of the imaginary White governmental dominance that has structured the discourse of productive diversity is its inability to conceive of this diversity at any level other than that of the managed object. Diversity is always assumed to be a diversity among employees, among those who need to be managed, those who need to be ruled. It is never conceived as a cultural diversity that needs to be promoted among employers, managers and rulers. Those are free from any recommendations concerning their own diversity and how productive or unproductive it can be. Thus, the *Productive Diversity in Business* discussion paper begins with: 'From a manager's point of view, the specific characteristics of a multicultural workforce are that the employee …' For Keating, as well, the issue was straightforwardly a matter of the diversity of the workforce:

> Managing a culturally diverse workforce may not be perceived as a challenge by managers and business owners, many of whom think that their workforce is able to speak and communicate adequately in English.[18]

A management representative, Robert Pritchard, in a paper to the Productive Diversity in Business Conference, revealed the White Management — culturally diverse employees polarity very clearly:

> The main message in this to all young Australians, but most especially to those whose cultural heritage is not Anglo-Saxon, is to develop your cultural and lingual ability to the stage where it can be exploited by you in your chosen career and utilised by your employer. The message in this for Australian employers is to invest in people with multicultural talents.

The White managerial imaginary behind all this becomes even clearer as one notices that the same 'worry' about numbers and concentrations is seen as a propeller behind the strategy. Thus, for another manager, Ivan Deveson, in his opening address to the conference:

> These changes are, of course, a two-way challenge. We must continue to ensure that, as a society, we avoid the prejudice and resultant violence that pervades many countries. We must ensure that we continue to integrate as a people, to avoid the ethnic ghettoes ...

Why 'ethnic ghettoes' are unproductive diversity can only be answered within the White governmental imaginary that perceives them as a problem in the first place. Northern Territory Chief Minister Marshall Perron states:

> However, we will never make the most of our opportunities in the region unless we learn Asian languages, become familiar with Asian history, geography, customs, and current events — and take in many more immigrants from the region to help us to do business with their countries of origin. There is nothing to fear in this.[19]

In this statement, Perron reveals the 'fearing' White governmental subject behind the whole construct. Indeed, if the addressee wasn't imagined to be a White Australian, why do we need to allay their fears at all. In a seminal report by Carmel Niland, *Towards Managing Diversity*, we can see how the very language used works to disallow the possibility of thought moving from the valorised 'managing cultural diversity' to the repressed idea of 'culturally diverse management':

> A managing diversity approach enables individual employees to be appreciated and valued. It begins by training managers to recognise the range of [cultural] differences that they have in their employees ... then it trains managers to tolerate and accommodate these differences and eventually trains them to see these differences not as a deficit but as an advantage.[20]

We can see here how the discourses of multicultural tolerance and valorisation fuse by conceiving of this tolerance as an interested mode of acceptance. This necessarily means that the object of tolerance cannot be seen in purely negative terms. Within this fantasy, it is because some benefits are derived from the objects of multicultural toleration, or at least from the act of toleration itself, that we tolerate them — go to the trouble of dominating them through tolerance — and accept them within our sphere of influence.

Rather than involving a negative evaluation of its objects, tolerance is guided by a process of evaluating both the benefits accruing from the act of toleration *and* what is perceived as negative and needs to be endured. However, and this is what has been emphasised in this chapter, what is important is that what defines the object of White multicultural tolerance is not that it is valued negatively or positively, but that it is constructed as an object of evaluation *as such*. It is because this evaluating process involves both the negative and the positive, what is appreciated and what needs to be endured that the positioning of White multiculturalism's other and the setting of the boundaries within which it can exist are far more complex than a mere search for protection from negativity as it is constructed in the nationalist practices of exclusion.

When reviewing all the managerial statements of valorisation in their totality, they add up to more than just a conception of a polarity between White national manager — non-White managed national object. If we examine their actual impact in the social field from which they emanate, we realise that they actually help shape the very ground that makes them credible. They help to ward off the possibility of a non-White national manager. In this sense, the discourse of valorisation raises an important issue regarding the relationship between the national fantasy of the White subject and the reality in which it is grounded.

For a fantasy to provide a solid basis for the construction of the White national self within it, it has to be well grounded in social reality. Such fantasies are not the products of wild imagination. To work efficiently as fantasies, to provide a relatively stable home for those who inhabit them, they have to support and be supported by the practical reality lived by the subject. If, as we have seen in the previous chapters, this practical reality has to be seen as lacking in comparison to the fantasy — otherwise the nationalist would not derive any 'existential purpose' from being positioned in it. At the same time, this relative lack cannot be too great or the fantasy would appear unattainable.

The fantasy of the White manager is grounded in a social reality where non-White Australians are clearly under-represented in the political, social and economic managerial class. It is this reality which gives credibility to the White Australian that positions himself or herself in the role of the valorising mixing manager. At the same time, there are clearly tendencies in Australian society for non-White Australians to assert themselves as equally empowered Australian national wills within the field. This is the reality that cannot be incorporated by White multiculturalism, the multicultural Real. Every fantasy has its Real.[21] It is that part of the subject's practical reality whose acknowledgment can lead to endangering the minimum of coherence and stability that the fantasy needs in order to reproduce itself.[22] This Real is the necessary result of the complex relationship between fantasy and practical reality outlined above. It is also why a fantasy does not merely 'represent' social reality, but also tries to shape it practically, in order efficiently to contain the changes that cannot be incorporated within it.

It is important to stress that containment does not mean exclusion. It involves a far more complex process of positioning. Let us look, for example, at the growing presence of the confidently Australian, but non-White nationalists among the migrant population. Because it is part of an Australian reality that undermines the national subject — national object/White nationalist — 'Third World — looking' migrant/tolerator–tolerated/enriched–enriching set of relations that underlie the fantasy, it is a reality that the practices emanating from within White multiculturalism aim to contain. What makes such a containment a complex process, however, is that White multiculturalism sees in the 'migrant' an enriching/tolerable presence, and therefore something exploitable that has to be included in national space. That is, such practices of containment cannot turn into practices of exclusion and aim at *regulating the modality of inclusion* of the Third World-looking migrants in national space instead. This makes for a far more complex spatial practice. It is an art of positioning which has its roots in the modes of regulating the presence of migrant labour to exploit it economically when such migrant labour was the dominant form of migration to Australia, and indeed across the world.

The Practical Logic of White Multiculturalism: On the Dialectic of Inclusion and Exclusion

As has often been pointed out, the history of the post-World War II wave of migration to Australia is essentially a history of labour migration.[23] The development of Australian capitalism following the war was accomplished with the help of an influx of workers from overseas imported by the state to meet local labour shortages. Employers gained directly, at least in the short term, from the presence of migrant labour. First, they gained from their mere presence as labour given existing shortages. Secondly, and more specifically, they gained from their presence as *migrant* labour.

The migrant workers, unlike the local workers, were unintegrated in society and its institutions. They could be subjected to highly exploitative working conditions without offering more than occasional, often individual, resistance. The reason behind this, of course, lay in their relative lack of social power emanating from their position as workers, from their inability to communicate in the dominant language and from the weakness of their links with an organised labour movement which looked after White workers and perceived migrant labour as a threat to White working conditions. This relative marginalisation of migrant labour was epitomised by the European guest-worker system.

As a set of mechanisms and rules which maintained the foreignness of the migrant worker while physically entrenching them as a structural component of production in the economy, the guest-worker system was chiefly a process aimed at maximising the exploitation of migrant labour. It put in place mechanisms through which migrants had to be physically positioned inside the nation, but, at the same time, also had to be symbolically kept foreign within it. It is those mechanisms which laid the ground for the peculiar position of migrant labour in these early periods of high exploitation.

In so far as employers needed migrant workers to work in their factories, they wanted them 'included' in national space. For these employers, however, the desirability of this *inclusion* lay precisely in the migrant workers being socially *excluded*. The distinctiveness of the migrant workers' position in this process is that while they were subjected to certain processes whose effect was their marginalisation and exclusion, these processes did not aim to marginalise to the point where they were driven outside social space as was the case with many Aborigines, for example.

The exclusion of migrant labour was not total, since obviously its aim was not to drive them outside social space, but to drive them to the point where it was precisely their *inclusion* (as cheap labour) that became viable. Thus, paradoxically, it is precisely the interest in their inclusion that activated the existing social processes of their exclusion, while at the same time setting limits on how far to the margin of society they ought to be excluded. Far from being mechanisms of exclusion, these processes activated a complex dialectic of inclusion and exclusion where cheap labour was positioned in a liminal space created by centripetal and centrifugal forces which activated each other — it was the very need for inclusion that activated exclusionary processes, while it was the exclusionary forces that allowed for the inclusionary ones to be activated.

It is often thought paradoxical, for example, how the virulent anti-immigration discourse that is dominant in California today is accompanied by an increase in the number of illegal Mexican immigrant labourers crossing the border. In fact, the two have to be seen as complementary processes. The anti-immigration discourse, by continually constructing the immigrants as unwanted, works precisely at maintaining their economic viability to American employers. They are best wanted as 'unwanted'.

Female labour in Australia and elsewhere in the West is increasingly subjected to a similar dialectic. It is often assumed that the re-emergence of ideologies that aim to reposition women in a traditional role within the domestic sphere contradict the fact that a greater proportion of women are entering the workforce relative to the number of men. In fact, far from being contradictory, this discourse operates to give this labour a marginal value such that it remains attractive from the point of view of the employers of this labour. Far from somehow sending women back into the domestic sphere, its main effect is to constitute the prism through which female labour is (de)valued. The social devaluation of their labour is part of the process of constructing its economic value for the employer.[24] It is this dialectic of inclusion and exclusion that constitutes the modus operandi of the technologies put in place to contain the multicultural Real through the positioning of Third World — looking migrants.

In his work on domestication, Geoffroy de St Hilaire, the famous French naturalist, analyses the difficult process of domesticating and exploiting a specific type of llama whose wool was only valuable (of good quality) while it remained in the wild.[25] As soon as it was included permanently in human settlements, the quality of the llama's wool deteriorated. Thus, the problem from the domesticators' point of view was that once domesticated, once included in the human settlement, the llama lost the value for which it was domesticated in the first place. Its value lied in it being excluded. At the same time, it could not be totally driven into the wild as this would mean its wool could not be exploited. Thus the problem was maintaining an in-between space where it could be neither totally included nor totally excluded.

De Saint Hilaire also gives us a further insight into this dialectic of inclusion and exclusion by pointing out that its aim was what he called 'la sauvegarde de la sauvagerie'. How does one tame (make less savage) something with a value which lies in its 'savageness' (i.e. in its non-belonging to the humanly defined social sphere) without threatening this very 'savageness'? To de Saint Hilaire, one needs to develop techniques aimed at safeguarding the savage state. This appears contradictory at first, for any savageness that is 'safeguarded' is no longer 'truly' savage. What de Saint Hilaire's analysis emphasises, however, is that the savageness that is needed is not the savageness of the llama's 'will', but the savageness of its woolly body. The techniques aimed at safeguarding the savage state are precisely those techniques which can maintain the savageness of the body (which is where the value of the domesticated other lies), while eradicating the savage will (which stands between the domesticator and the exploitable body).

As we have seen in examining White multiculturalism, it is precisely the eradication of the migrant will that constitutes the very basis of the White Australian capacity for tolerance and acceptance. As such, White multiculturalism activates a dialectic of inclusion and exclusion, similar to the above, in order to position Third World-looking migrants in the permanent spatial in-between where their will is excluded, while their exploitable 'savage' body/culture is included. This constitutes the essence of the technologies aimed at the containment of the multicultural Real and which have been chiefly present in the settlement policies of the White Australian state.

The closest the dialectic of inclusion and exclusion in Australia came to resemble its mode of operation under the European guest-worker system was under the policy of assimilation, when migrant workers were at their weakest. Undoubtedly, the resemblance is limited given that even under the policy of assimilation Australian migrants had full formal legal, political and social security rights after a relatively short period of residency. Nevertheless, the effect of the assimilation policy was similar to the guest-worker system in that it positioned the migrant workers in a process of mere *economic* inclusion in the workplace and of *socio-political* exclusion both in the workplace and elsewhere in society. As I argued in chapter 2, the real effect of the prevalence of the ideology of assimilation was in fact *exclusionary* for non-White migrants in the socio-political spheres of society. It only served as a system of classification through which the accusatory category 'non-assimilated' served to construct and reproduce the tenuous nature of the migrant's inclusion within the nation. This category did not only indicate the division of the population between two sections — one seen as central/assimilated and the other as marginal/unassimilated. More importantly, it also constructed non-assimilation such that it empowered the 'assimilated' to see in the unassimilated a negative, problematic group and actively to exclude them from the social, political and cultural spheres of society. To use de Saint Hilaire, we can say that the policy of assimilation operated as a technology aimed at constructing the migrant into a perpetual 'internal savage'.

While state multiculturalism distinguishes itself from preceding settlement policies in the extent of the inclusionary social/cultural spaces opened up by the state for non-White Australians, it was nevertheless a refining of the processes through which settlement policy regulated the dialectic of inclusion and exclusion. This is most clearly embodied in the notions of enrichment, tolerance and acceptance examined in this chapter. Indeed, through the way they promote an open arms approach to the non-White Australian population only to reposition it as a dependent 'will-less valuable', these categories were a perfection of the dialectic of inclusion and exclusion.

One further distinctive feature of the White multiculturalism of the state is the way it opens up cultural spaces of inclusion *as a substitute* to effective inclusion in mainstream political processes. The closest the non-White middle classes come to political participation is in the closed circles of welfare politics, or, more precisely, the politics of regulating and distributing 'multicultural' welfare funds made available by the White state. The very nature of this 'political' involvement reproduced the paradigm of tolerance and acceptance by promoting a conception of multiculturalism as something granted, a kind gesture White Australians in which were good enough to engage.

As it can be seen, the dialectic of inclusion and exclusion at work within White multiculturalism constantly works at laying the practical ground on which it can sustain itself as a White fantasy. It also lays the material foundation for the fundamental ambivalence that is constitutive of the White multicultural gaze towards the 'ethnic other'.

Conclusion

In his much referred to work on cultural diversity, the philosopher Charles Taylor defines multiculturalism as involving the demand that 'we all *recognize* the equal value of different cultures; that we not only let them survive, but acknowledge their *worth*.'[26] For all its sophistication, Taylor's approach exemplifies the White multiculturalism that we have examined in this chapter. This aspect of Taylor's argument is criticised by Susan Wolf, who points out that the issue is well beyond a question of acknowledging worth. More importantly, it 'rests on the claim that African or Asian or Native American cultures are part of our culture, or rather, of the cultures of some of the groups that together constitute our community.'[27] Criticising the idea that multiculturalism is an invitation to recognise, for example, the equal value of the literary works of the 'other cultures' present in the United States, she argued that:

> The most significant harm to which the previous failures of recognition in our libraries contributed was not that we were deprived access to some great folktales, as great as or even greater than the ones represented on the shelves.... The most significant good ... is not that our stock of legends is now better or more comprehensive than before. It is, rather, that by having these books and by reading them, we come to recognize ourselves as a multicultural community and so to recognize and respect the members of that community in all our diversity.[28]

It is this recognition that we are a 'multicultural community in all our diversity' that is evaded by White multiculturalism, for it is in the opposition between valuing diversity and *being* diverse that the White nation fantasy operates to reproduce itself. The 'we appreciate' diversity, 'we value' ethnic contributions, etc. attitudes which abound in the dominant political discourse in Australia create a gulf between the 'we' and that which is appreciated and valued. In so doing, they work to mystify the real possibility, grounded in the very composition of Australian society, of a national 'we' which is itself diverse. It is this 'we' that is at the core of the multicultural Real: we are diversity. It is a 'we' associated with the verb 'to be', while it is the verb 'to have' (which always presupposes a subject that has and an object that is had) that structures the imaginary of White multiculturalism. Indeed, 'to have' others is a necessary precondition for 'appreciating' them.

'To have' and 'to be' are both what Benveniste calls *verbes d'état*, verbs delineating a state of being. However, Benveniste asserts — in a complex argument that one needs to read in full to capture its strength — that while they both indicate a state of being, they don't indicate the same state of being.

> *To be* is, the state of that who is being, the one who is something. *To have* is the state of the possessor, the one for whom something is. The difference appears thus. Between the two terms it joins *to be* establishes an intrinsic relation of identity: it is the consubstantial state of being. On the contrary,

the two terms joined by to have remain distinct ... it is the relation between the possessor to the possessed.[29]

This is the crucial difference between the multiculturalism of being and the multiculturalism of having. While the former establishes a unified Australian 'we' where Whites and non-Whites fuse in a 'consubstantial state of being', the latter always establishes an extrinsic relation between a White possessor and non-White possessed. The White multicultural 'we' which appreciates diversity seems continuous with the old Australian 'we' that did not appreciate it. Diversity simply does not affect the nature of the White 'we'. It remains extrinsic to it. It is in this sense that White multiculturalism's 'to have' is set against the verb 'to be'. For if we *are* diversity, there would be nothing to 'appreciate' and 'value' other than ourselves. This is the difficult imaginary domain of the multicultural Real.

chapter 5

White National Zoology:
The Pro-Asian Republic Fantasy

… just as we would like to be masters of our destiny,
so too we would like to be masters of our own international image.

(Greg Sheridan, *Australian*, 14 June 1995)

There is a consensus in Australia that multiculturalism and
Australia's attempts to move away from Europe and into Asia
are naturally complementary. If multiculturalism is the
antithesis of the assimilationist drive to subject all
Australians, regardless of their background, to Anglo cultural norms, then surely multiculturalism, by its very nature as
an anti-Eurocentric discourse, lays the ground for a redirect-
ing of Australia towards Asia.

The argument that interests me here is not so much the
one built around the anti-Eurocentric nature of multiculturalism, but the idea that Australia's drive to be 'part of Asia'
today, what I will call for the sake of simplification the 'pro-
Asia discourse', is necessarily 'multicultural'. This is the idea
that Australia's reorientation towards Asia is inspired by, and
articulated from within, Australia's multicultural experience.
This idea is strongly expressed in the narratives of the dominant pro-Asia discourse, such as seen in the 'Australia as a
Euro-Asian republic' campaign of the Australian Labor
Party. The narrative begins with the 'story' of postwar migration and the fundamental changes it brought to both the

everyday nature of Australian society and to Australia's national identity. Indeed, this narrative goes so far as to see these multicultural changes as the 'cause', or at least the main condition of possibility, of an Asia-orientated Australia today.

I would like to argue that despite, and through, this narrative, the dominant pro-Asia discourse remains (paradoxically) animated by a White nationalist problematic. I will show that the narrative of migration, cultural diversity and change, rather than being at the roots of the pro-Asia discourse, is a deployment within it. That is, pro-Asian thought in Australia is not multicultural, rather official multiculturalism should be seen primarily as a White nationalist strategy directed towards Asia. In the argument that follows, I will be concentrating on a particular instance of the articulation between the Labor Party's 'pro-Asian' republicanism and multiculturalism.

Republicanism is above all a discourse of national home-building. As Malcolm Turnbull sees it: 'The most important thing is to keep discussing these questions of Australia's identity, its destiny and its development into an independent nation.'[1] Such a discourse, like all discourses of nation-building, is dialogic.[2] It contains two overlapping, sexuated sub-discourses. The first, the sub-discourse of the motherland, is directed internally towards the Australian people. It is the homely nation discourse we have been examining so far. Here, it is about the capacity of the 'pro-Asian republic' to provide a better 'home' for Australians to live in. The second, the sub-discourse of the fatherland, is an internationally orientated sub-discourse. It defines the identity of Australia as an active (inter)national subject/body to both Australians and to other international subjects (nations and nationals).

Multiculturalism plays a different but related role within each of these discourses. In the second half of the 1970s, when it emerged as a state ideology, multiculturalism was above all a 'homely' discourse. It helped to define the Australian nation to its nationals as a more tolerant, egalitarian and culturally richer place in which to live. In the 1980s, however, state ideologies of multiculturalism increasingly became part of an internationally orientated discourse aiming to define Australia's international identity, particularly to its regional neighbours. It is on this particular 'internationalist' articulation that I want to concentrate. I will show how the dominant pro-Asian republican discourse reveals the White nation fantasy within it in the very way it positions multiculturalism vis-à-vis the Australian (inter)national body.

Who's Afraid of Asia?: On the Whiteness of the Dominant pro-Asian Discourse

The nationalist sub-discourses centred on the emergence and the presence of nations as active international subjects do not only abound in bodily metaphors. They also abound in related metaphors of birth, growth and maturity. The development of the Western capitalist world, the colonial ventures it engaged in, and the newer nation-states these ventures gave rise to created a distinct division in the way nations are imagined in this regard.

First, there are the imperialist nations themselves, imagined somewhat like gods (and like fathers and mothers in the child's imaginary), either as immediately and forever adult, or as born in a past somewhat discontinuous with the present where their adulthood is unquestionable. Secondly, there comes a host of nations imagined to be in various stages of development on the way to 'adulthood'. The national 'maturity' of all these nations was or is still seen as problematic, by themselves and by the rest of the world, especially by the imperialist power under whose wing they have grown into recognised nation-states. In this context, 'adulthood' and 'maturity' were taken to be a type of cultural measure of both independence and the capacity of using one's independence 'wisely'.

Australia, a nation born out of the imperialist system, has always fallen into this second category. Its nationalists have often, through a discourse of adulthood and maturity, perceived its degree of independence as problematic. Ideas of an independent and mature Australia emerged in the process of federation. They also have a strong presence in the war mythologies of Gallipoli. They have always, however,

suffered from the weight of acknowledged political and economic dependency, and the 'fighting other people's wars'
syndrome.

Lately, the idea of Australia as a 'truly' independent international actor has become increasingly important within
Australian nationalist discourse. It has accompanied an
important shift in the process of symbolising the nation.
Along with the passive, internally directed mode of imagining Australia as a motherly/homely place (variations on 'the
lucky country'), there has been an increasing emphasis on a
more active and internationally directed mode of conceiving
Australia's existence. This shift coincides with the disarticu-
lation of the Australian economy from its traditional English,
and then US-centred, networks and its articulation to the
'Asian' economy.

This new articulation brought with it the emergence of a
number of 'before and after' discourses along the lines of:
before we were a 'semi-colony', a dependent protectorate, and
now we are truly independent. An important instance of this
before and after discourse has also come to exist within economic culture, where we find a very clear dichotomy between
the active and the passive. The 'European/American'
Australia of 'before' was perceived as an essentially passive
provider of raw materials; the 'Asian' Australia of 'after' is an
active producer/competitor in the region.

Against this background, one can also discern in the
Australia of the 1980s, and even more so in the 1990s, a
much higher profile given to the foreign affairs initiatives of
prime ministers and foreign affairs ministers. This is accompanied by a more active and relatively independent role
played by the Australian government in the world's, and particularly in the region's, affairs — from the pacification of
Cambodian politics to Asian or intra-Pacific economic sum-
mits. It is in this context that the discourse of 'maturity', of
being 'on our own' and 'out of the colonial shadow', has re-
emerged, finding only one of its expressions within the
republican discourse, but continuing in different guises
under the present anti-republican government.

This active international posture has led to a fairly recent
mode of presentation of multiculturalism within Australian
nationalist discourse. At the time of its emergence, and well

into the Hawke prime ministership, multiculturalism was predominantly an internally directed discourse. That is, 'we are a multicultural society' was largely an answer to the question: 'What are we?' This is a question that nationals ask themselves about themselves: let us look at ourselves and discover what we are. More recently, 'we are a multicultural society' has also become part of a new internationally directed discourse: 'Look at us, people of the world, we are a multicultural society.'

Within this discourse, multiculturalism is presented as a central component of Australia's new international identity. More specifically, it is conceived as important in allowing the Australian nation as an international body to reorientate itself and assume a non-Eurocentric posture and identity, and to imagine itself as an independent international subject in Asia rather than in Europe. For Paul Keating: 'Multiculturalism has done much to break down our fear of cultural difference, and therefore our old fear of Asia.'[3] In this discourse, Asia is the 'Real' that the immature self could not face. Armed with its multiculturalism, however, the new mature (and secure) self can now face the Asian Real which in the very process is no longer beyond being symbolised and, as such, loses it Real-ness.

It is statements such as the above that can lead one to believe that the pro-Asia discourse is deeply and irrevocably multicultural. I would like to take Keating's statement as a point of entry into some of the basic structures of this pro-Asianness. From this position, I will argue that, despite the apparent centrality of multiculturalism in this drama of bodily re-orientation, maturity and independence, pro-Asianness remains primarily a discourse from within the White nation fantasy.

My starting point is an unease and a suspicion with regard to the nature of the 'we' implied by the 'our fear of cultural difference' and 'our old fear of Asia'. As a non-Anglo-Celtic person who does not identify with the history of the White Australia policy and assimilation, I have had no fear of 'cultural difference' or, more precisely, of the cultural differences implied here — and, most certainly, I have no *old* fear of Asia. Paul Keating is using the national 'we', but he is not speaking for me, nor could he be speaking to the millions of

Australians like me. The 'we' is a strictly Anglo-Celtic White affair: it refers to an *old* White history and deals with a present White problem. I would argue that this is not an isolated utterance. In fact, the centrality of the discourse of 'maturity', the idea that Australia has 'matured' enough to break its colonial ties with Britain, is itself the clearest indication of the Anglo-Celtic White identity of the pro-Asian 'we' of the republican discourse.

Discourses of 'maturity' are only discourses of change in a limited sense. Post-revolutionary societies do not usually perceive themselves as a maturation of the older societies they replaced. Maturity is essentially an evolutionary discourse. It is a discourse of change within a deeper continuity. Those who have matured are no longer the same as those who were immature, but their remaining fundamentally the same people is the condition of possibility of their experience of maturity. Here we have one of the paradoxes of the republican discourse of maturity. If Australia has matured, even if it has matured 'because' of multiculturalism, an essential continuity between the immature and the mature Australia has to exist as a necessary condition of possibility of any utterance concerning national maturation. This continuity cannot be other than that of an Anglo-Celtic White Australia.

The Australian High Court judge Michael Kirby has argued that rather than being a sign of maturity, the pro-republic discourse is a sign of immaturity.[4] This is true to the extent that those who are confident about their maturity do not perceive it as a problem. Their maturity *goes without saying*: we do not remember our parents having to declare themselves mature, or trying to convince us of their maturity. This does not mean, however, that the discourse of maturity is a sign of immaturity. From a purely descriptive and behaviourist perspective, it is more a sign of a perceived transitional stage towards maturity. It is a stage where maturity is seen as a problem because it is perceived as possible. This is why the discourse of maturity is specific to the middle to late teens: the stage where the young person perceives the possibility and the necessity of becoming 'independent', and usually does so in a successive series of break-up dramas and generational wars with the parents.

What should be noted here is that these often stormy teenager–parent dramas that accompany the transition to maturity have an important symbolic value. Most often, they are rituals unconsciously reproducing the imagined inaugural violence of birth. In this sense, they are symbols of the 'birth' of a phase of change that has already been happening. In the very process of symbolising change, however, the symbolic practice itself becomes a *sui generis element* of the process. There has always been a stigma attached to those teenagers who merely slide into adulthood without having had such a symbolic dramatic confrontation with their parents — as if they live without having really been born.

I am dwelling on this point because it leads us to a distinctive aspect of the dominant pro-Asian and pro-republic discourse. Its emphasis on a *break* with the monarchy is an important part of its discourse on maturity. Indeed, many republicans seem to be more interested in the break than in what happens after it. I would even suspect that many are seeking the break even though they know that nothing much will change.[5] Behind this need for a break is a very old and powerful White nationalist discourse — which often appears as if it is a mere observation, but, if one listens carefully, is in fact a lament — that Australia has had no civil war, no war of independence. Within this discourse, like the teenager who has not had its symbolic violent rebirth, 'Australia' remains an unborn living being yearning for its normalising 'violent' adult beginning. This is why no matter how many people argue, and with good reason, that we are already independent regardless of the monarchy, they will not be heard by those who need such a break.

Furthermore, and as with all teenagers wishing to assert the birth of their mature self, for the break to happen at all, it has to be witnessed by those it is intending to break away from as a 'mature' being. There is no point breaking with mum without her being there. This is why, for republicans, it is not good enough to wait for the Queen to die, as some have suggested. There needs to be a *drama* in which the break is *willed* by the new 'mature' being and is watched by those from which the latter is breaking.

In much the same way as the maturing Australia is the maturing of White Australia, the break is also, and necessar-

ily so, a White family affair. First, while everyone desires a
break or a new beginning, the desire for the 'violent' re-birth
that has not yet happened is specifically White Australian,
particularly Anglo-Celtic. For example, as a Lebanese-born
Australian, I have already seen more violent rebirths than I
care to experience. Secondly, and most obviously, the object
of the break, the Queen, is an Anglo-Celtic Australian object
of affect (even if in a different and a more complex way in
the case of Celtics). If assimilation aimed to force on non-
Anglo Australians a 'mother' to which they had no affective
ties, the republican expectation that these same Australians
feel the 'teenage thrill' of breaking with her seems the
height of assimilationism.

The dominant pro-Asia discourse as it emerges in republicanism then, is clearly centred on a White subject and a
White perception of a problem. Consequently, the apparent
centrality of multiculturalism in this discourse cannot be the
centrality of a subject. Looking back at Keating's statement,
in light of the above, it becomes clear that multiculturalism's
apparent centrality is the centrality of a function: it 'has done
much'. Multiculturalism is not central because the national
subject *is* multicultural. It is central because it figures as a
solution to a White problem. The relationship between the
two remains at an important level, like the relationship
between the cook and 'the stew that grew', *a relationship of
exteriority* between self and other.

Indeed, because of this relation of exteriority, Whites can
only experience multiculturalism positively as a function. The
positive function of multiculturalism in reorientating
Australia within the international nationalist discourse is an
extension of the positive function of culturally 'enriching'
Australia which it is seen to play within the internally oriented White nationalist discourse.

Sydney/Australia's presentation of itself in the bidding for
the year 2000 Olympic Games provides a clear illustration of
the mode of existence of multiculturalism in the international arena and the way it is shaped by the structure of decision-making in Australia. As it was widely reported in the
media, Australia's presentation of itself as a multicultural
society was crucial in shaping the image that overseas people
had of it. While this presentation was crucial and even dom-

inant, however, it was striking how White the Australian Olympic subject was. That is, while many cultures were deployed on the stage to 'show off' the diversity of Australia, very few non-White Australians were part of the managerial decision-making team. Multicultural Australia did not come to represent Australia, it came to be *presented* by White Australia. All the 'multicultural' performers, from the ethnic dancers to the Prime Minister's wife's multilingual prowess, were objects/functions that White Australian decision-makers used in presenting 'Australia' (themselves) to the international community. In this sense, despite its 'multiculturalism', the performance was an actualisation of a White nation fantasy.

It should be clear from the above how, rather than being imagined as an essential part of the national body, multiculturalism is imagined as an object performing a function for that body. Once again, we see how in this White performative fantasy, 'ethnics' are not part of the national *will*, which remains essentially White. Multiculturalism here becomes an instrument used to special effect by a White Australian will in the process of presenting the Australian national body on the international scene. In other words, it is imagined as a technology of the (inter)national body. Here again we see the importance of the structuring effect of *having* rather than *being* on the White nation fantasy. In so far as it is an exhibition of cultural diversity, it is less an exhibition of a culturally diverse Australia than an exhibition of the cultural diversity that (White) Australia *has*. It is as such that multiculturalism is present within the dominant pro-Asian republican discourse.

It is important, however, to examine further this subject/object, body/technology of the body dualism and its consequences on what I have termed a relationship of exteriorisation in the dominant White imaginary of the relationship between multiculturalism and 'Australia'. These dualisms are helpful in perceiving as a problem the relationship of exteriorisation, but they are insufficient to help us explain its complexity. While multiculturalism is imagined, experienced and activated by White Australians as an object in the presentation of the national body, it also remains imagined and, in a more obvious way, it is presented as a *part* of that body. That is, rather than in terms of a dualism, it is perceived as both a technology of the body and an extension of the body. Here, it operates within the White fantasy dually as an exterior object while being, at the same time, an interior extension of the national subject.

Olivier Burgelin, in an excellent article, 'Les outils de la toilette', provides us with an engaging anthropological examination of the many tools we use to control our appearances. I think that his analysis can help us to better conceptualise multiculturalism's dualistic 'presentational function'. Burgelin begins by pointing out that:

> It is in fact impossible to succeed in controlling appearances without having at our disposal a differentiated range of tools. Most of our everyday tools of the body aim (or one of their aims is) to allow the person who applies them or to whom they are applied to control his/her physical appearances and to make it conform to a social norm or to the idea he has of it.[6]

He starts his analysis by pointing out that he does not want to 'distinguish between "tools" as such (hair brush, scissors, comb) and "materials" (soap, shaving cream)', since his aim is to distinguish between functions.[7] Most of the examples given by Burgelin such as scissors or soap are technologies of the body that have a straightforward external relationship to the body. We use them to present our body, but they are not part of the presentation of the body. In fact, they are mostly used in private spaces so that only the effect of their usage is available to the public gaze. Clearly, the imaginary exhibitory multiculturalism of the White Nation fantasy does not fall in this category of technologies since, as we have argued, it is part of the presentation.

It is when Burgelin proceeds to examine clothing which he singles out for a special treatment that his analysis becomes of specific interest to us. Clothes, he argues, have a special status as far as being specific technologies of the body. Unlike other technologies such as shaving equipment, the hair brush or the scissors, they are not simply applied to modify the body, and then left behind. They are also applied as relatively enduring extensions. As he puts it: 'in relation to other tools of the body, clothes are both tools and body'.[8] On the one hand, they are technologies of the body, since they have a function (protection from the cold, veiling etc.) and they can modify the body's appearances and even sometimes its internal structure (bras). On the other hand, they are also body in the sense of being the prolongation of the body/its substitute. Thus, they end up requiring themselves specific technologies of maintenance and presentation (iron, washing machine, sewing kit etc.) and their appearances have to be maintained in the same way as the appearance of the rest of the body.[9]

There are limits, of course, to the extent to which the analogy of the clothes–human body relationship can apply to the White imaginary multiculturalism-Australian (inter)national body relationship. At the same time, it is clear from the above that there are important ways in which this White imagined exhibitory multiculturalism stands in relation to the Australian national body in the same way as clothes stand to the human body. Above all, like clothes, this multiculturalism is perceived to have a external relationship to the body while being an extension of that body. It is also, on the one hand, a tool in the presentation of the self and, on the other, a part of the presented self.

Consequently, while I have argued above that multiculturalism figures within this dominant White nationalist discourse as an exhibition of the cultural diversity that Australia has rather than the presentation of a multicultural Australia, it is important not to see this difference too simply as one between what Australia *is* and what Australia *has*. Rather, it is better understood as an exhibition of what White Australia is *through* the exhibition of the cultural diversity that White Australia has.

From such a perspective, this exhibitory multiculturalism can be seen to belong to a long, White colonialist tradition of exhibiting the national self through the exhibiting of otherness. Such a tradition goes beyond the exhibition of human otherness and has its historical roots in zoos and royal menageries. In what follows, I will examine some aspects of this tradition that can help us better understand the way multiculturalism operates as a technology of the national body within the dominant White nationalist/republican imagining.

Otherness and the Presentation of the National Self in International Life

The deployment of otherness in the presentation of the self has a very long history. From the Pharaohs to today's dog owner, an important dimension of the relationship between the owner and the animal was its being a mode of exhibiting the self (what one is) through the otherness that one has. This process is not confined to animals that have no direct 'practical' function. Roland Barthes's suggestion that every usage tends to turn into a sign of that usage is true well beyond the usage of objects. Horses as a means of transport are an obvious example of objects of practical usage that can be simultaneously objects of exhibitory usage. One can also take the less obvious example of oxen and donkeys, whose owners might both use them for a 'practical' task *and* derive prestige from owning them. What is important is that, in all of these cases, even though it is the animal and its characteristics (beauty, strength etc.) that are 'on show', it is really the owner that is exhibiting himself or herself through the exhibited otherness that they possess.

Nor is this process confined to the usage of objects and animals. 'Used people' like used objects (perfume, clothes, watches, etc.) have always had a symbolic value that derives from their usage. A slave owner can show off his or her slaves while simultaneously exploiting them. A factory owner can derive prestige from the size, the productivity or any other characteristic of his or her workforce, even from things such as its cleanliness. The classical historical case here is the exhibitory usage of servants which has been, and remains, a common practice by the ruling classes.

S. C. Maza, in *Servants and Masters in Eighteenth Century France: The Uses of Loyalty*, gives us a fascinating look at the many exhibitory usages of the servant that ultimately aim at exhibiting the power of the masters. A striking example, referred to in chapter 3, is the ornamental deployment of black servants around white middle class women, aimed at emphasising their paleness.[10] Here the black servant clearly operates as a technology of the body with the clear function of 'producing' paleness. Another example which appears to be more *genetically* linked to multiculturalism is the exhibition of *foreign* objects and people. As Raymond Corbey explains:

> In all cultures, political and religious elites tend to accumulate and flaunt their rare and precious objects from faraway places in order to gain prestige and to display their knowledgeability. Everyone, from Renaissance princes and cardinals to Chinese emperors, owned collections of exotic animals, objects, and even people.[11]

The above examples should give us sufficient insight into the general structure of the practice of exhibiting the self through the exhibition of otherness (whether this otherness is one of class, sex, race or species). Essential to this structure is a relationship of power between the exhibitor and the exhibited. It is, in fact, this relationship of power that is on show and from which the exhibitor derives his or her cultural capital. That is, what fascinates more than the exotic otherness is the capacity of the exhibitor to control and exhibit it. It is because the exhibited is an extension of the power of the exhibitor that it can also figure as an extension of exhibitor's body.

To move closer (empirically speaking) to multiculturalism as an exhibitory practice, we first need to begin examining the way nations can exhibit themselves through otherness, rather than the individual practices we have examined so far. Secondly, in so far as multiculturalism is an exhibition of cultural *diversity*, we need to move from examining the usage of a single other (horse, cat, servant etc.) to the exhibition of simultaneously presented otherness. To begin with, we have to start examining the mechanics of the presentation of the national self.

To help answer this question, or more precisely to help order such an answer, I have turned to Erving Goffman's *The Presentation of Self in Everyday Life*,[12] for, after all, this is what the deployment of the national body is about: the presentation of the national self in everyday international life.

While Goffman begins his analysis with individuals and individual performances, he is quick to move on to what he calls teams and teamwork. He defines a team in a classically Durkheimian manner as a *sui generis* collective reality that equals more than the sum of the individuals that constitute it:

> Whether the members of a team stage a similar individual performance or stage dissimilar performances which fit together into a whole, an emergent team impression arises which can conveniently be treated as a fact in its own right ...[13]

This seems to me crucial if we are to understand the presentation of the national self as an intrinsically collective phenomenon irreducible to the reality of the individual performers that may be involved in the presentation. This is why, in the case of Australia's bid for the Olympics, the sole presence of 'multicultural' performers on the stage does not make the performance multicultural except in an individual sense. It is only when seen as part of a collective presentation of the national self — that is, as part of a system of relationships between individual performances — that its significance can be fully understood.

Goffman's analysis of teams has important limitations, however, when it comes to the analysis of collectives such as nations. Given that they are 'imagined communities' that cannot be experienced empirically in their totality, and whose identity is often contested, nations cannot be understood outside the relationships of power that give certain groups the possibility of simultaneously representing, constructing and, most importantly for our purposes, staging the nation.[14] As we have seen, power relations are of crucial importance in the exhibitory process. Such a systematic examination of power relations within teams and the way they shape collective performances is absent in Goffman's work. Paradoxically, many of the particular examples he gives of teamwork show a considerable appreciation of the effect of power relations on the shaping of such performances. With the above in mind, let us now proceed to examine what I have called the mechanics of the presentation of the national self.

One of the crucial differences that Goffman emphasises in his analyses of 'performances' is between what he calls 'front region' and 'back region'. In all presentations of the self, the front region is where the 'fostered impressions' are played out. As Goffman defines it:

> Front, then, is the expressive equipment of a standard kind intentionally or unwillingly employed by the individual during his performance ...

First, there is the 'setting', involving furniture, decor, physical layout, and other background items which supply the scenery and stage props for the spate of human action played out before, within, or upon it. A setting tends to stay put geographically speaking ...[15]

Secondly, there is the 'personal front', which refers to:

the items that we most intimately identify with the performer himself and that we naturally expect will follow the performer wherever he goes. As part of the personal front we may include: insignia of office or rank; clothing; sex, age or racial characteristics; size and looks; posture; speech patterns; facial expressions; bodily gestures; and the like ...[16]

Goffman's distinction between an immobile setting and a mobile personal front is only relevant in the case of individual performances, where the distinction was initially made. If, as we have argued, we are treating the nation as a *sui generis* collective representation, clearly such an order of reality lacks 'mobility' in the sense implied above. The nation as a collective can only present itself as a setting, physical or symbolic. At the same time, however, this setting has to function so as to include in its representation of the nation those elements which are part of the personal front and that may be relevant to the nation. For example, it is in elements of the setting, such as preserved historical architecture, that the nation can present its 'age'.

As far as the back region is concerned, Goffman points out that it is not only the place where aspects 'which might discredit the fostered impression are suppressed',[17] but it is also where 'illusions and impressions are openly constructed'.[18] That is, this is also a place where instruments which are necessary for the construction of the self, but which are not part of the presentation of the self, are usually kept.

Already, this helps us begin to grasp an important aspect of the positioning of otherness in the presentation of the self, including the imaginary positioning of multiculturalism in the presentation of the White Australian self as pro-Asian on the international arena. Such otherness, in being an instrument or a technology of the 'self', performs a function that is often associated with the back region. It does not, however, belong to the back region, since it is *part of* the presentation and belongs to the front region. It is both a technology of the presentation and a part of it. That is, it performs a back region function while *and by* being in the front region. But what is the front region of an imaginary nation? What do nationalists and those speaking for the nation have at their disposal to present their nation, and how do they do it?

First, it is clear that part of the imaginary nation's presentation of itself occurs at a purely symbolic level. The dominant information made available about the nation, whether by government agencies or tourist bureaus, plays an important part in creating particular impressions of what the nation is like. Other national symbolic productions such as literature, art and film also play an important role. On the whole, a nation's symbolic front plays a far more important part in its presentation than it does for individuals or smaller teams.

Secondly, in so far as imaginary nations are 'homes' for their nationals, they constitute private spaces more like what Goffman refers to as 'back region'. Like all 'homes', however, they have the equivalent of the 'living room', which is that part of the private space that is available to the public gaze of those allowed in it. It is in the living room that the 'household' as a collective entity presents itself to the public and it is from the experience of the living room that most people form ideas about what a specific household 'is like'. I think that the equivalent of the 'living room' for nations is tourist space. Tourist space is precisely that part of national space that is made available to non-nationals in order to experience the nation. It offers, like all living rooms, a reasonably controlled physical setting and a reasonably controlled visibility. It is so arranged as to minimise the capacity of the tourist to see anything other than what the host wants the tourist to see. That is, it is precisely a space in which a national 'front' is literally staged for an international audience.[19]

Thirdly, historically speaking, there have always been specific arenas in which nations are allowed to exhibit themselves and their products before the rest of the world. The Olympic Games present such an occasion. Along with their individual prowess, the athletes of a nation as a totality are seen to exhibit the health and prowess of the nation. The world expos and their historical forerunners, the colonial world fairs, are even more important. They allow nations to exhibit themselves in more diverse fields than would the Olympics, or any other mono-thematic international gathering. In many ways, such spaces can be perceived as extensions of the tourist spaces of the nation. The colonial world fairs were far more important when tourism was not as generalised a practice as it is today. It is, in fact, in those fairs that we find the roots of multicultural exhibitionism.

Zoology and the Colonial Art of Collecting Otherness

Tourist spaces exhibit the nation metonymically in that the tourist is given an intimation of what the whole nation is through an experience of a part of the whole nation. In the world fair, however, the nation is represented metaphorically in that the representation aims to reproduce, within a limited space, the totality of the nation conceived as the sum of, and the relation between, its various distinguishing characteristics. Of course, one of the distinguishing characteristics of colonial nations was the possession of colonies, and it is here that we find the national exhibition of human otherness at its best. As Benedict Burton explains:

> Apart from showing piles of colonial produce, exhibition organizers constructed pavilions in 'indigenous' styles. Such 'exotic' exhibits were popular. They also provided an arena in which each colonial power could flaunt its possessions to its rivals.[20]

Raymond Corbey provides us with a further indication of what these 'exotic' exhibitions entailed. He points out that these exhibitions were by no means confined to the world fairs:

> At these gigantic exhibitions, staged by the principal colonial powers, the world was collected and displayed. Natives from a wide range of colonised cultures quickly became a standard part of most manifestations of this kind. Together with their artefacts, houses, and even complete villages, so-called savages or primitives were made available for visual inspection by millions of strolling and staring Western citizens. Comparable places of spectacle such as the zoos,

botanical gardens, circuses, temporary or permanent exhibitions staged by missionary societies and museums of natural history, all exhibited other races and/or other species and testified to the imperialism of 19th-century nation-states.[21]

With these colonial 'ethnographic showcases',[22] we move closer to the multicultural exhibition, not only because it involves a national exhibition of 'other cultures', but also because it is presented as a *collection* of otherness. Thus, as Corbey relates:

The Great Britain Exhibition of 1899 included a 'Kaffir Kraal — A Vivid Representation of Life in the Wilds of the Dark Continent,' an exhibit featuring African animals and 174 natives from several South African peoples brought under control only shortly before.[23]

The lumping of the animals and 'natives' together attests to the empirical continuity that existed between the collection of animals and the collection of natives. Often the 'exotic natives' appeared side by side with the 'exotic animals' in European zoos such as the Jardins d'Acclimatation in Paris. It was also the very people who 'dealt' in the import and export of wild animals and the direction of zoos and circuses who also 'dealt' in the import and export of 'natural peoples' (*Naturvölker*), as they were known in Germany.[24]

More important for our purposes than this empirical continuity was the structural and logical continuity between the zoo and the circus, and the exhibition of 'natives'. Above all, they were an exhibition of the nation that exhibited them. More precisely, they were an exhibition of the power of the nation that exhibited them.

The powers exhibited at the zoo in the late nineteenth century made it both a specifically modern and a colonial construction. It was modern in that it exhibited a nation's mastery/power over nature, which was crucial in defining a nation's civilisation within modernity. It was colonial in that sometimes the animals collected reflected the power that the exhibiting nation had over the parts of the world from which the animals originated.

The 'exotic peoples' exhibitions at the colonial world fairs operated much like the zoo in that those exhibited were seen as both part of subjugated 'nature' (natural people) and as colonial 'artefacts'. Through such 'exotic people' was exhibited the greatness and the colonising, taming and domesticating power of the nation exhibiting them. Like all the exhibited otherness we have examined so far, there was a relation of exteriorisation between the exhibiting colonial power and the exhibited colonised such that the latter operated as a technology of the colonial power. At the same time, the exhibited otherness was presented as an extension/part of that colonial power (the empire).

What particularly facilitated the process through which these exhibitions functioned as an extension of the colonial nation exhibiting them was their quality as a *collection* of otherness. More often than not, they were presented either as a collection of people and artefacts constituted into a 'native village', an ethnographic showcase, or as a larger collection of various exotic people from various parts of the world.

As I have already argued, what makes the exhibited an extension of the exhibitor is that it is primarily an extension of the latter's power: it comes to exist as it does *because* of the exhibitor's power over it. If collections constitute by their very nature 'ideal extensions' of the exhibitor, it is precisely because they embody the power of the exhibitor/collector in a way no single object does.

As many commentators have emphasised, the world of the collection is the world of commodity fetishism par excellence. Walter Benjamin saw the world fairs, in particular, as 'pilgrimage sites of commodity fetishism.'[25] The elements that constitute a collection tend to lose any meaning derived from their original context of usage and, instead, obtain their significance from their presence within the collection. Thus, not only is the Indian carpet, which was originally intended by the producer for use on the ground, transformed into a pure object of exhibition by being hung on the wall, but also, when hung with other carpets from other locations, it derives its meaning from its difference within the collection rather than from its history and the value of its initial use.[26]

Not only does the principle of organisation behind the collection end up giving each item its specific meaning, but that principle of organisation is also itself as much a part of the exhibited collection as its elements. Thus, as Benedict

Burton points out, in many exhibitions of 'native people', what was also exhibited was the western colonial modes of classification of those native people:

> People could be arranged to explicate theories, as they were in the evolutionary sequence of 'villages' at St Louis where Pygmies were placed in sequence with Patagonians. Typology took precedence over geography.[27]

As Susan Stewart has argued: 'The collection is not constructed by its elements; rather, it comes to exist by means of its principle of organisation.'[28] Furthermore, 'the collection replaces history with *classification*.'[29] What is the collection's principle of classification and organisation, however, but the objectification of the collector/exhibitor's power?

This is how the significance of a collected object becomes a function of the power of the exhibitor in a way no other object is. In that very process, it becomes an extension of the exhibitor/collector *tout court*. As Stewart has put it:

> When one wants to disparage the souvenir, one says that it is not authentic; when one wants to disparage the collected object, one says "it is not you".[30]

It is in this sense that the exhibiting nation completes the circle of using the collection as an instrument in the presentation of itself, while this instrument is being presented, at the same time, as an extension of itself.

Multiculturalism, Zoology and 'Ethnic Death'

As I began by suggesting, it is precisely as an exhibition of a collection of other cultures that the function of multiculturalism, as it is present in the dominant White republican pro-Asian discourse, can be best understood. In light of the above, it can be argued that this exhibitory multiculturalism is the post-colonial version of the colonial fair. For, if the exhibition of the 'exotic natives' was the product of the power relation between the coloniser and the colonised *in the colonies* as it came to exist in the colonial era, the multicultural exhibition is the product of the power relation between the post-colonial powers and the post-colonised as it developed *in the metropolis* following the migratory processes that characterised the post-colonial era.

Everyday White discourses on multiculturalism abound with utterances and practices alluding to the world of collecting. To begin with, one can detect a characteristic competitive preoccupation with 'numbers' somewhat different from the number pathology examined in chapter 4. 'In Australia, we are one of the *most* culturally diverse countries in the world' or 'We have *x* cultures living here together' is a typical introduction to the collection. This discursive form is also played out in everyday life at the level of streets or neighbourhoods, with their proud cosmopolitan White residents boasting about the *x* number of different ethnic restaurants *they have*. The logic of enumeration reaches its climax in the process of enumerating/exhibiting the number of Aboriginal languages Australia *has*.[31]

More important than the logic of enumeration — and not unlike the principle behind the stew that grew — there is the crucial function of the principle of organisation behind the multicultural collection: the principle of 'peaceful coexistence'. As we have seen, far more than its elements, it is precisely the principle of organisation behind a collection that constitutes it. It is also that principle of organisation, in being that of the collector, which allows the collection of 'otherness' to operate as an extension of the collector. As in the preceding chapter, while White multiculturalism requires a number of cultures, White culture is not merely one among those cultures — it is precisely the culture which provides the collection with the spirit that moves it and gives it coherence: 'peaceful coexistence'.

Here again, however, for exhibitory purposes this time, left to themselves 'ethnic' cultures are imagined as unable to coexist. It is only the White effort to inject 'peaceful coexistence' into them which allows them to do so. Like all elements of a collection, 'ethnics' have to forget those 'unexhibitable' parts of their history and become living fetishes deriving their significance from the White organising principle that controls and positions them within the Australian social space. As I have argued, it is by virtue of the capacity of the collection to be an embodiment of the collector's power that it succeeds in becoming an extension of the collector.

In commenting on the private collecting practices of an English civil servant in India, Carol Breckenridge argues:

> For individual colonial officials, the act of collecting and the building of a collection created the illusion of cognitive control over their experience in India — an experience that might otherwise be disturbingly chaotic. Since many officials collected, it can be argued that collections promoted a sense of moral and material control over the Indian environment. At the same time, collected objects could be fed into the two growing institutions of the second half of the nineteenth century, the exhibition and the museum, thus allowing this sense of knowledge and control to be repatriated to the metropolis. In the metropole, fairs and museums could serve, over time, as reminders of the orderliness of empire as well as the exoticism of distant parts of the Victorian ecumene.[32]

As such, the collection operates as a space of fantasy, a mode of exhibiting oneself through idealised images of the self. More specifically, it is a fantasy of total power, a yearning for complete control where such control is impossible.

Such a fantasy of order is definitely played out in the multicultural fairs and festivals organised throughout Australia. These fairs, with their well-ordered and well-arranged ethnic stalls, are indeed a far cry from the disorderly and chaotic lives of most of the migrants involved in them. They are also a far cry from the real power of the White centre to arrange and order these migrant lives. They are the clearest objectification, within Australia's tourist space, of a White fantasy of how Australia's many cultures ought to be positioned.

The fact that multicultural policy 'allows' non-Anglo–Celtic ethnics to 'maintain their culture' does in no sense make it less of a fantasy of total control. Multicultural language in this regard is merely moving along with the language of zoology. A recent entry under 'zoo' in the *Encyclopedia Americana* points out that:

> Concepts of how animals should be presented to the public in a zoological garden are constantly changing in the direction of more natural surrounding and greater liberty for the animals and special exhibits or situations are created to demonstrate the animals' normal way of life.[33]

It is not because of the above that zoos and botanical gardens are no longer the ultimate objectification of the classificatory order of the collector. Indeed, despite and because of this, they remain the purest incarnations of power/knowledge. In starting the Jardins d'Acclimatation in Paris, Geoffroy de St Hilaire was merely giving life to his system of classification.

Most important for us here is that in giving life to a system of classification, to a fantasy space embodying an economy of one's desire for power and control, the collection 'kills' everything that exists within it. That is, all its elements can have no being of their own, but merely a being derived from the limited life-giving logic of the collection. Here again we are faced with the 'ethnic object with no will' that is at the core of all White fantasies of the nation. When people are positioned within such spaces of fantasy, they are 'killed', such that no will can emerge from them; they exist through the collection and for the collector. This is why spaces of fantasy, in so far as they are spaces of total control, cannot be other than spaces of social death.

We have seen in a previous chapter how Slavoj Zizek explains fantasy space through the story a woman who exhibits her deceased pets in her garden.[34] Something akin to this exhibition of 'dead valued others' is operative in White exhibitory multiculturalism. All ethnic cultures within the White fantasy of the multicultural collection are imagined as dead cultures that cannot have a life of their own except through the 'peaceful coexistence' that regulates the collection. This is what Marc Guillaume and Jean Baudrillard mean when they argue in their work *Figures de l'Altérité* that Western thought thrives on reducing alterity to a tamed otherness:

> Western Societies have reduced the reality of the Other through colonisation or through cultural assimilation. They have abolished what was radically heterogeneous and incommensurable in the other.[35]

As they put it, the new legitimisations of the 'exoticisms of the interior' go hand in hand with the 'measures of control and normalisation which lead to the rapid or progressive disappearance of these popular cultural forms as living cultures'.[36]

It is precisely such a process of control and normalisation embodied in the multicultural collection which makes every multicultural celebration of difference in Australia operate paradoxically like a mourning ritual. Every celebration becomes a tomb to the difference it is celebrating.

Conclusion

The polarisation produced by the popular debates about multiculturalism between those who are for and those who are against creates an illusion that multiculturalism is a single reality that one can either like or dislike, be part of or reject. Such a polarisation obscures the fact, emphasised by Bourdieu, that, given the constructed nature of the social, all struggles within social reality are also struggles for defining and constructing that very social reality in which those struggles are occurring.

To be 'for' multiculturalism in no sense guarantees that those who are for it share a common social/discursive reality. Multiculturalism constitutes a field of struggle for its definition and construction by the various interests of those who are positioned within it.

In the above, I have attempted to examine a particular construction of multiculturalism that exists within the dominant White imaginary. It would be ludicrous to take this to mean a simple, straightforward: 'within multiculturalism migrants are treated as if they are animals in a zoo'. It would be just as simplistic, however, to see this construction a mere presence in the 'brains' of those who share the dominant White nationalist discourse.

In being a party involved in the struggle to define and construct multiculturalism as a social reality, the White nation fantasy is constitutive of this reality. While no 'exotic' Third World — looking migrants are merely part of a multicultural zoo, the social existence of those migrants positioned within the multicultural field cannot be understood outside of the very real processes that tend to 'zoologise' them.

chapter 6

Ecological Nationalism: Green Parks/White Nation

This chapter is concerned with the relationship between certain modes of ecological thinking and White governmental nationalism as they have emerged in Australia. For many people, at least until recently, the idea of a relationship between ecological thinking, racism and nationalism could appear as absurd. The initial rise of ecological struggles has been primarily experienced within left and liberal popular culture as a specifically 'radical left' phenomenon and, as such, ecologists are perceived to be immune from a thought uncritically associated with the radical right.

In recent times, however, a number of groups have formulated within a framework of ecological concern their opposition to particular 'kinds' (read: races) of people, such as 'Asians'. For some of these groups, such as the Australians Against Further Immigration (AAFI), so-called ecological concerns are but a very thin veil for a more-than-obvious racist nationalist agenda of excluding a particular part of the world population from the White-imagined nation. In fact, the links between AAFI and more explicitly racist organisations such as the League of Rights has been exposed by journalists.[1]

There are, however, a number of groups with what appears as a primarily ecological concern who have voiced their opposition to 'increased immigration' without explicitly targeting a specific group of people. While openly defining themselves as 'non-racist', such groups have been perceived by anti-racists as a type of 'closet racists'. Such is the group Australians for an Ecologically Sustainable Population (AESP).

In examining certain modalities of ecological thinking, and AESP's work in particular, I am particularly interested in examining the way White nationalist fantasies emerge (implicitly or explicitly) within ecological thought. I want to show how a specific ecological fantasy, a specific mode of being and thinking ecologically and of imagining ecological space, presents us with another variation of the White nation fantasy.[2]

The Ecological Fantasy and its Others: Nationalism and the Logic of Domestication

Beyond the naive and impressionistic belief in the impossibility of a 'radical leftie' being racist, there are some good reasons for seeing ecological thinking as intrinsically anathema to nationalist thinking. The history of modern 'biological' racism, its practices and its essentialist and hierarchical conception of 'race' that have been part of the luggage of nationalism everywhere are a continuation of the initial development of this conception in the categorisation of the natural, and particularly the animal, world. 'Race' was part of the 'interconnected concepts of breeding, differentiation, specialisation and hierarchy',[3] directly grounded in the domesticating practices of animal breeding that are often the target of ecological critique. Nationalist practices are similarly structured to the practices of domestication to which most ecologists are opposed.

The nature of the nationalist–racist fantasy analysed in the preceding chapters emphasises the continuity between it and the 'classical' modes of imagining nature. Indeed, well before the emergence of the nation as a dominant fantasy space where people realised their being, it is domesticated nature that has historically been the ultimate Thing for so many people, generating the key narratives that have driven the never ending dreams of, and attempts at, 'overcoming nature' that are so integral to the 'civilising process'.

The national 'home' fantasy is in many ways a secular version of one of the oldest fantasies of domestication available to us and which is primarily an ecological fantasy of domesticated nature: the Garden of Eden. It is precisely as a space of ultimate domestication that the Garden of Eden functions as a 'paradise'. Indeed, its chief characteristic as described in Genesis is that it was an *a priori* domesticated space. There was no need to engage in practices of subjugating nature since everything was always readily available. Adam and Eve merely fitted into it. They were totally at home.

It is obvious that what characterises the Fall in Genesis — or, more precisely, what characterises the state of *being* on earth after the Fall — is the *loss* of this constant and already domesticated space and a condemnation to *a life of never ending domestication*. As Keith Thomas has put it:

> By rebelling against God, man forfeited his easy dominance over the species. The earth degenerated. Thorns and thistles grew up where there had been only fruits and flowers (Genesis, iii.18). The soil became stony and less fertile, making arduous labour necessary for its cultivation. There appeared fleas, gnats and other odious pests. Many animals cast off the yoke, becoming fierce, warring with each other and attacking men. Even domestic animals have now to be coerced into submission.[4]

That is, Genesis clearly pictures 'being' (on earth) as structured by a fundamental lack produced by the Fall: the loss of the womb-like 'perfect fit' between humans and nature. Life on earth becomes an endless attempt at recovering that 'perfect fit' on earth.

Ecological Fantasies and their Other

While it is obvious that most radical ecologists explicitly aim to position themselves in opposition to such narratives of domestication, such a mode of thinking still manages to creep into the ecological thought of the left, as exemplified by certain sections of a recent work of Ted Benton:

> Landscape features, woodland paths, established patterns of urban settlement, even factories, pits and slag heaps consti-

tute the texture of the lived biographies of those who pass their lives among them. They carry reminders of past moments of pleasure or fear, come to represent whole way of living, working and enjoying to communities of people. They are in short significant among the means by which we come to understand who and what we are. A threat to them can be felt a threat to our own continuous and stable identity.

... the fight to preserve features of one's environment from destruction is not (or not solely) a form of instrumental action, in which some external object is protected because it is contributory to one's interests (the value of one's property, the quality of the view from the back window, or whatever), but rather because it is included in one's sense of self and so is inseparable from one's personal well-being.[5]

The problem with Benton's theorising lies in its inability to recognise the fantasy element in such images of homely space. Uncritically, it ends up laying the ground for the commonsense construction of the 'perturbing other', without perceiving the necessity of the presence of this 'other' for the very construction that is being described. More importantly, such a conception bears an uncanny resemblance to nationalist modes of ecological thinking where Benton's unspecified social becomes the social of national space.

Indeed, it is mainly nationalist ecology that often operates the fusion between the national and the natural fantasy, seeing the nation as both a social and a natural domesticated space. In such a space, otherness exists as a social and/or a natural value for the domesticator. Nature is perceived as a national value that needs to be exploited and/or saved, depending on how it is classified by the domesticators. This tendency is best exemplified by Nazi ecological thinking, where the wilderness was conceived as a 'German cultural good'.[6] Nazi writing is interesting in this regard for the explicit links it makes between the existence of a domesticated German space and a fulfilled German self. Thus, for Wilhelm Heinrich Riehl:

The German people need the forest. And as much as we need the wood to warm the human exterior ... the forest is also necessary to warm the human interior. We ought to protect our forests, not simply to keep our stoves hot in winter but so that the pulse of the people can continue to beat with a joyful vital warmth and for Germany to remain German.[7]

In such thought, the ecological fantasy is part of the national fantasy and vice versa. Consequently, the 'undomesticated' other is imagined as someone that can disturb both the social and the natural national home. This ecological nationalism is not altogether absent from modern ecological thinking in general, and it is certainly present in the writings and formulations of AESP. According to the so-called Ehrlich equation, approved by AESP:

(environmental impact = population x affluence x technology) or $I = PAT$ where P = population size, A = affluence, which is the average individual consumption, T = an index of environmental demand a technology imposes to supply goods consumed.[8]

Within such a narrow nationalist framework, otherness becomes both something that disrupts national ecological sustainability and a non-national/foreign otherness. Thus, in the pamphlet-like article in the Bureau of Immigration and Population Research Bulletin in which this formula is presented, it is argued that:

Each nation has a primary responsibility to manage its own environment, industry, agriculture and population to ensure a sustainable long term balance between population and resources. Nations that neglect this balance cannot be allowed to export the consequences as environmental and economic refugees. Such refugees may ultimately transfer to their host countries the problems from which they thought to escape.[9]

Despite the above, it would be unfair to treat these tendencies in AESP's thought as more than just a minor element within it. For it is certain that the main thrust of their work is moved by an anti-domestication logic. And while the relationship between racist nationalist practices and the domestication of nature was easy to establish in the light of the spatial conception of nationalist practices we have developed, the relationship between nationalist practices and anti-domestication is far from obvious. Nevertheless, as I would now like to show, such a relationship does exist.

In introducing the Lacanian concept of fantasy, I pointed out that the fantasy is propelled by a Thing, a yearned for object-cause of desire. It is crucial to stress here that the Thing, as far as the relationship between humans and nature is concerned, has never been domesticated nature as such. The Thing is the imagined plenitude and bliss that would result from the 'perfect fit' between humans and nature. More than the domesticated status of nature, it is this perfect fit that characterises 'paradise'.

Domestication is only *one* of the ways, even if it has been historically the dominant way, in which the goal of recovering paradise is pursued. Another way of pursuing such a goal has been the attempt to 'return to nature', to mould the self so as to fit 'back' into nature. In this fantasy, it is the constant subjugation of nature which has led human beings to move away from the state of bliss in which they existed when they lived in paradise. Here 'civilisation' becomes the other standing between the human and the 'natural state' of 'fulfilment'. This fantasy of a return to the golden age of an '*original* perfect fit' with nature has always offered the key narratives of opposition to the domesticating drive of civilisation.

It figures in Plato in the *Protagoras* and is still played out in popular culture by the 'hippie type', but no one has articulated it as clearly as Jean-Jacques Rousseau. As he puts it in his *Rêveries*: 'I feel transports of joy and inexpressible raptures in becoming fused as it were with the great system of beings and identifying myself with the whole of nature' [10]

It is precisely this state of fusion that characterises what Rousseau calls *l'état de nature*, the state which was 'lost' with the rise of civilisation and which, as Guy Playret points out, is equivalent to the 'original unity'.[11] What is interesting here is that Rousseau recognised that the status of the yearning for such an original perfect fit between humans and nature was not a yearning for something that ever existed. In this sense, his conceptualisation of this *état de nature* constitutes in many ways an embryonic theorisation of it as fantasy:

> … a state which no longer exists, which perhaps never exist-ed, which probably never will exist, and yet about which it is necessary to have accurate notions in order to judge prop-erly our own present state.[12]

The Rousseau-ian fantasy is certainly different from the fantasy of domestication. It is, in fact, explicitly 'anti-domestication'. In *Reveries*, Rousseau clearly attacks the utilitarian conception of nature. In his fantasy space, the interest of the self takes the back seat: 'No, nothing that is personal, nothing that involves the interests of my body, can truly possess my soul'.[13]

Current ecological thinking is grounded in this Rousseau-ian tradition, but it also goes beyond it in some important respects. While the Rousseau-ian fantasy is different from the fantasy of domestication in relation to its *aim*, it is the same in relation to its *goal*.[14] Both yearn for an overcoming of lack through the reaching of the final stage of a perfect fit between humans and their environment. As importantly, and as a result of the above, the Rousseau-ian fantasy not only shares the same goal, but also has the same premise of a dualism between humans and 'nature'. For even though Rousseau's subject is pictured as a subject which has no utilitarian interest in its interaction with nature, what is meant by this is that this subject has no 'mundane' practical interests. In fact, that subject continues to occupy centre stage as a subject with an affective interest. Instead of 'I want to control', we have 'I want to feel'.

It is the decentring of this 'I' — but only at an explicit discursive level, as we shall see — that characterises the current dominant tendency in the ecological movement. Rather than perceiving itself as separate from nature, the modern ecological subject becomes merely the voice of nature in its totality, yearning for a lost balance brought about by the processes of exploitation of nature. Thus, if this ecological subject opposes this exploitation and domestication of nature, it is not merely on the grounds of a perceived personal interest, or a wish to 'feel good' personally as Rousseau does. Exploitation is opposed so that 'nature on the whole' feels good.

Unlike the fantasies of a 'perfect fit' based on a dualism between humans and nature, this construction claims radically to transcend such a dualism. It no longer stages the individual as an 'I' pursuing that perfect fit with nature, it stages him or her as merely traversed by a nature that has lost and is seeking herself back. The ecological subject is merely the instrument of nature rather than a subject that perceives nature instrumentally. Thus, AESP does not see itself as just a subject with a human interest, rather it is a subject voicing the interest of the 'integrity of the creation'. As the BIR pamphlet explains:

> Christian theologians are increasingly recognising that humankind has an obligation not only to just one species, namely itself, but to the integrity of creation.[15]

Although this construction presents itself as a transcendence of the fantasies of domestication that preceded it, I want to argue that it actually restages this fantasy in a roundabout way. In fact, it stages what Lacan defines as a *perverse* fantasy — a fantasy within which the subject's view coincides with the view of the big 'Other'. It is when the subject, as Lacan puts it, 'confuses his contemplative eye with the eye with which God is looking at him'.[16]

In his poem 'The Masters', Mark O'Connor, one of AESP's poets/intellectuals, yearns for a nature unperturbed by the imperative of the human gaze and by the centrality of human presence. His evaluation of old landscape painters goes like this:

> As if no rock or bush could stand
> without a human ornament. Infants
> like cherubs scattered all around:
> one fights, another reaps, so that each field
> can show the range of human nature. Here
> by the darkening storm, a woman's milked
> while her belly swells once more. Her man
> stands stoutly by; and you can bet
> the distance shows more forms. The age could not
> conceive God's Hills as good unreaped.[17]

In the poem 'The Discovery', O'Connor is describing a place where the human is not supposed to be a disruption in the beautiful landscape. Among other things, 'he' notices:

> Trunks with no leaves in sight
> rose like columns from the gully floor.[18]

But where does this 'sight' come from if the nature described by O'Connor is not perturbed by human presence. It is here that the perverse gaze reveals itself. The gaze is the imagined gaze of O'Connor, but he wants us to believe otherwise; he wants us to believe that it is the gaze of nature on itself, as it expresses itself, through O'Connor.

It is within this configuration that the perverse domesticating subject emerges as a subject in pursuit of/constructed via a new fantasy space: the integrity of the creation in pursuit of itself. That is, the new domesticator does not appear as a subject of domestication as such, he or she tries to stage his or her own disappearance behind the big Other — the logic behind things, the integrity of the creation itself, Nature. The domesticator, however, still determines the value of everything and everyone according to the extent to which they help in or obstruct achieving the goal of the fantasy — the ecological balance, etc.

As Zizek points out, the perverse fantasy is typified by the Stalinist fantasy of the Party:

> Stalinist communism consists in the fact that the view by means of which the Party looks at history coincides with history's gaze upon itself.... Communists act immediately in the name of 'Objective laws of historical progress'; it is history itself, its necessity, that speaks through their mouth.[19]

This is perceived by Tom Regan in his critique of what he calls 'environmental fascism' as 'the view that moral value resides in properties such as stability, diversity and beauty of ecological communities'. Regan bases his critique on his rejection of anything that 'would override the rights of individual living beings in favour of the collectivity'.[20]

Sociologically speaking, however, there is never an 'in favour of the collectivity'. Rather, there is the particular interest of those who have obtained the right to speak in the interest of the collectivity. While it is possible to argue logically that there *may* be something like the interest of the people, of humanity, of the working class or of nature, there is no necessary link between such logically possible interests and those who claim to have found out what they actually are. Sociologically speaking, what we have as given is only the interest of those who speak in the name of the people, humanity, the working class or nature. It is here that the White nation fantasy begins to emerge, for while AESP claims to speak in the name of the ecological balance, it never really goes beyond speaking in the name of a White ecological balance.

Australia is currently pledged to reduce by 20 per cent its contribution to the greenhouse effect. If our population doubles over the next 40–50 years, the per capita allotments of petrol, coal etc. will have to be halved.[21]

Suddenly, instead of the integrity of creation, it is the consumption of 'Australians' that seems to be in need of protection. But who is this 'Australian' imagined by AESP? We know it from knowing its other — the other that constitutes a threat to the ecological balance (and to consumption):

An extra person in Australia uses about 100 times more energy than a person from Bangladesh, for example.

An overpopulated country is not necessarily a crowded one. Even India and China have large areas that are sparsely populated. Overpopulation is better defined as a condition in which the community cannot live on its environmental 'interest' and so must deplete its 'capital'.[22]

One of the key elements of AESP's discourse which allows it to believe in itself as a non-racist organisation despite such pronouncements is their explicit pro-Aboriginal politics. It is in this very 'pro-Aboriginality', however, that AESP exhibits the extent of its perverse domesticating logic to the full.

It is important at this point to remind ourselves, as I have argued above, that nationalist domestication is not necessarily about excluding/destroying otherness, but primarily about regulating the modality of its inclusion. This can also mean a strategy of preservation. That is, the ecological struggle to preserve specific species can easily be part of, not in opposition to, the logic of domestication, especially a perverse domestication interested in promoting and preserving the diversity of nature.

The Nazis, for example, despite being most popularly known for their politics of extermination, strongly promoted a logic of preservation within their project of domesticating both the social and the natural world. That is, they advocated the preservation of both natural species and 'primitive cultures'. As the fascist theorist, Schoenichen, put it:

It is the old theory of liberal exploitation which has always constituted the background of French colonial politics, such that there was no room for a treatment of the primitives which goes in the sense of a thought that is protective of nature.[23]

In trying to explain the range of the Nazis' racist practices — aiming on one hand to exterminate the Jews and on the other to preserve the culture of 'the primitives', while at the same time conceiving of both as 'inferior races' — we encounter some of the explanatory limitations of the theorisation of racist nationalism as a variant of the inferiorisation, essentialisation and stereotyping discourses. For while this theory may correctly reflect that inferiorisation etc. are a feature of racism in both cases, it does not explain why preservation should occur in one case, while extermination is advocated in the other.

The conception of nationalism as driven by a fantasy of domesticated space does account better for this variety of racist nationalist practices and categorisations. Within such a conception, each categorisation, as well as the practice in which it is grounded, is specific to the evaluation of the other as an object of domestication: one exterminates what is conceived as harmful and preserves what might be harmless and useful, even if its usage value is as an exotic spectacle. As Schoenichen wrote:

> For the natural politics of national socialism, the road that needs to be followed is clear. The politics of repression and extermination, as exemplified by America or Australia in their beginnings, are just as much out of the question as the French theory of assimilation. A development of the naturals which would conform with their racial specificity is the only convenient strategy.[24]

Consequently, it is a logic of domestication which differentiates between the harmful Jewish other and the harmless exotic 'primitive' other that governs the Nazis' advocacy of the recognition of differences. AESP's supposed pro-Aboriginal politics and its anti-migrant stance are linked in a very similar differentiation. This clearly reveals that AESP's thought, despite its claims, shares with the Nazis and other White nationalists the same White-centred preservationist/domesticating logic.

For AESP, elements of nature are perceived as worth preserving because they are 'unique' and/or 'scarce':

> The surviving remnants of our unique native species and natural habitats are the more precious for their scarcity and

need to be carefully guarded for their own sake and in trust for all humanity.[25]

Uniqueness and scarcity, however, are far from being nature-centred concepts. Indeed, the whole notion of a nature-centred concept is absurd. There is no such thing as uniqueness and scarceness except as human values, as categories of nature for humans — that is, as categories of domestication. In fact, the domesticating logic becomes explicit when it is revealed that the whole aim of the exercise is the benefit of 'humanity'. And just as this preservationist logic is extended to human 'primitive species' within Nazi thought, it is extended to Aborigines in the writings of AESP. That is, their pro-Aboriginality is nothing other than a naturalistic categorisation of the Aborigines as harmless (as far as AESP's ecological fantasy is concerned). Thus:

> Immigration and population growth over the past two hundred years have profoundly affected and continue to affect traditional Aboriginal communities. Almost all immigrants belong to the dominant economic culture, which contrasts with the 'forever culture' of the first Australians.[26]

Here, Aboriginality is constructed within a logic of domestication as a harmless part of the landscape that needs to be preserved. This is especially so since Aborigines, like other 'harmless animals', only 'fit into' nature rather than being a burden on the environment. That is, their 'value' lies precisely in that they would not disrupt the fantasy of the 'ecological balance'. This is how O'Connor perceives Australia in one of his ecological poems:

> My native land, that vast dry continent which was certainly not put there for human use, and whose centre still defies all attempts to allegorize, Anglicize, or humanize it. If Europe (and much of the USA) is the planet disguised as a human possession, Australia is the thing itself.[27]

As I have argued, psychoanalytically speaking, Australia in this writing is indeed the *Thing* itself, more so than O'Connor and AESP realise. It is clear from the above, how an unconscious relation between humanisation and Anglicisation is established, as the Aboriginal presence in the Australian centre fails to 'humanise', leaving an unperturbed fantasy space for the very human and very White O'Connor and AESP.

Conclusion: Multiculturalism and Eco-Nationalism

This 'ecological' thinking, then, is not far from other forms of White nationalist domestication except at a rhetorical level. Instead of a White subject positioning herself as the master of the Australian space domesticating otherness in her own interest, we have a White subject positioning himself as the rightful domesticator of the Australian space in the name of nature, but still effectively in the perceived interest of White Australians.

Looked at from this perspective, AESP's claims of not being 'racist' are somewhat ridiculous. A more serious aspect of their claims, however, is that they seem to be accepted within governmental circles for what they pretend to be. AESP's pamphlets were published in the journals of the official multicultural establishment, such as the Bureau of Immigration and Population Research journal. While this certainly did not mean an official multicultural endorsement of AESP views, it was certainly an endorsement of their 'respectability'.

The fact that AESP manages to acquire such a respectability lies in the affinity —but this does not mean a complicity — between it and the White multiculturalism of the dominant culture we have examined in previous chapters. This affinity helps us explain further the nature of the White national fantasy delineated by White multiculturalism. It shows us how the latter stands vis-à-vis traditional pre-multicultural White nationalism in much the same way as the new ecological thought stands vis-à-vis the traditional fantasies of domestication. That is, rather than constructing a White subject within a fantasy of a socially domesticated nation full of tamed otherness, White multiculturalism stages a perverse fantasy in which the White subject disappears behind a big 'other' perceived here in terms of the multicultural balance. What this perverse multiculturalism entails is not a White subject domesticating non-Whites in the name of a White-centred Australia, but a (still) White subject acting on behalf of 'The Multicultural Balance' (or, as it is popularly known, peaceful coexistence), and domesticating non-Whites in the name of that balance. Within this multiculturalism, the otherness, as for the eco-nationalists, is primarily one that disturbs the 'balance'. It is the ethnic conflicts that migrants 'bring with them' — religious fundamentalism, political clientelism, the ghetto — that upset the status quo. All of these are seen as multicultural evils — they are all dangers emanating from non-White Australians and it is still the task of White Australians to make sure they are tamed or weeded out of the Australian space.

chapter 7

The Discourse of Anglo Decline 1: The Spectre of Cosmopolitan Whiteness

The changes to Australia's social and cultural landscape brought about by the increased immigration from Asian countries in the 1980s and 1990s, as well as by the global economic transformations of that period, have generated among certain people of British background a specific genre of White discourse. This discourse either passively mourns or actively calls for resistance against what it perceives as a state-sanctioned assault on the cultural forms that have their roots in the British colonisation of Australia. This is what I will be calling in this chapter the 'discourse of Anglo decline'.

Elements of this discourse can be found as far back as the gold rush era, during the first serious wave of White fears of being 'swamped by Asians'. In more recent times, however, it has started to reassert itself as part of national discourse, beginning with the 'Blainey debate' of the early 1980s. Geoffrey Blainey himself, in addition to worrying about Asianisation and 'the mix' (see chapter 4), voiced his explicit worries concerning the fate of Australians of British background. He also, more specifically, expressed his concerns for what he saw as the devaluing, by historians and intellectuals, of the positive British Australian contribution to the making of Australia and a concentration on negative aspects such as racism and genocidal tendencies towards the Aboriginal people. This critique of the so-called 'black armband' view of history, which has been currently taken up by the Prime Minister, John Howard, clearly falls within the tradition of the discourse of Anglo decline.

Since the Blainey debate, the discourse of decline has been taking up an increasing proportion of prime media space every time similar 'debates' have raged in Australia.[1] It is, however, Pauline Hanson's One Nation Party that has given the discourse its most systematic political articulation.

In what follows, I propose to analyse the discourse of decline and to show it to be a specific modality of the White nation fantasy. Before doing so, it is useful to see the various ways in which the sentiment of decline is expressed within Australia's everyday life.

The Discourse of Anglo Decline

At the height of the debate generated by the Keating Labor Government's push for an Australian republic, Joan Sutherland, Australia's famous diva, contributed to the anti-republican cause by expressing her yearning for a time when, as an Australian, she held a British passport. She also expressed her concern at the prospect of having to be interviewed by 'Indians and Pakistanis' at the post office to obtain her passport. In a series of letters to the editor in the *Sydney Morning Herald* that followed her intervention and the general outcry it generated, one could read statements such as:

> Apparently, if one's ancestors came from England and/or Scotland, successfully settled here and helped to develop our country, raised large families and were loyal to our Constitution and the elected government, we, their offspring have no right to espouse our love and respect for our ancestors' homelands.[2]
>
> Dame Joan may be forgiven for being out of touch with Australia's multicultural society, but after reading today's Herald letters, she will now realise that the only race in Australia that one is allowed to insult and vilify with impunity are [sic] the British.[3]

Another letter warns against surrendering 'without a struggle our language which enshrines the culture whose freedoms we gladly offer people of any racial origin who choose to enjoy them'.[4]

Exactly a year before this exchange, another series of letters appeared in the *Sydney Morning Herald* when a correspondent, Syd Cauveren, wrote after a trip to Britain, complaining of his treatment by 'turban-attired immigration officers' and being 'brushed past by Africans and Indians, and other exotic origins', concluding that Australians have been rejected by 'Mother England'.[5] Another correspondent replied that:

> Syd apparently cannot remember that it was our Mr Whitlam who exacerbated the prevailing anti-English attitudes within Australia with the creation of an Australian passport — which forced the writer onto the alien queue at Mascot when returning from the UK shortly after. Messrs Grassby and Whitlam then turned immigration on its head with preference to the ASEAN communities, resulting in our own government departments providing employment to many non-English–speaking nationalities. Personally, I would like to see a revival of trade with the UK and to drive some British cars and motorcycles again. The alternative, as I see it, will be the eventual loss of our Anglo-Saxon heritage.[6]

This sense of Australia's dominant ethno-cultural grouping being under siege has also been expressed by politicians, particularly in the Liberal Party, conservative academics and radio commentators, each in their own specific language.

When the great claimant to the position of national worried cook, Geoffrey Blainey, worried publicly about the Asian mix, he also anointed himself a spokesperson for those Australians who are, culturally speaking, of British background. He felt that the latter were losing the right to maintain their own culture:

> If the people of each minority should have the right to establish here a way of life familiar to them, is it not equally right — or more so, in a democracy — for the majority of Australians to retain the way of life familiar to them?[7]

For talkback radio star Ron Casey, the loss is metonymically expressed by the decline of Anglo-Australian idioms:

> I suppose it's too much to ask Australians to use words like 'bonzer'. In another 10 years, with all the blinking Japs and

slopes we've got coming into this country, it'll be 'Bonzai, Bonzai'. Wait until the white-born Australian becomes the minority, mate, the world will be ours. We'll be able to get housing commission flats, we'll be able to do anything we like, but first of all we've got to get enough slopes in here so that we become the minority.[8]

Pauline Hanson expressed similar themes in her 'maiden speech' to parliament following her election:

We now have a situation where a type of reverse racism is applied to mainstream Australians by those who promote political correctness and those who control the various tax-payer funded 'industries' that flourish in our society servicing Aboriginals, multiculturalists and a host of other minority groups.[9]

In a newspaper interview she declared that: 'the most downtrodden person in this country is the white Anglo-Saxon male'.[10]

From the interview material I have collected, it is clear that the discourse of decline is not only voiced by those who have a capacity to articulate it in the public sphere. Similar themes and fears were also expressed by less articulate Anglo-Australians. One unemployed person declared to an interviewer: 'We're a dying race now, and I think most of us agree with that.'

In analysing the discourse of Anglo decline, we come face to face again with the way White multiculturalism thrives on portraying itself as the anathema of what it pictures as a living example of 'evil racist nationalism'. Indeed, White multiculturalists have easily denounced the discourse of decline as hopelessly racist, Anglophile, out of touch and old-fashioned. In turn, they have posited their multiculturalism as clearly urbane, anti-racist, cosmopolitan and non-Anglocentric.[11] It is symptomatic of this negative affinity today that the greater the media exposure given to the Hansonites' view, for example, the more we hear about 'tolerance'.[12]

Taking the critique of the White multicultural conception of 'evil nationalism' developed in the early chapters as a starting point, I want to examine some further weaknesses inherent in the attempts at an academic categorisation of the discourse of decline as just 'racism' or 'new racism', and stress instead the importance of the spatial imaginary that moves it. More precisely, I will argue that it is a specific modality of the White nation fantasy taking root among a group of Anglo-Australian Whites who feel unable to reproduce their imaginary spatial power within the nation. I will argue that their crisis reflects a devaluing of Angloness in the field of Whiteness in favour of a wider cosmopolitan Whiteness.

The Discourse of Anglo Decline between 'Racism' and 'Anti-Racism'

In criticising the *academic* analysis and understanding of actions like the tearing off of a Muslim scarf or statements such as 'Wogs go home' solely in terms of 'racism', I emphasised the spatial nature of these practices. I argued that considerations of race alone do not help us to understand their practical logic, which was, above all, a spatial national logic. In dealing with the discourse of decline we encounter a further problem. This is due to the fact that the explicit and persistent rejection of the accusations of racism that have been directed against its proponents is part and parcel of the discourse. While some of these rejections take the form of the now cliched 'I am not racist, but ...', there often is far more consistency in the rejection than this.

The Members of the Pauline Hanson Support Movement, writing in defence of Pauline Hanson, begin with:

> Before engaging in this debate it is worthwhile to set out the thoughts of Pauline Hanson. The reader of unbiased mind may disagree with some or most of the following sentiments, but it is absurd, we believe, to seriously claim that Hanson is a 'racist'.[13]

They use explicit statements made by Hanson that are worth quoting precisely for their explicitness: 'I am not racist. I know in my heart I am not racist ... I take people on who they are', 'I must stress that I do not consider people from ethnic backgrounds currently living in Australia anything but first-class citizens' and 'I am not saying that I want all Asian immigration to cease. There has always been an Asian presence in Australia and there always will be.'

Ron Casey, a like-minded radio commentator who has attacked multiculturalism and immigration is also adamant:

I want to make the point right now that I am not a racist. A racist is someone who believes his own race is superior and I do not believe that. I believe all people are equal.[14]

'I am not racist', 'I am not discriminative', 'I believe all people are equal' were common statements made in interviews by people who went on to attack multiculturalism, migrants and immigration.

The difficulty arises because once the category 'racism' becomes an object of struggle in the social world, it becomes far more imperative sociologically to understand the way each specific meaning arises rather than aim at producing a more 'sophisticated' theory of racism in order to continue maintaining that someone like Pauline Hanson is racist. In light of the argument I developed in chapter 1 concerning the importance of recognising the specificity of sociological categories, I firmly believe that it is a vacuous exercise for academics to attempt to enter the debate on 'racism' by producing 'superior' academic understandings of it designed for political consumption.

It is precisely this sort of enterprise that leads academics to forget the specificity of their own intellectual products and to sustain the illusion that they can 'decide' the meaning of disputed categories and make the parties to a dispute agree to their learned understanding of it. As I have argued, this means proceeding as if the only reason people deploy certain categories and classifications of others is to understand them academically.

It is with this in mind that, as a starting point, I want to take seriously the fact that many, but by no means all, of Hanson's supporters *really* do not want to be associated with any form of racism. Such people see racism as something ugly and bad, and they do not perceive themselves as ugly and bad. To somehow propose a different understanding of what racism is in order to convince them at any cost that they are 'ugly and bad' is not only bad academic practice, but, it seems to me, also ridiculously bad political practice.

While there are clearly journalists and intellectuals who have understood that there is nothing to gain from a 'Yes you are/No I'm not' type debate on racism,[15] it is clear that the attitude of a number of White multiculturalists with high media exposure to the likes of Pauline Hanson and Ron Casey has been vacuously moralising and accusatory, as well as being marked by ironic disdain. This is well exhibited in much-used categories of abuse such as calling Hanson the 'Oxley moron', and her party 'One Notion'. Rather than a considered search for how to make Hansonites reflect critically on their own beliefs, the aim of such public intellectuals seems to be more to put down the Ron Caseys and Pauline Hansons of the world and establish their own capacity for 'tolerance', as well as their impeccably sophisticated 'anti-racist' credentials. Despite all the high-sounding rhetoric, the effect of such 'sophisticated abuse' is ultimately conservative. For not only will it have no effect whatsoever on the abused, but it also works uncritically to legitimise White multiculturalism as an anti-racist cultural alternative.[16]

The point is not, of course, that those operating in the political field, and who perceive Hansonite-like arguments as racist, should not counter it with anti-racism. Indeed, many do. As I have already pointed out, intellectual labour is not an alternative to the struggle of anti-racist activists. It seems to me, however, that it is ethically imperative, if nothing else, that this intellectual labour should strive to add something other than 'laboured abuse' to the already abuse-saturated political field of racism and anti-racism.

Consequently, I want to begin this analysis by concentrating on a set of more 'socio-existential' questions such as: what kind of crisis in social being is expressed by the discourse of decline? This seems to me crucial if we are to achieve any understanding of the phenomenon and proceed according to Spinoza's already mentioned precept: 'Not to deplore, not to laugh, not to detest, but to understand.'[17] Or, as the Spinoza-inspired Pierre Bourdieu has put it:

> I have constantly denounced the tendency of social science to think in terms of the logic of the trial, or the tendency of the readers of works of social science to make them operate this way ...
>
> These warnings seem to me especially necessary since, in reality, social science, whose vocation is to understand, has sometimes been used to condemn.[18]

I want to contend that by examining the discourse of decline as a specific instance of a White nation fantasy in crisis, we can achieve a far richer understanding of the anxiety suffered by those who articulate it, and the kind of politics that has come to express their plight.

The Logic of National–Spatial Disintegration

If we examine carefully the very statements with which the proponents of the discourse of decline try to distance themselves from 'racism', we find that they are far more propelled by an urgent and systematic concern with national spatial control than with a concern with race as such. In this sense, they present themselves as typical of the nationalist discourses we have examined so far.

Invariably, they articulate a spatial imaginary typical of an ideal, to-be-achieved nation and which acts as a propellant for the nationalist's political motivations and the backdrop for determining who is to be included or excluded from national space. They are also typical in their excessive numerological concern, as well as a concern with the 'mix' and the 'balance'.

Pauline Hanson's discourse clearly embodies a fantasy of herself as someone with a unique managerial right over national space. Thus, when she states: 'I am not saying that I want all Asian immigration to cease. There has always been an Asian presence in Australia and there always will be', she immediately adds: 'All I want is the balanced restored.' Pauline Hanson's fantasy of a balanced nation is also a fantasy of herself as someone with a prime responsibility as far as restoring the balance is concerned.

The key word to the fantasy of domination that propels her discourse becomes not the racial category 'Asian', but the spatial category 'presence' with its intimations of a containable, tame and tolerable otherness. For Hanson, Asians as a 'presence' in her balanced nation are not a problem. This is why she can *credibly* claim that her discourse is not racist. According to her logic of what racism is, if she had a problem with Asians as a race, she would be opposed to *any* kind of Asian presence. Nevertheless, this insistence on presence doesn't augur well for 'the Asians' for, if they become something more than a presence, with Hanson responsible for maintaining the balance and the mix, then they *do* become a problem. Asians are welcomed in Pauline Hanson's One Nation as long as they don't mind Pauline checking up on their numbers every now and then. Thus, Pauline Hanson may not be racist according to her own criteria, but she certainly has an unshakeable belief that it is a White Australian like her who *ought to be* in control of the Asian numbers. As we shall see, her sense of crisis emanates from the fact that she does not feel that she actually is in control as someone who ought to be.

This logic runs throughout the discourse of decline tradition. If one examines the whole text of Geoffrey Blainey's *All for Australia*, as well as other books — such as Ron Casey's autobiography *Confessions of a Larrikin* or *Pauline Hanson, The Truth* — one cannot avoid recognising that there is a far more urgent and pervasive preoccupation that runs through them than a preoccupation with 'race'. This preoccupation has more to do with a loss of governmental power within the nation.

In the conclusion of his now famous speech to the National Press Club in November 1983 — and that he chose to highlight in his polemic, *All for Australia* — Blainey's governmental concern is clear: 'We should continue to welcome a variety of Asian immigrants, but they should come on our terms, through our choosing, and in numbers with which our society can cope.'[19] We can see here how the usage of the national 'we' allows the nationalist to present his governmental aspirations as an already national constant, for what Blainey really means, of course, is through *his* White terms, *his* White choosing, and in numbers with which *he*, as a White Australian, can cope.

In the logic of the home-builder that should be familiar to us by now, Blainey approvingly quotes Charles Price as saying:

> Just as the family has the right to decide whom it invites to visit or live in its home, so a nation has the right to decide its own ethnic composition and the kind of people it invites to visit or live permanently within its borders. This principle underlies the refusal of Malaysia and Sri Lanka to admit more Indians for permanent settlement and the similar refusal of countries all over the world to admit large num-

bers of persons of widely differing backgrounds and customs. In only a few countries, such as Australia, or the USA or the UK, is such a principle castigated as 'racist' by unrealistic and insensitive ideologues.[20]

For Hanson, as well, the issue is primarily a control over the 'home':

> I can invite who I like into my home, but I have no say in who comes into my country. This situation must change.[21]

The right to have one's views with regard to the organisation of the nation treated as legitimate — that is, worthy of considering — is also the overwhelming issue in Ron Casey's autobiography. He wants people to consider what he calls his 'legitimate worries about the future of this nation'.[22] His legitimate worries concern what he sees as 'the unrestricted flow of people from other countries into Australia',[23] that is, an absence of government. Indeed, he stresses that his worry is a governmental one by pointing out that he is not against immigration as such. Instead, as he put it: 'I am for controlled immigration; I am against *invasion*.'[24] It is important to notice that what characterises 'invasion' as opposed to 'controlled immigration' is not that invasion merely means 'too many', but more essentially that it means too many entering with *a will of their own* rather than according to the will of the national domesticator.

What Casey is about, then, is 'the right to check' and 'the right to stay in control'. What bothers him is not really the fact that there are Chinese or Asians coming to Australia. It is the fact that they are coming in a process that appears to him as beyond his control. It is this loss of a capacity to control that constitutes the main element of his 'racism'. In fact, Casey cannot understand why, by merely asking a governmental question — 'trying to learn how many Asian migrants would be coming to Australia' — he came to be considered a racist.[25] For him, racism is when one explicitly declares their hatred and opposition to Asian migration. He, on the other hand, was merely 'a concerned citizen'. This is when he declares the above-quoted:

> I want to make the point right now that I am not a racist. A racist is someone who believes his own race is superior and I do not believe that. I believe all people are equal.

Immediately after, however, he states:

> But I also believe we should strive for social harmony and this cannot exist when you allow Asians to come to Australia in large numbers with no intention of ever assimilating into the ways of old Australia.[26]

We can see how, in exactly the same way as Hanson assumes the role of the worried guardian of the national balance following the denial of her 'racism', Casey's 'I am not racist' is immediately followed by the construction of the self in the role of the worried nationalist responsible for upholding national 'social harmony'.

The above makes it clear, then, that the discourse of decline is a discourse moved by governmental aspirations similar to the White national fantasy we have examined so far. Casey's arguments, however, point beyond this similarity to what makes the specificity of this discourse. Casey is not the normal nationalist who aims at *maintaining* the control of his nation. He is a worried nationalist who perceives that things are *already* on the way to being out of control. He stresses that his question is legitimate, but if he actually felt it to be unarguably legitimate, this would have gone without saying. The fact that he has to insist on qualifying it as legitimate shows that he is experiencing a crisis in his sense of legitimacy as a governmental nationalist.

When examining Hanson's statement in the beginning of this section, I stressed the clear similarity between her national fantasy and other governmental fantasies of national/spatial control. When she claims, however, that all she wants is the balance *restored*, this clearly means that she perceives that the balance has *already* been lost. This is the crucial difference between the Hansonite fantasy and White multiculturalism. White multiculturalists talk about the balance and they position themselves as the guardians of this balance, They do not, however, speak of restoring the balance; they speak of *maintaining* it. Hanson-like fantasies, on the other hand, are propelled by *a fear of having already lost control.* Talking about the Gold Coast where she worked as a cocktail waitress in the early 1970s, Hanson worries that:

> ... the average Aussie out there is saying, 'It's not the Surfers Paradise that we used to know.' People are sort of feeling

that they're losing something that was theirs. Like you're in your country but it's another world. By all means allow investment into the country, but I think we've got to be selective. If you're not an Australian citizen I don't believe you should be able to own property in this country. We're losing control of this country.[27]

In this sense, finding themselves in the process of losing control, nationalists constructed by the discourse of decline are faced with either despair or the far more heroic task of re-establishing national order against what is perceived as a chaotic situation. To the extent that the imaginary national order, in so far as it is *their* national order, is what gives the nationalists their own sense of stability and power in facing the threat of its disintegration, the nationalists face the threat of their own disintegration. This is why, when examining the discourse of decline, we are faced with an abundance of apocalyptic statements à la 'we're a dying race now'. The Pauline Hanson's Support Movement wrote in *Pauline Hanson, The Truth*: 'In our opinion the real "genocide" which is occurring in Australia today is the dispossession of the majority of Anglo-Australians.'[28]

While this discourse obviously reflects a change in the status of Anglo-Australianness as a dominant national culture, it is equally obvious that it tends to *exaggerate* it. If White multiculturalism operates with a denial of any loss due to the presence of non-White Australians, the discourse of white decline seems to experience a significant, but nevertheless minor, change overdramatically and even traumatically. After all, even if we assume that their power is being undermined by migration and multiculturalism, Anglo-Australians and the cultural forms they have generated continue to be comfortably dominant within Australian society.

No matter how much it is maintained that multiculturalism reflects the 'reality' of Australia, the visible and public side of power remains essentially Anglo-White: politicians are mainly Anglo-White, customs officers, diplomats, police officers and judges are largely Anglo-White. At the same time, Australian myth-makers and icons, old and new, are largely Anglo-White, from shearers and surfers to television and radio 'personalities', to movie actors and rock stars. What this creates for those positioned in this public space is a lasting impression that the field of power in Australia, even if it is open for non-Anglos to accumulate Whiteness within it, remains above all an 'Anglo-looking' phenomenon. Anglo-ness remains the most valued of all cultural capitals in the field of Whiteness. After all, it is precisely on such fertile ground that the White nation fantasy manages to maintain its credibility for so many Anglo-Australians. That is why the discourse of decline appears at this descriptive level as an exaggeration.

Even if it is likely that some politicians such as Hanson and intellectuals such as Geoffrey Blainey use it for strategic purposes, the exaggeration that is part of this discourse is neither manipulative nor strategic. It is pathological. It reflects the neurotic character of the gaze that is collecting the empirical data, so to speak. To understand this gaze, we need to examine the position from which it appears to be viewing the rest of society.

Clearly, no one under the new multicultural order has abdicated the right to control who comes to the nation. What those White Australians are experiencing as 'lack of control' is merely a different modality of control. It is, as I will now argue, a new topography of the national field, instituted by a new dominant group that has successfully challenged the old group for the dominance of the nation and is aspiring for the status of national aristocracy.

This raises a crucial question. If possessing 'Anglo-ness' allows certain White multiculturalists to retain a sense of governmental belonging and maintain a fantasy of Australia as a White nation, why is this Anglo-ness not enough for subjects such as the above to retain their sense of control over the nation? To deal with this issue we need to examine briefly the history of the national significance of possessing Anglo-ness as a form of national cultural capital within the Australian national field of Whiteness.

The Rise and Fall of the 'Anglos' as a White National Aristocracy

As is often recognised, the Australia of the post — World War II assimilation era was a relatively homogeneous society. White Anglo and Celtic Australians, despite the struggles of valorisation among them, developed a privileged identification with an Australian national identity imbued with primarily Anglo-Australian national ideals. In this period, a clear White Australian national aristocracy emerged where Anglo-ness was a highly valued national cultural capital. This aristocracy reinforced its symbolic violence through the policy of assimilation which, as with all such assimilation policies, constructed Anglo-Australianness contradictorily as the inimitable centre that migrants had to strive, nevertheless, to mimic.

In what follows, I want to examine the complex and peculiar way White multiculturalism has threatened the aristocratic status of *some* 'Anglo-Australians'. I will argue that White multiculturalism has undermined the traditional 'aristocratic' status conferred on people who possessed Anglo-ness as national capital by giving rise to a new modality of aristocratic White dominance. Consequently, I will suggest that there is more than just old-fashioned racism and Anglophilia to the discourse of decline, and that its critique cannot be separated from a critique of the nature of the new White multicultural governmental aristocracy that has threatened those who identify with this discourse. Understanding the nature of this threat will allow us to explain better the neurotic nature of the Hansonite fantasy.

As I argued in chapter 2, the national capital one needs to accumulate in order to maximise homely belonging to the nation is not the same as that which one needs to accumulate to maximise governmental belonging. The identity traits and characteristics that need to be accumulated in order to feel at home in Australia are not enough to constitute their holders into a national aristocracy. To maximise one's governmental belonging, there are further specific elements that need to be accumulated, and it is only by naturalising its hold on those elements that a group can achieve aristocratic status. In doing so, a group would have succeeded in imposing its symbolic violence on the national field by naturalising its aspirations and ideals, and then transforming them into *national* aspirations and ideals by naturalising their own topography of the nation, the positions that constitute the national field and the subcapital needed to occupy them.[29]

The common idea that the early history of 'Australian

identity' can be seen as a struggle between Australianness and Britishness, between what Richard White terms 'the impulse to be distinctively Australian and the lingering sense of British heritage,'[30] while faithfully reproducing the categories with which the struggle was fought, does not provide any sociological clarification as to the change embodied in these categories. This is not simply because 'this attitude to the development of an Australian identity only became common towards the end of the nineteenth century, when self-conscious nationalists began to exaggerate what was distinctive about Australia.'[31] It is also because it creates too radical a cultural break between Australianness and Britishness. This tends to perceive the close relationship between the two cultural formations that has endured that struggle as unproblematic.

Asking who constituted the national aristocracy within the field of Whiteness during each of these historical formations can help us to identify both the important differences and the important similarities between the two that the categories Australian and British leave, at best, underemphasised.

Britishness, of course, constituted one of the dominant identities within Australia during the colonial and immediate post-colonial era. As Robert Hughes puts it, during all this period, 'the official voices of Australia would continue to stake their claim to respectability on their Britishness.'[32] For all its importance, however, Britishness, as is obvious but not clearly articulated sociologically, was not enough to constitute respectability, let alone a governmental class.[33] While to be born British was enough to make a person feel at home in Australia (to the extent that the British did feel at home in it), one needed to accumulate something more specific within Britishness to acquire aristocratic governmental power. That something else was class (in its socioeconomic sense). It was only by being born upper-class British that one felt and was considered an aristocrat within the national field.

It should be specified that the 'national' field during that period was more imperial than national. That is, the topography in which the British upper classes situated themselves, and which constituted the imaginary of the territory they considered *theirs*, was the British Empire as a whole. This included Australia as a mere locale within the field.

While there was a local population that felt more or less at home in distinct parts of the Empire, only upper-class British individuals felt at home throughout the Empire, as well as considering themselves to have a governmental right within it. While Australians, Canadians and so on felt mostly part of the Empire and minimally as if they had a right to that Empire, only the upper-class British felt it to be innately their Empire. As such, the very fact that 'national' identities were constituted within an imperial context was itself part of the reproduction of upper-class British dominance within the field, since the imperial topography was precisely theirs.

That this continued to varying degrees well into the twentieth century is undoubted and has been documented in many literary and social scientific works. Even after World War II, C. J. Koch could write in a piece from his book of essays *Crossing the Gap*:

> We were left in no doubt of what we were and where we were; being Australian was secondary, and at the top of the map, in the south of that dragon-shaped island we had never seen, the great web of London waited for us to come to it.[34]

He later states that:

> We who lived [in Tasmania] between the thirties and the fifties were living in the half-light of a dying British Empire; but we only slowly came to realise it. The culture based on London was the imaginary pole star of our world.[35]

It was the innate acquisition of the upper-class British cultural essence — which found its utmost actualisation in 'London culture' — that constituted the capital needed to acquire aristocratic governmental power. This virtually meant that even if Australian-born descendants of British-born convicts managed to accumulate enough cultural capital (enough elements of British upper class identity) to allow them to maximise governmental power, they could not be constituted into an Australian aristocracy by the very logic of the field. Consequently, the culture of the dominant in Australia remained for a long time an aspiring ruling culture which, like all non-aristocratic cultures, was torn between what Bourdieu terms a hyper-identification, which reveals one to be an aspirant, and despairing revolt, which is that of those who give up or feel they cannot aspire.[36]

As such, both the acceptance of the category 'convict' or 'ex-convict' and the attempt to rise 'above it' were merely the signs of the symbolic violence upper-class Britishness exerted on the field. The very movement of transcending the convict culture — whether by some elements of the working class who felt it realistic to aspire to do so, or by upper-class Australians — indicated the sway of the upper-class British ideal on the field. This is why Hughes rightly points out:

> What the convict system bequeathed to later Australian gen-
> erations was not the sturdy, sceptical independence on
> which, with gradually waning justification, we pride our-
> selves, but an intense concern with social and political
> respectability.[37]

Again, this search for upper-class, British-defined respectability continued well into the twentieth century. As Koch relates, although admittedly in the extreme case of Tasmania:

> The convict past is like a wound, scarring the whole inner
> life of Tasmanians. It's taken lightly nowadays; but
> Tasmanians of my generation remember when the suspi-
> cion of convict ancestry was a matter of real shame and
> anguish — even up to the 1950s.[38]

Undoubtedly, the English upper-class, like all governmen-tal aristocracies, aimed at essentialising its hold on its cultur-al capital and essentialising the inability of others to acquire it. Thus, as Hughes points out:

> … the late nineteenth century was a flourishing time for
> biological determinism, for notions of purity of race and
> stock, and few respectable native-born Australians had the
> confidence not to quail when real Englishmen spoke of
> their convict heritage.[39]

The sneers directed by the British upper classes at the criminal ancestry of Australians and 'which continued with a waning intensity well into the sixties' and which 'would send upper-middle class Australians into paroxysms of social embarrassment'[40] is proof of the strategies of essentialisation that the British imperial aristocracy continued to deploy to protect its declining cultural power. The Australian 'quailing' is, however, proof also of the belatedness of the decline of the symbolic violence that this aristocracy exercised on the Australian middle class in particular.

To emphasise the sway the British upper-class culture continued to hold over mainly upper class Australia is to recognise that while the latter remained positioned in the current identified by Bourdieu as that of 'anxious hyper-identification', the other current Bourdieu mentions — that of 'the ostentatious assertion of difference' — had already been developing from the late nineteenth century, leading up to Federation. This was the current, well known to contemporary, Australians and based on its elevation to the status of national capital by the local middle class and intellectuals of representations of an 'Australian', partly working class, partly Irish encounter with the 'Australian' natural environment.

As I have already argued, it is misleading to see this new current simply in terms of an Australianness as opposed to a Britishness. It is mainly in opposition to upper-class Britishness rather than Britishness as such that the newly elevated Australian-specific national capital was deployed. So, rather than being non-British, the new national capital was, above all, a new modality of Britishness within and outside the Empire. That is, the new national capital was clearly the product of a frustration with the constant inability of Australians to accumulate British upper-class capital and a strategy aimed at valorising a different capital. This remained, however, a search for distinction within a wider field of Britishness, rather than a break with it.[41]

This is the emphasis, for example, of Judith Wright's introduction to *Preoccupations in Australian Poetry*, published in 1965. She begins by examining the early European encounter with Australia exemplified by Marcus Clarke's 'In Australian forests no leaves fall ...' and moves to show how, increasingly, Australian novels and poetry revealed an 'uneasy movement from Australia to England and back to Australia again. In them, not only the characters but the writing itself seems never at home in either country — nostalgic in both yet settled in neither'.[42] She concludes that:

... if we reject outright the literature of nostalgia, we fail to understand something important about ourselves, and will not be able to set about making Australia into our real spiritual home. In the same way, if we accept it too wholeheartedly, and take too seriously the notion that ours is a transplanted community, we deny the second aspect of our situation as Australians, to turn Australia into a reality, to become something new in the world; to be not, as Hope puts it, 'second-hand Europeans' timidly pullulating on alien shores, but a people who have seized the chance to make a new kind of consciousness out of new conditions.[43]

Wright is clearly advocating and celebrating a change in the national aristocratic culture. She clearly sees the attachment to the 'old culture' in class terms: 'the European culture to which the upper strata of society clung has had to change, and has made way in important respects for something new.[44] It is not, however, anti-'Europeanness' (a more valorised term for Britishness within the field of White national power among intellectuals) that is advocated. Rather, it is a new kind of 'Europeanness' which brings to an end the Australian status of a constant aspirant to culture ('second-hand Europeans') and allows Australians to be cultural aristocrats ('first-hand different Europeans') in their own right. It is because the old aristocratic Britishness was so infused with class-based values and because it remained chiefly pursued by the Australian upper class that the new aristocratic Britishness — the specifically Australian one and what I have referred to as 'Australo-Britishness' (the fact that it was heavily laced with Irishness was part of what made it an *Australo*-Britishness) — was conceived as culturally classless (drawing on representations of so-called Australian egalitarianism). It precisely operated as an opening for White male Australians to accumulate 'what was needed' to experience the aristocratic feeling of innate governmental belonging.

As is commonly acknowledged, albeit in a different language, it is this 'democratisation' of the aristocratic national identity that characterises the Australian modality of Britishness. To be an Australian national aristocrat, one only had to be born into this new cultural identity. To feel that one had the right to take a governmental posture towards Australia, one no longer needed to be born to a socioeconomically defined upper-class family. One's Anglo-Celtic background was a necessary and sufficient national capital. That is, by removing any class qualifier from the Anglo-ness needed to assume a governmental position vis-à-vis Australia, it paradoxically removed all social qualifiers and transformed this Anglo-ness into an essence. It is as such that Australian Anglo-Celtic Whiteness became in itself the aristocratic national identity. In the post-colonial Australia of the mid-1960s onwards, coming from an Anglo-Celtic background was enough to make one feel that one had the capital to maximise both homely and governmental belonging as an innate right.

That the valorisation of this non-class–based modality of Britishness as national capital was one of the key moves away from colonial Britishness to Australo-Britishness can be clearly seen in the autobiography of Ron Casey. There is in Casey's text a very significant passage — in which he debunks his mother's fantasy of origin — that is very indicative of the change in the *dominant* national capital that had occurred in the transition from his parents' generation to his:

> I have spoken before of my mother's flights of fantasy. Well, she also liked to believe and to tell Frank and me that we were descended, at least on her side, from aristocratic English stock. For years she told us that our maternal grandparents were blue-bloods. I have done some digging on the subject in recent years, and found the opposite to be true. Grandad, she told us, was a seafaring man, a proud ship's captain. In fact, he was a ship's purser — a glorified waiter. And Grandma Edith Mayer was of Jewish stock.[45]

Ron Casey's unceremonious puncturing of the class ideal of his mother's fantasy is at the same time a puncturing of the very modality of Australian nationalism centred on the class-based ideal of aristocratic Britishness and a 'killing' of the very national subject to which it gives birth. As importantly, it shows how radically *unaffected* Casey is by this class ideal. He does not care. Unlike Koch's Tasmanians and Hughes's upper-class Australians, stories of working-class origins do not *shame* him.

Casey, the nationalist, is part of a different fantasy centred on an egalitarian White idealisation of the 'mate', born out

of the specific male Irish/British experience in Australia. In
this world, it was enough to possess the capital required for
one's recognition as a mate to feel legitimately empowered
to consider that you belong to Australia *and* that Australia
belongs to you:

> It fell to the people in the surf club to teach me Australian
> mateship — how to stand by your mates, how to earn their
> respect, how to pay your way, the time for work and the time
> for play. I believed then, and do now, that this is the very
> fabric of Australian life — what sets us apart from the rest of
> the world and what will lead us into the next century.[46]

Further:

> After drinking ourselves rotten, we'd plan the evening's mis-
> chief, usually the club dance or maybe a night in town. It
> might sound rough and ready, but it gave me an education
> in the ways of life that I never received at home. No-one ever
> welched or tried to cheat his mates. Everyone paid his way.
> It was one-in, all-in. These are the values that distinguish the
> Australian way of life that I came to cherish. They are values
> I would hate to see die.[47]

As it has often been argued, except maybe for the surf club
and the drinking component, there is nothing specifically
Australian about this almost universal idealisation of male
bonding and friendship. What is specifically Anglo-Celtic
Australian is its elevation into a national ideal precisely
because it represented an antithesis of the image of the
upper-class British national aristocrat that it historically
aimed to dethrone. This is why it can only be understood as
an opposition *within* a wider field of Britishness. Despite his
lack of attachment to the British class ideals of his mother,
and even though his dad was 'of Irish stock' — who knew
'what the English had done to his people', and who 'thought
there was no way his kind should be made to give any help at
all to the British Empire'[48] — Casey is far from being anti-
British:

> Bands, marches, memories of the war, and the traditions of
> Britain — the feeling being instilled in us that we lived in an
> outpost of Britain — these are the feelings that stick so vivid-
> ly in the memory about growing up in a country town in the

30's. It wasn't so bad to have been colonised by the Poms.
The older I get, the more rooted in the British traditions I
seem to become. I suppose it's just a hang-up from those
early days in Lismore — the Light Horse Brigade members
always marching so proudly at the front of the Anzac Day
march, and only 20 years after the end of World War I, still
fitting handsomely and snugly into their uniforms. The
effect on a young person was indelible. This you remember
most, plus the good times.[49]

Casey's valuing of both his Britishness and his capacity for
mateship is the quintessential modality of his generation's
White Australian aristocratic identification. It is only in the
post–World War II era that male Australo-Britishness, in no
need of further class specifications, becomes the necessary
and sufficient condition for national aristocratic status.
Casey clearly values those elements that he feels he possesses
and which make him believe that he has an unquestionable
aristocratic right to the nation. Throughout his autobiography, Casey's most unquestioned assumption is that he naturally fits into the Australian nation and that he naturally has
the right to ask questions about how this country is managed. Of course, Casey is also trying to communicate a sense
of crisis, the perceived crisis behind what we have identified
as the discourse of decline:

> I need the opportunity to express my fears and concerns for
> Australia's future if this crazy policy of multiculturalism and
> unlimited Asian immigration continue unchecked.[50]

It is here that we arrive at the issue that concerns us most.
What is it about the rise of multiculturalism that has made
someone like Casey, who strongly claims an unequal *right* to
governmental belonging in Australia, feel that the nation is
left 'unchecked' and that somehow he is 'on the outer' as far
as his *actual* sense of governmental belonging is concerned?

In most literature on Australian nationalism, while each
period is defined with the help of a description of a dominant 'social type' (e.g. the mate), the multicultural era is far
more often defined by a national principle of organisation
such as tolerance or respect for diversity, or an overall
description such as the existence of a plurality of cultures.
This is not because there is no such thing as a national type

within the dominant multicultural discourse. Implicit in the language of White multiculturalism — the capacity to appreciate and productively exploit diversity, the capacity to operate in a number of cultural milieu, etc. — is a new dominant figure in the history of Australian nationalism: the figure of the White cosmopolite. This is the figure that makes an explicit emergence in the Fitzgerald inquiry on multicultural Australia where multiculturalism and cosmopolitanism were sometimes used as synonyms. It is on that basis that I have referred to this White multiculturalism elsewhere as cosmo-multiculturalism.[51]

The cosmopolite is an essentially 'mega-urban' figure: one detached from strong affiliations with roots and consequently open to all forms of otherness. Referring to one of the 'personas' adopted by Malinowski in his ethnographical writings as that of 'the Absolute Cosmopolite', Clifford Geertz, defines it as 'a figure of such enlarged capacities for adaptability and fellow feeling.'[52] This is, indeed, a crucial aspect of the cosmopolite, but, because he is writing about an anthropologist, Geertz leaves out a crucial domain in which the cosmopolite is defined in everyday life, and that is the domain of refined consumption. Just as important as his or her urban nature, the cosmopolite is a *class* figure *and* a White person, capable of appreciating and consuming 'high-quality' commodities and cultures, including 'ethnic' culture. That is, it is a class figure in a cultural sense. There are some traditional and provincial middle and upper classes who would not rate highly as possessors of cosmopolitan capital.

In this sense, White multiculturalism continues the White Eurocentric quest for a distinctive form of Europeanness begun by the Australo-British. Following the colonial 'We are here as British' and the Australo-British 'We are British Europeans who have been changed by the Australian environment', we now have 'We are cosmopolitan Europeans who have been changed by migration, have become multicultural and are turning to Asia.' The crucial difference, however, is that the dominant White cosmo-multiculturalist type is no longer simply any White person, but necessarily a classy one.

There has been an increasing number of mainstream Australian movies with a portrayal of this new national ideal and whose very structure is based on an opposition between an archaic, restricting Anglo-Australian culture and a living, promising White cosmo-multiculturalism. This is clearly played out in *Strictly Ballroom* in the struggle between the promising and creative Anglo-Australianness laced with 'Spanish-ness' and a claustrophobic Australo-British tradition. Likewise, *Death in Brunswick*, as described by Graeme Turner:

> ... involves a weak but sympathetic hero, Carl, whose attempts to get his life in order involve him in ... a risky but rewarding romance with a Greek-Australian girl, Sophie, and the attempted murder of his dominating mother. The film places Sophie's ethnic/sexy vitality ('She looks like Gina Lollobrigida' says an awe struck Carl) in direct opposition to the dead hand of Anglo values symbolised by Carl's elderly middle-class mother.[53]

It is important to notice that, in both these movies, the crucial struggle is happening *among* Whites. While ethnic culture plays a vital function, it is not an 'ethnic' *subject* that plays the hero. The hero is a classy male White subject who has enough cosmopolitanism in him to embrace ethnic difference and to use it to 'beat' his archaic and unsophisticated Australo-British opponent. Thus, the 'ethnic element' is included and even welcomed into the world of the White multiculturalist. That is, it is allowed to feel at home within it, but only for as long as it knows and keeps to its place as a function for the newly central White cosmo-multicultural subject.

On the other hand, the merely Australo-British are beaten not only because an element of otherness has been included in a space in which they previously assumed control, but also because they appear as lacking the necessary *class* cultural capital to make the leap made by the cosmo-multiculturalists and to embrace difference (by using it).

It was Paul Keating who presided as prime minister over the period in which White multiculturalism was becoming increasingly entrenched as a new natural national order, weaving its symbolic violence into everyday national life. He was also perceived as the very symbol of the White cosmo-multiculturalist. Indeed, the extent to which the classiness of

Paul Keating was a subject of popular and media discourse was reminiscent of the discourses surrounding Robert Menzies. While Menzies's classiness was established by his outdoing the British with his Britishness, Paul Keating's classiness is a far less nation-specific one. It is, precisely, open, urbanite and cosmopolitan. Let us hear what a journalist had to say about him, in what had become a very typical discourse during Keating's prime ministership:[54]

> Mr. Keating is equally passionate about music, which he sees as an intellectual and emotional release from the stress of political life. He still tries to give up his Saturday afternoons to the pleasure of music, and yearns to conduct an opera.
>
> His current favourite pieces of music include Brahms' German Requiem and Beethoven's Fifth Symphony.
>
> With Dr. Kohl, he fell into an animated discussion about the merits of German conductors of the past ...[55]

It is the 'denial of lower, coarse, vulgar, venal, servile — in a word, natural — enjoyment, which constitutes the sacred sphere of culture', according to Bourdieu. It 'implies an affirmation of the superiority of those who can be satisfied with the sublimated, refined, disinterested, gratuitous, distinguished pleasures forever closed to the profane'.[56] It is precisely by ruling on the basis of projecting an image of himself as a priest of the sacred, a member of a cosmopolitan elite, that Keating culturally distinguishes himself.[57]

This has created the interesting situation where it is conservative politicians wanting to maintain the dominance of Australo-Britishness, such as the current prime minister John Howard, who are decrying the decline of the egalitarian spirit in Australia under Keating. It is rather quaint to hear the culturally and *economically* conservative John Howard declaring, while systematically destroying the Australian welfare state:

> The great egalitarian innocence, that egalitarian spirit which was the birthright of most Australians only a short time ago, has significantly disappeared under his [Keating] stewardship and it will be his political epitaph that the Labor man from Bankstown in Sydney did more to betray the battlers of Australian society than any other prime minister that this country has had.[58]

In a peculiarly Australian way, the call for 'equality' was emptied of its socio-economic significance and became effectively a call for the reassertion of the old Anglo-Australian order and for assimilation. There was no hypocrisy here, for egalitarianism was precisely a yearning for the time when Anglo-Celtic males could credibly, despite their class differences, imagine themselves as just 'mates', and where they could all feel that they had an equal right to the nation.

It is something of a paradox, then, that with White cosmo-multiculturalism there is a reverting to include class identity as a necessary component of the ruling national culture, as in the days when colonial Britishness dominated. It could also be argued that the dominant cosmo-multiculturalist is more of a Celtic-Anglo than an Anglo-Celtic in that the changes to the configuration of power between the Anglo and the Celtic have themselves contributed to the move away from Australo-Britishness.

Above all, however, it is the class aspect of the new national multicultural 'ideal of the dominant' that separates it from the 'matey' ideal that preceded it. In *Distinction*, Bourdieu argues that 'a work of art has meaning and interest only for someone who possesses the cultural competence, that is, the code, into which it is encoded'.[59] In much the same way, White multiculturalism raises the crucial question: who has the competence to enjoy ethnic cultural diversity? The very language of White multiculturalism (diversity, difference, etc.) presupposes a 'cultured' and sublimated approach to otherness devoid of a too materialist functionality, which the upper classes use to distinguish themselves and exclude less 'cultured' people.[60]

The classiness required by cosmo-multiculturalism is not only the product of accumulating money capital. In researching cosmo-multiculturalism in the culinary field, for example, it was also clear that those who possessed the capacity to appreciate ethnic cuisine were not necessarily the richest, although the possession of money capital was clearly significant. The inhabitants of Lane Cove in Sydney were perceived generally as richer than the inhabitants of Balmain. They were seen as less cosmopolitan and less capable of appreciating ethnic diversity, however, than the Balmain inhabitants. What the latter possessed over the former was a

specific cosmopolitan capital accumulated through exposure to a certain 'sophisticated internationalism' which gives
the cosmopolitans a global consciousness of the field in
which they are operating.[61]

It is through such processes that 'class' is reintroduced as a
necessary *cultural* component of the male Anglo identity
aspiring for national aristocratic status within Australia, thus
dethroning the likes of Casey from the governmental tower.
Casey is very conscious of this when he sees the multiculturalists as 'looking down on him': 'They [the supporters of
multiculturalism], along with Bob Hawke, look down from
their high and mighty perch on me.'[62] We can see here how
Casey is experiencing a change in the *position of his imaginary
body* that accompanies the changes in his position of power.
He becomes someone *down* at whom one can gaze.

This class consciousness is clearly exhibited by Pauline
Hanson and her supporters, who see the 'cosmopolitan intellectuals' as the real enemy. Indeed, the neurosis resulting
from the loss of *their* national reality leads the Hansonites to
construct a whole conspiracy theory which has behind it a
kind of omnipotent New Class cosmopolitan elite.

> Ordinary Australians do have a common enemy, but it is not
> Aborigines, Asians or people of any particular colour, race
> or creed. Our common oppressors are a class of raceless,
> placeless cosmopolitan elites who are exercising almost
> absolute power over us; like black spiders above the wheels
> of industry, they are spinning the webs of our destiny. We
> can only escape these webs by organised action.[63]

This neurotic sense of disempowerment should not, however, lead us to dismiss the *actual* loss and disempowerment
from which it has resulted. As far as cultural politics is concerned, whatever forms of inclusion and 'democracy' White
cosmo-multiculturalism grants to ethnic people, it takes away
from the more insular White working- and middle-class people, who are perceived as unable, by definition, to appreciate
and value otherness, let alone govern it. Indeed, deprived of
the capacity of appreciating other ethnic cultures, and with
Anglo culture decreed as uninteresting and provincial by the
multicultural order, those possessors of Angloness are left
without even a stall in the multicultural fair.

Conclusion

The undermining of the aristocratic status of an unqualified Whiteness by class does not mean that it is no longer capable of aspiring for the dominant position. To lose one's aristocratic status means that one's cultural capital no longer operates as symbolic violence. As Moi points out in her excellent reading of Bourdieu:

> If explicit ideological or material struggle between groups or classes develops, such as class conflict or the feminist struggle, symbolic violence maybe unmasked and recognised for what it is. In the very moment it is recognized, however, it can no longer function as symbolic violence.[64]

In such cases, the dominant cultural capital is no longer taken for granted and, consequently, it goes back to being a party in the struggle within the field rather than the natural governor of a natural order. It is interesting to notice how the discourse of decline is constantly wavering between reassuming a governmental posture (asking questions about what is good and not good for the nation) and an interested posture (with questions à la 'What about us from a British background?').

Geoffrey Blainey, as quoted earlier, can, on the one hand, adopt a partisan line, worrying about Anglo-Celtics as such:

> If the people of each minority should have the right to establish here a way of life familiar to them, is it not equally right — or more so, in democracy — for the majority of Australians to retain the way of life familiar to them?[65]

On the other hand, he can reassume a governmental position, worrying about social harmony:

> The pace of Asian immigration was accepted, reluctantly, by average Australians so long as they believed that it was temporary and so long as economic conditions were not too depressed. But in what proved to be the last full year of the Fraser Government, unemployment jumped, preparing the way for a change of government and also further undermining the acceptance of strong Asian immigration. When the Hawke government was elected in March 1983, it faced the most serious unemployment for nearly half a century. It was committed to fighting unemployment, but, apparently,

it was also committed to continuing the strongest wave of Asian immigration seen in more than a century. To aggravate the situation, the Asian immigrants were becoming numerous in many suburbs where the unemployment was highest. Here was a sure recipe for social tension. An immigration policy that for one third of a century had been one of the most successful in the history of any modern land was slowly drifting into serious trouble.[66]

It is because the struggle to impose the dominant capital that defines the national field between Australo-Britishness and White cosmo-multiculturalism within the field of White national power is still inconclusive that both of them continue to be perceived as interested struggles by specific parties. At the same time, they both also aim for the governmental high ground. Under the Keating government, it was clear — although it is less clear today — that it was White multiculturalism that had the upper hand in this struggle for supremacy.

In the institution of new forms of symbolic violence, the possessors of the dominant cultural capital strive to present themselves as the governmental enactors and guarantors of the national *doxa* (everyday common sense) and assume the power to deligitimise those who challenge the *doxa*. As Toril Moi has explained:

> The right to speak, *legitimacy*, is invested in those agents recognised by the field as powerful possessors of capital, such individuals become spokespersons for the *doxa* and struggle to relegate challengers to their position as *heterodox*, as lacking capital, as individuals whom one cannot *credit* with the right to speak. The powerful wielders of symbolic capital becomes the wielders of symbolic power, and thus of symbolic violence.[67]

It is to such a heterodox position that the White multiculturalists have slowly succeeded to relegate the older form of dominant Australo-Britishness. The discourse of decline is the ultimate sign that the latter are increasingly becoming a heterodoxy, with its bearers slowly losing whatever vestiges of aristocratic governmental power they had. Keating, as we have noted, already, *credibly* to many, described his Australo-British opponents as irrelevant Anglophile dinosaurs. He even described them as 'un-Australian' — the height of national illegitimacy.[68]

In this sense, the discourse of decline is above all the revolt of those who always felt their legitimacy to be beyond question, as they face their newly acquired sense of illegitimacy. Ron Casey, for example, does not only see himself fighting to regain control of the nation in the face of increased lack of control. He is also fighting for the right to have his questions considered as legitimate. It is this that he experiences most dramatically. Describing a television debate on the issue of migration, he says:

> The 20 minutes that went to air were edited from 90 min-utes of wide ranging debate. So much was left out, includ-ing my questions, which I believe go to the very heart of the immigration debate : such as 'How many Asian immigrants constitute enough?' If anyone will answer that, I will happi-ly drop off the campaign trail. But no one has ...[69]

What Casey is unable to cope with is the newly acquired *ille-gitimacy* of the very question he is asking. This is what the loss of governmental power is ultimately about. It is not merely about losing control, nor is it about being given answers to one's questions that one disagrees with, it is about the inabil-ity to make the dominant culture consider that your ques-tions are even worth answering: 'If anyone will answer ...' It is not the trauma of the speaking subject who is not listened to, but the trauma of the subject who is not being heard. That is the spectre of national insignificance.

The Discourse of Anglo Decline 2: The Role of 'Asians' in the Destruction of the 'White Race'

What characterises the White multiculturalism and the White ecology examined in earlier chapters is that they exemplify a fantasy's adaptive capacity. They represent the way a socially and historically grounded fantasy of White dominance, which emerged from the history of the White colonisation of Australia, was adapted by its subjects to the changing social and demographic constitution of Australia. A fantasy's capacity for adaptation means its ability to sustain itself despite the change in the practical social reality in which it is grounded. In so doing, it offers the subject who inhabits it a relatively stable and viable sense of themselves — in this case, a credible and continuing sense of White dominance.

In labouring to adapt their fantasies to changing realities, subjects aim to 'persevere in their own being', as Spinoza would put it. Fantasies constitute the conatus of their being as subjects. White multiculturalism operates as an adaptation of the assimilation fantasy of postwar Australia which allows the White subjects to retain their governmental position within the nation. It does so through a process of incorporating Australia's multicultural reality by constructing it into a reality of tamed ethnicities structured around a primary White culture.

It is not the case, however, that everyone is either willing to and/or capable of engaging in this labour of adaptation. The capacity to maintain one's fantasy requires a certain disposition, and even a certain sophistication, that is often related to socioeconomic, educational and cultural background. Some subjects, instead of adapting their fantasy and incorporating the social changes around them, end up perceiving those changes as a threat. This has largely to do with the way they imagine their position in the field of power, and how secure they feel it to be. It is this phenomenon that we come face to face with when analysing the discourse of decline and which I want to analyse here.

On Being Swamped by Asians

It is important to insist that, on the whole, the perception of national chaos — of being swamped, of losing control — described in the previous chapter is not merely the political construct of opportunist politicians. Although it can be that *as well*, it is primarily a lived reality for some Australians who, because of their specific social and cultural background, have not been able to incorporate into their national fantasy space the migrant presence that has resulted from the immigration of the 1970s, 1980s and 1990s. Instead, they vividly experience it as a loss. This was evident in many highly emotional interviews conducted with White Australians articulating various aspects of the discourse of decline. To understand this experience of loss, we need to further examine a crucial aspect of aristocratic identity so far left unexplored.

One of the crucial qualities of an ethnic identity that allows it to work as an aristocratic identity is its capacity to be essentialised. It is such a capacity which allowed 'having Anglo-ness' to work as an aristocratic identity during a certain phase in Australia's history. What does this mean? Clearly, to say, as we did in the previous chapter, that before White multiculturalism 'having Anglo-ness' was in itself enough to experience governmental belonging to the nation does not mean that those who actually accumulated high governmental belonging were classless. As is found everywhere, it is the upper and middle classes who are in a position to maximise the accumulation of governmental belonging by adding to their identity various forms of economic and cultural capital.

Nevertheless, to say that Anglo-ness operated as an aristo-cratic capital does mean that its possession, even on its own, by otherwise impoverished White Australians did allow them to feel that they had at least some natural governmental right over the nation. What allowed these impoverished White Australians to experience this governmental belonging is that, by essentialising their Anglo-derived Whiteness, they could identify with the more capital-endowed classes who were in the highest positions of governmental power. That is, a working-class White Australian who was not in a position to accumulate much else as far as national capital was con-cerned could still experience a sense of governmental belonging by experiencing his Whiteness as an essence or a potential: 'It is true that I do not have much at the moment, but I have my Anglo-ness.' The fact that Anglo-ness can be experientially perceived as a *positive* essence is due in large part to the fact that most middle-class and upper-class people were Anglo Australians. This is how the essentialisation works: 'I have the identity of those who are middle class and who are in power. While, in material terms, I may be not much better off than the Aboriginal or Hungarian family next door, at least I have an essence/identity which gives me, unlike my Aboriginal, Arab, Hungarian or Chinese neigh-bours, the *possibility* of accumulating more capital. I belong to the 'race' of those who rule, even though I am not actual-ly ruling. This means that I could rule.' Identity embodies, in this case, a principle of hope that ensures the viability of its adoption.

Consequently, processes of essentialisation, such as the conception of one's identity as a 'race', allows potential to become a form of capital and, through identification with the existing governmental class, allows for governmental strategies of distinction even by those who have nothing other than this potential. As we can see, however, what the above entails is that this essentialisation has its specific con-ditions of possibility. And the most crucial of these condi-tions of possibility is the capacity to experience an ethnically homogeneous middle class with a quasi-monopoly over mid-dle-class positions. This gives the possessor of the identity a concrete sense of the capacity of realising its 'potential'.

It is here that we encounter one of the main causes of the crisis exhibited by the discourse of decline. If there is one thing that the development of multiculturalism and the recent wave of Asian migration to Australia has entailed, it is the diversification of the middle classes. That is, multiculturalism and Asian migration have undermined the very conditions of possibility of experiencing White identity as a potential, as a race and/or as embodying a hope of social mobility. This is how 'the Asians' have inadvertently led to the destruction of the 'White race' in Australia. While the political discourse of Hansonism talks about Asians in general, nothing has been made as explicit in the interviews we have recorded as the traumatic experience by White Australians of *middle-class* Asians.

Alan works as a storeman at a major computer store; he's been doing the same job for seven years. He dreams of a more prestigious position: 'I started a computer course at TAFE, but I had to leave.' He tried to get a loan from the bank to start his own business. He was unsuccessful. Alan has totally racialised the frustration of his desire for social mobility. The bank manager was 'Asian' and he refused to give him a loan 'because I'm an Aussie'. For Alan, what happened was the proof that 'we're going under' and the 'Asians will soon take over the whole place'. In fact, 'we' are 'so hopeless' that 'we're giving it to them on a plate'.

> Those fucking middle-class Asians ... have you seen the look in their eyes?... I know this look really well ... more than half of the people who come in to buy a computer are Asians ... they give you this look as if you ought to kneel and kiss their feet and thank them for coming here ...

Even if we cannot generalise too much from the interviews conducted in suburban Sydney where people expressed a sense of White decline, it is striking that all of them articulated a crisis of social mobility using a racialised anti-Asian discourse.

Let us listen to Paul, who had worked 'in the meat industry' (he did not specify any further) for a long time ('forever'). Paul is fifty and has never married, but he's got nieces and nephews whom he sees regularly. Paul's fantasies of social mobility are generational. He does not seem to hold much hope of himself moving into a better job, but he clearly sees his nieces and nephews as the ones who could better the lot of 'the family'. His hopes for them, however, are clouded with worries:

> *Paul:* I sort of look at my nieces and nephews and think *God, they'll never have a job.* I mean, not only do they keep bringing in more people to do manual labour and we're going through that at work, but the unis and all that, you know, even, even the kids that want to go to uni again, they're bringing more Asians into, in Universities because they've got the money. What about the legit people here? They're all going back, I went to the doctor's around the corner last night, the first, this is the first time I've been there ...
>
> *Interviewer:* Right.
>
> *Paul:* and ... I went up there last night and one's, one's Indian and another one's some other bloody thing, and I thought, *Stuff it, I'm not coming back here again, I'll go back to the general hospital.*
>
> *Interviewer:* Hmm, hmm.
>
> *Paul:* You know, but where are our doctors? I mean, a place as big as Marrickville, sure fair enough, you know, have a, have a couple ...
>
> *Interviewer:* Yeah.
>
> *Paul:* ... because you, you need the ethnic doctors to, to speak and that but, you know, if you go anywhere ... I think it was Westmead hospital, well nearly all the doctors and nurses are Asians ...

These interviews give us a window onto the kind of experiences people such as Paul and Alan have undergone following the arrival of the Asian middle classes in the 1980s and 1990s. I think the analysis of essentialism above sheds some crucial light on the reasons why these experiences being so traumatic. The 'Asian' middle and upper classes make being an upper-class Australian no longer a strictly White affair. By the same token, there can no longer be a privileged essential link between being White and the national dreams of social mobility.

A similar feeling of crisis is derived from the international 'rise of Asia' discourse that dominated the Australian media until the recent Asian economic crisis. This is often seen as unjustified and the interviewees find many reasons why they don't find the discourse convincing. For Joan, who works in a milk bar in Penrith:

> Well, I guess there must be many people in Asia doing really well. My sister lives and works in Katoomba. She says it is unbelievable how many Asians seem to be able to afford coming here … She hates them [giggles] … She's not good for our tourist industry … She is really rude to them, but she said that doesn't stop some of them from wanting to take a picture of themselves with her.
>
> … [but] I am sick of everyone telling me how well the economy in Asia is doing. If it is doing so well, why is it that it's their people who keep wanting to migrate here. I mean, I am not the one dying to migrate to Asia, am I?

Ross who owns the same milk bar agrees:

> The government has sold out to Asian investors. Why is it so hard for them to say that bloody Suharto or Mahatir are fucking dictators? I mean, we live in a democracy and they're bloody dictators, but every time an Australian politician visits it seems as if it is we who have to apologise for something … 'No, no, we shouldn't say that … it's racist.' All we hear is 'Asia's economy is growing' and 'the importance of Asian investment and the Asian market'. I mean, something is wrong here, don't you think? We can't even be proud of our English democratic heritage. I mean, why should we not say to Mahatir, like that, straight in his face, 'We are superior because we are a democracy and you're a dictatorship.' Why should we restrain ourselves from saying what we know is true and wipe that smug dictator's smile of his face? All of this is because 'Asia's economy is growing'.

Ross and Joan's views capture quite well some of the contradictory aspects of the way in which the 'rise of Asia' and the 'need to be part of Asia' is constructed in Australia. What is important to us here, however, is the clear competitive framework within which they present their critique. Their critique reflects a fear of losing that sense of distinction derived from having a White European identity.

Interestingly, tourism operates as a link between the sense of White decline derived from the presence of the Asian middle class in Australia and the one derived from the international images of a growing Asian capitalism.

I am not familiar with the growing body of research done on tourism, but the few works I have examined do not seem to capture in any way how tourism seems to lead some people — those who clearly do not have the opportunity to travel — to experience a peculiar relation of power between themselves and the tourists. Not only does the visitor appear to be someone who is 'better off' economically than they, but he or she is also in the position of the voyeur who reduces the Australian into an object. This is why the discourse on tourism feeds into the feared imaginary reversal of the relation of power between White Australians and 'Asians' that characterises the discourse of decline.

The tourists and the 'Asian' investors — just as much as the 'Asian' doctors, students and bank managers — take away from these White Australians their capacity to experience their Whiteness as a privileged essence. They rob them of its potential and, in the process, rob them of their aspirations of social mobility on the basis of this identity. Alan makes this even clearer:

> Every Mercedes and BMW in Sydney is driven by an Asian. You know how they say 'The rich are getting richer and the poor are getting poorer.' They forget to add that the rich are becoming Asian and the poor are becoming Australian. No wonder all government decisions go their way. You can only influence government decisions if you've got money … and who's got money? Not me, I can tell you that much …

Alan, more so than Paul, experiences the arrival of the Asian middle class not just as something that has thwarted his desires for social mobility, but, probably on the basis of his 'bank experience', he also sees it as signalling a power reversal within the nation. Such experiences lead to the disintegration of one's sense of privileged belonging to the nation on the basis of cultural identity, and the subsequent experience of 'losing control' and 'being swamped'. This was made most dramatically explicit in an interview with Scott, a middle-aged unemployed man in Marrickville. Scott did not have any immediate dreams of social mobility, but he spoke at length of the many occasions whereby his family had a chance to 'make it', but '… Dad blew them one after the other'. His dad 'even had a chance to work for a Jewish man-ufacturer in Surry Hills' who wanted him because he knew that 'Dad could sell a Jewish cap to Hitler if he wanted to'. Instead, his dad ended up 'spending all his money and his time on the races'. Scott is now a very worried man:

Scott: … You know that, as I said, I never considered myself bias, umm, biased like, or, um, discriminative.

Interviewer: Sure.

Scott: But I think in some ways I am a bit, and for me that's bad, but I, I blame the government for that because they're the ones that are, are setting the people against each other … if you sort of look at it deeply.

Interviewer: Why's that?

Scott: Well, they've given up on keeping things under con-trol. I mean, twenty years ago you wouldn't have caught me dead saying something nasty about Lebanese, Greeks, Vietnamese or anybody. But now, I do … Well, I'll be hon-est with you, I can't stand many of them. They're all so fuck-ing arrogant, you know. We Australians, mate, are plain stu-pid. They've come and we looked at them, and all we've done is smile … and now … see, I am getting angry … you think it's alright? …

Interviewer: No worries. Keep going.

Scott: Well now, they fucking act as if they own the place and as if you're the one who's in the way. How the fuck did they become so arrogant? Well, we've let them become arrogant with all this fucking multiculturalism and God knows what …

Interviewer: It is … it is … interesting that you … as you said, you … didn't feel like this before. When … when do you think you started feeling like this?

Scott: I don't know, about ten years ago maybe. I am not racist, you know. I know about racism. I know about South Africa and the Holocaust, you know … I am not a racist and yet sometimes I think, Shit, you know …

Interviewer: Yes.

Scott: I go to … in the morning, I catch a train now, and sometimes I look around me and I might be the only White person in the whole damn place …

Interviewer: Right.

Scott: The only white person in the whole damn place ... yeah ...

Interviewer: Yeah.

Scott: You know, and, what all of a sudden, say when they get there and they're yapping away and I'll think to myself, *Sh ... For Christ's sake, why don't you ... You're here, speak English or shut up, you know.* See what I mean, it's the government's fault. How did we get to be in this situation?

We can see, in the above, how an everyday life experience such as 'being the only white person in the whole damn place', coupled with a sense of power reversal because of the migrants who have become 'arrogant', takes on a traumatic dimension and is experienced by the subject as a loss of his national reality. That this traumatic experience by the subject is seen as caused by 'the government' gives us an important insight into the nature of the White neurosis we are analysing.

The subject's crisis is clearly a governmental crisis. He no longer sees the state as enacting his will. Indeed, he no longer sees the state as enacting any will — 'They've given up.' The migrants becoming arrogant is a symbol of a general disintegration of the traditional national hierarchies. We can also, however, see behind this loss the fantasy of power that informs it. It is a yearning for a nation where migrants 'knew their place' and where the subject's Whiteness yielded a clearer sense of conceiving Australia as his home. The order of things (in the nation) is no longer his order of things, the language (of the nation) is no longer his language, and there is no coercive apparatus, no National Father, no God, no Other, to use Lacan's term, willing to impose and guarantee his language and his order.

It would be a mistake to see Scott's crisis as the product of his experience on the train. It is more likely that the causality is exactly the reverse here. Many people can travel on the train and not perceive that 'they are the only White people' on it. Alternatively, they may perceive it and explain it sociologically as the result of the train passing through a specific geographical location. It is *because* he is suffering from a crisis in his Whiteness that his experience on the train is so traumatic. This is why, before anything else, it was imperative to understand the nature of this governmental crisis. That such a crisis is a crisis of social mobility is made totally clear, even if with a certain degree of ironic self-criticism, by an unemployed university drop-out in Newtown (an Australian-born person of Greek background):

> Let's not beat around the bush. I am envious. I am envious because of the cars they drive. I am envious because of the women they go out with. I am envious because of the houses they are buying. They're living the life I dream about, damn it! They've come all the way from I don't know where and they've stolen my dreams.

White Neurosis and Fears of Disintegration

For the national subjects to derive a meaningful and satisfying identity from defining themselves as nation-building subjects, as builders of a specific imaginary, to-be-achieved nation, such an imaginary nation has to be experienced as partly existing — and partly achievable. That is, the national ideal has to be experienced as having a basis in the experienced reality of the subject, of being *credibly* worthy of pursuit. If they are not to suffer from an identity crisis, nationalists have to be faced with constant 'empirical' confirmations of the adequacy of their conception of themselves, their nation and their national yearnings. These vary according to the nationalist subject, but constitute the minimum condition for the self-reproduction of their national fantasy.

Enduring fantasies, such as nations and national selves, are therefore *well-grounded subjective realities*. This is why it is important to stress that the nationalists' loss of their privileged sense of governmental belonging is not something that they acquire from the outside, from a politician or a radio commentator who 'convinces' them to feel in a specific way. They experience the loss through the specific take they have on their everyday experience.

As we have argued in earlier chapters, fantasies have an 'existential' dimension in that they provide the means of staging the subject constructed within them into a meaningful subject — a subject whose life has a purpose which makes it worth living. Because of this, a threat to one's fantasy is experienced as a threat to one's own viability as a living subject. This is why, in such cases, perceived threats to one's fantasies lead to deep anxieties about the capacity of reproducing one's own significance as a subject.

The threat to the fantasy becomes a fear of insignificance. The more the fantasy is central to the being of the subject, the more anxious the subject becomes in the face of the threat. This is why statements of the 'genocide' and 'We're a dying race' type, quoted above, abound in this discourse.

In the examples examined in chapter 7 of the Australian ruling class's relation to the British national aristocracy in the colonial period, categories of affect seemed to be often used to describe the Australian feeling of a lack of national aristocratic status due to their convict ancestry when faced with 'real Englishmen'. Robert Hughes uses categories such as 'the Stain'[1] and talks of Australians 'quailing' when reminded of such a history;[2] Koch very explicitly refers to the 'scarring' of 'the whole inner life of Tasmanians'.[3] That is, it seems that not having, or losing, 'what it takes' to be a national aristocrat for those who aspire to such a status is not treated in a utilitarian manner as a mere practical functional or dysfunctional aspect of one's life, but as a phallic loss affecting the way one experiences one's whole being.

Having identified the national order as their own, national aristocratic subjects experience the loss of governmental belonging as a loss of the national reality that has acted as their support. Contradictory imagined states of chaos, conspiracy and invasion lead to a precarious experience of the self and consequently to the formation of a deeply paranoid subject. Casey, imagining himself pursued by 'ethnics' out to get him because of his views, expresses this quite clearly, even lucidly:

> At about the time of the second Jana Wendt interview I became a little paranoid about my safety and that of my family … I could sense the hatred welling in the ethnics …
>
> I would walk quickly to the car, but I don't mind saying that not a morning went by for weeks that I didn't turn the ignition key without a sense of foreboding. Once or twice, I even checked under the car for bombs.[4]

Even some of its more intellectually sophisticated proponents become prone to conspiracy theories. Thus, in Geoffrey Blainey's account of the Asianisation of Australia, we are told that:

Unknown to the public, unknown probably to parliament, but certainly known to ministers for immigration [and Geoffrey Blainey, I might add], a secret room lies inside the scoreboard. The sign on the door says: 'Keep out.'

Inside the room are devised plans that run counter to the immigration principles announced to parliament ...[5]

In a similar vein, Ron Casey maintains that:

... the conspiracy exists among prominent politicians to stifle any debate on the immigration issue, and among ethnic leaders in the community to defuse any opposition to unlimited Asian immigration. The facts are plain to see. The majority of Australians are against it, but nothing is done to ensure that their wishes are fulfilled. I spoke out and was vilified. Professor Blainey spoke out and lost his job. John Howard spoke out and was dumped as Opposition Leader. Bruce Ruxton spoke out and was labelled a racist loony.[6]

Within this clearly neurotic imaginary, the migrant other begins to assume sub- or super-human proportions. For Geoffrey Blainey, the 'Asian threat' takes the allure of an 'irrational' tide with which one cannot possibly reason. As he relates in *All for Australia*:

I have been at formal dinners in China when the conversation has turned to Australia, and the Chinese present say with animation: 'All that space and so few people!' When we explain that much of Australia is desert and that the longest rivers would seem like half-dry canals to anybody who has sailed down the Yangtze, the Chinese blink. It can't all be desert, they say. And if it is desert, then perhaps water should be sent to the fertile soil along new irrigation channels. Where, we reply, will the water come from? A map of Australia is produced by a diligent Chinese, and there stands the lakes — Lake Eyre, Lake Torrens and many others. And we have to explain that the lakes are usually dry and when they are filled with water are salty. The Chinese are not altogether convinced ...[7]

For Blainey, the overwhelming trait which makes the Asians a threat to the predominance of White Australians is a negative one. It is their lack of rationality, compared to the rational White Australian, which constitutes them into such a dangerous 'unthinking matter' inexorably moving to over-take Australia and which no reasoned argument can stop. For others, however, what makes the 'Asians' a threat is that they are 'too good'. Here, the imaginary of the 'Asians' as other shifts so that they are perceived in excessively positive terms. This, however, also works to dehumanise the 'Asians' and make them appear as if they are superhumans:

Greg: They're getting more powerful. Mainly because of the younger kids growing up and they're all either brothers or cousins or ...

Interviewer: Right.

Greg: ... That is typically ethnic, everyone's a brother, a cousin or ...

Interviewer: [Laughs.]

Greg: Family, you know, I mean, I ... I, I admire them for that, because, Australians have never ever been, well if you think of it, family oriented. Could you imagine, um ... Well, I can't imagine me living with my cousins at, in, in another house. Bugger them, I'd rather go somewhere else, but like, the place across the road you don't even know who, who lives there ...

Interviewer: Hmm.

Greg: ... and one of the units up here, um, they've been dif-ferent, um, Vietnamese or Chinese, whatever they were, you know, or Asians anyway, um, they just seem to thrive, you know. They'll be a day shift, they'll be a night shift, they'll have a hundred in there if they could, you know, but there's ... How, how many Australians could you imagine doing that? Not too many at all.

Interviewer: No, that's true, I can't imagine living even with my brother, he'd give me the shits.

Greg: So ... This is about the only thing I, I, you know ... you got to give them guts for, because they work like this, they live like this, and that's probably how they can do it. That's why they're much better off than the rest of us.

Whether because of such negative or positive features, the 'ethnics' are invariably perceived as having become, or as about to become, the masters of the situation. Ultimately, the most distinguishing feature of the loss of national reality is the fear of the other turning the tables and reversing the imaginary master–slave relationship that constituted the basis of the nationalist governmental fantasy. One of the unvarying characteristics of the discourse of decline is precisely its perception of the ethnic presence in Australia as an untamed presence. Indeed, not only are 'ethnics' and particularly 'Asians' perceived as beyond control, but they are also perceived as having reversed the relationship of power that underlies the White nation fantasy. Not only are the 'Asians' in control, but they are also specifically in control over Anglo-Australians.

This imaginary power reversal was expressed on many occasions in the interviews we conducted in Marrickville. It was perceived by different interviewees to affect various areas of their everyday life. Thus, for Glenn, who works as a security guard in a shopping centre, the 'Asians' simply work among themselves, and the 'Aussies' are left out. Furthermore, it is the 'Asians' who are increasingly in a position to employ workers, but only employ people from their own 'race'.

Glenn: They import their own stuff from Asia. They, they buy from other Vietnamese out here. Asians buy only the stuff that they, they get. Um, and, so, so and they employ ... I ... I don't think — talk about being prejudiced, come to think of it — I don't think I've seen any Aussie or anything in any Asian shop whatsoever, or in an Asian warehouse maybe ...
Interviewer: Hmm.
Glenn: Now, I mean, can you honestly say that you'd know people working for an Asian firm?
Interviewer: Hmm.
Glenn: And I mean, some of them have got pretty big places ...
Interviewer: Hmm.
Glenn: ... but would the government ask them to employ people from other races? No way.
Interviewer: Hmm.

Glenn: You try that one time. Just see. Walk into a place and say, 'Right, yeah, you got a job here?' They'll say, 'No! You're White! You're too bloody White!'

For Dave, a factory worker and a union delegate, the power relationship reversal occurs in the workplace, where he perceives that anti-discrimination rules set up to help migrants counter racism are now used by them to get away with being racists themselves against the 'Australians':

This thing with now, um, uh, what is it? ... discrimination. No one'll touch it, and they won't touch it at work. We've got a lot of trouble there and the only one that really, who's been discriminated against, and people are finding out now, is the Australian, because we can't say a thing. This anti-discrimination rule, I don't know how you feel on this, but it really irks me because, um, I'm a union delegate, so we've had trouble from some of the guys at work about this. They'll stick up for the ethnic, because one time, one time we went down there and it was quoted that, oh sure, it was okay for him to call you an Aussie bastard or something, but for you to call them, 'Oh you, you're ... anything at all', um, somehow turns around that you're not having a go at him, you're having a go at their race. But, they can say it to you, doesn't work the same way here. So, I mean it's making a lot of people unhappy ... You know, in some ways, the anti-discrimination's great, but it's going overboard, I mean it's, it's really, you know, it is really, really going overboard ...

This imaginary power reversal can be 'detected' in very different areas of social life. For the Hansonites, it is demonstrated by the way Asians are wrecking the Anglo moral order and controlling the sexuality of young Australian girls: 'In our cities, girls as young as 14 sell sex for as little as $10 to buy drugs from Asian gangs.'[8] For Scott, on the other hand, the proof of the power reversal is in the fact that Australian kids are encouraged to learn Asian languages:

Scott: America's far from great ... but at least they say, 'We've got a problem.' I mean, but the thing is Australia's young and we should be learning from them as we should be learning from the English. I mean, I've been to France once ... I hate the French, I loathe them, they're the most arrogant people in the world. Now, that I know, I am biased because I just don't like them.

Interviewer: [Laughs.] Fair enough.

Scott: But, I've reason for saying that, because the French, one thing I do admire them for, as far as they're concerned, French is the number one language, you go there, you obey French laws there, no matter what, you've, you've sort of, um ... go and settle there, then you're a Frenchman, you live under French laws, you speak French. Now I, they don't even want to talk to tourists over there if you can't speak it.

Interviewer: I know, I know.

Scott: But I agree. I can see why.

Interviewer: Hmm.

Scott: Really. I mean, we're a Western country and what happens now? The poor young kids of today have to now take up an Asian language, they've got to take up a bloody Asian language in their own country ... a bloody Asian language in their own country [punctuated] ... You go on, you tell me that's right ...

Interviewer: Hmm. Oh, I won't, I won't say anything. [laughs]

Scott: No, no, you probably, no but honestly Australian kids have got to take up Asian languages ... Why aren't the people coming out here learning English? Might as well give up.

It is the loss of reality generated by this imaginary power reversal which explains some of the more hallucinatory fantasies one finds in the discourse of decline. In Casey's autobiography, the 'analysis' of the effect of Asian migration reaches truly phantasmagoric proportions:

In 2020, the entire east coast of Australia, from Cairns in the north to Melbourne in the south, could be overrun by those of Chinese and Japanese extraction. The north, from Broome across the Northern Territory to the Gulf of Carpentaria, could be populated almost entirely by Indonesians and Malays, and the west coast from Broome in the north to Perth in the South could be home to millions of Indians. Those of European extraction, the ordinary white Australians, could live in small enclaves in South Australia or be driven back to Europe or to parts of the United States. There could be sporadic fighting from guerilla groups of 'dinkums', but this insurrection won't have a snowflake's chance in hell of reversing the Asianisation of

Australia. Ghettoes of Australian labourers — or 'white coolies' — could live in outer metropolitan areas to service the Asian factories.[9]

It is an updated version of this hallucinatory imaginary, historical antecedents of which can be found as far back as the 1840s Anglo-Asian encounters, that we find in *Pauline Hanson, The Truth.* Here we meet the president of what is imagined to have become the 'Republic of Australasia' in the year 2050: Poona Li Hung, 'a lesbian ... of multiracial descent, of Indian and Chinese background' who is also 'part machine — the first cyborg president. Her neuro-circuits were produced by a joint Korean-Indian-Chinese research team.'[10]

Embodied in this discourse is both the actual fear of national insignificance and the strategic whipping-up of this fear. The fear of reversal, because it is perceived as a reversal, also reveals the imaginary ideal of the way the likes of Ron Casey and the Hansonites believe that things ought to be if they were straightened up. Behind the fear of becoming transformed into white coolies is the subliminal idealisation of a reality where the Asians themselves were *just* 'coolies'. Poona Li Hung, on the other hand, is also the reversal of what the Hansonites would fantasise Hanson herself to be, a 'straight woman, monoracial, of British descent' and, maybe, a 'woman of steel', produced by BHP.

The Real of the Discourse of Anglo Decline

Despite the loss of reality it entails, and probably because of it, the discourse of decline is not overwhelmingly a discourse of defeat. If it were, it would not be able to constitute the ideological ground for a political movement as it has done. While there are clearly those who see Anglo decline as irreversible, the majority still see it as an aberration of a normal state of affairs that ought to be restored. What constitutes the discourse of decline into a fantasy space is that, in using the images of national and personal disintegration it promotes, as well as the fear of insignificance that propels it, it successfully promotes it as a drama of survival and heroism. It invests in those images of disintegration to weave the story of a desperate rearguard action by a disintegrating nationalist trying at all cost to save a disintegrating national order.[11] For the subject interpellated by it, it constructs significance out of insignificance.

In Pauline Hanson's discourse, this quest for significance is made possible particularly through a fantasy of the Anglo self as still constituting 'the mainstream'.

> Mainstream Australia must be allowed to have a say in how this country will look in a hundred years' time! (Pauline Hanson, *The Truth*, p. 17)

> Abolishing the policy of multiculturalism will save billions of dollars and allow those from ethnic backgrounds to join mainstream Australia ... (Pauline Hanson, *The Truth*, p. 9)

> Along with millions of Australians, I am fed up to the back teeth with the inequalities that are being promoted by the government. (Pauline Hanson, The Truth, *Pauline Hanson's Maiden Speech, 10 Sept. 1996, p. 3*)

> As you all know, the debate that has been denied mainstream Australia for so long, is now well and truly on. (Pauline Hanson, *The Truth*, p. 14).

While the concept of the 'mainstream' appears as secondary to statements such as the above, it is in fact the core on which the fantasy is constructed. Its power lies in the naturalness with which it is put forward. It is as if it goes without saying that the mainstream is speaking through the discourse of decline. If the experience of decline was seen as based on the mere fact that Anglo-Australians are simply declining in number and influence in Australia, then there would be nothing about which to be outraged. Consequently, 'mainstreaming the Anglo' becomes a necessary strategic deployment aimed at giving the discourse its moral legitimacy and the sense of moral outrage from which it gains much strength.[12] This is how it becomes perceived as the discourse of a majority that is not being taken into consideration. It is also here, however, that the discourse comes face to face with its Real, that part of social reality which it cannot incorporate.

Pauline Hanson still likes to fantasise herself as someone

who can decide who does and does not deserve to be
Australian. I have already cited a well-known example of this:

> I must stress at this stage that I do not consider those peo-
> ple from ethnic backgrounds currently living in Australia
> anything but first-class citizens, provided of course that they
> give this country their full, undivided loyalty.[13]

Udayan Prasad's film *Brothers in Trouble* is a story of the evolution of a migrant's sense of governmental belonging in
Britain. Towards the end of the film, Amir, the migrant, is
picking wildflowers near a hospital when, assuming the
nationalist role of spatial police with which we are now familiar, a nurse tells him that he is trespassing. Amir, however, has
reached a stage of nationalist accumulation where he can
answer back. 'Are you the owner?' he asks. ''Cos if you're
not, please to mind your own bloody bastard business.'[14]

In Australia today, many non-White migrants' sense of
national belonging has evolved much further than Prasad's
hero. I am not only referring to the postwar European
migrants, but also to many Asian migrants who have arrived
here in the past twenty years. They have accumulated
enough national belonging to tell even those who approach
them with an unnecessary 'You're welcome' to 'Mind their
own bloody bastard business.' They have grown to know the
difference between being told 'You're welcome' on the day
they first arrived at Sydney airport, and being told 'You're
welcome' five or ten years later.

In one of a number of interviews I conducted recently with
some Lebanese Australians concerning the rise of Pauline
Hanson, this is what a 46-year-old Lebanese engineer said
referring directly to Hanson's comment above:

> I came to Australia twenty-six years ago. I was twenty. I love
> Lebanon and I love Australia and that's how it is. What I
> can't stand about Hanson is that she thinks that I have to
> choose. Actually ... no ... let me rephrase this. What I can't
> stand is her acting as if I have to give her some account
> about how Australian I am. You know that really irks me. It's
> not when she's going on about how there are too many
> migrants, and all that stuff, that upsets me. It's when she
> says 'I don't consider migrants anything other than first-
> class citizens.' This really gets to me, you know, as if she's

doing me a favour or something. I mean who the hell is she to consider me or not consider me. I certainly don't need anyone like her to tell me whether I am a nice Aussie boy or not. I am an Australian and that's all there is to it. Look … I have two boys, one is seventeen and one is nineteen and, if ever there's a war, they are the ones who will be fighting for this country. So, really, I wouldn't even have Howard question or supervise how Australian I really am, let alone Hanson.

The 'Real' of the matter is that feelings that they had no time for those who want to call their Australianness into question are quite widespread among migrants. As an indication of how far the market for accumulating national capital has evolved over the past twenty years, there were others who thought *they* were in a position to question the Australianness of Hanson herself. As this middle-aged woman, a university graduate who owns a pastry shop, put it to me:

I mean, I often hear racist views around me, and not only by Australians from British background, I hasten to say. I never really feel it's as bad as people make it out to be. You know, the old man next door can be really abusive, especially when he comes home drunk in the evening. But his daughter is going out with my son and we treat him a bit like a family problem. I still talk to him and he talks to me. Now, you might laugh, but I think there is an Australian way of being racist. I think Australians, and I include here ethnic Australians, are more virulently racists [sic] towards Aborigines. That's where it's really bad. I think it is a bit different towards migrants. I've grown up with that. It's sort of, you know, you mutter a few words and you go to sleep, or have a beer or something. [Laughs.] But, you know, this Hanson thing … organising and talking of civil war and I don't know what … I mean, how un-Australian can you get!

It is this increased refusal to see one's presence as dependent on the acquiescence of a White Australian governmental subject that Hanson cannot actually acknowledge. It constitutes the Real of her fantasy which the discourse of decline is striving to avoid facing. For this Real would make Pauline Hanson and her like face the *unavoidable* basis of their anxiety. It would also deprive them of the ground on which they have attempted to reconstruct their political significance, as well as make them face their national irrelevance. It shows them that the 'mainstream' is no longer the Anglo affair they like to think it is and that Australia can no longer have, and Australians simply do not need, any special ethnically defined group, Anglo or other, to police the borders of national belonging for them.

States of Entrapment and the rise of the White Shamans

Have you ever underestimated one man's will to live,
Have you ever been inspired as to what one heart can give,
in the darkness of an hour when the world has fallen down
In the loneliness of silence, when pain is all around?
Have you ever felt the spirit that can rise to find a way,
That can fight its way through anything to see another day,
Where hope is held unsparingly, despite the clouds of doubt,
Have you ever seen a miracle — a voice that reaches out?[15]

Although it could have easily been the case, this poem was not written by a One Nation Party supporter. It is not even a political poem. It is the poet Jason 'Rupert' McCall's tribute to Stuart Diver, the famous sole survivor of the fatal landslide at the ski resort of Thredbo. Nevertheless, there is something very interesting in the public construction of Stuart Diver's heroism which does make his story of particular relevance to an understanding of the politics of White decline we are examining. It is this something which makes the above poem appear as if it has been written by a Hansonite.

Stuart Diver did not climb any mountains or cross any sea. Most of the time, he simply lay there, almost unable to move.[16] His was not the active heroism of the great achiever. It was the passive heroism of the trapped. How well can you endure being trapped? How well can you cope when you are 'stuck' under a concrete slab? The construction of heroism around a state of entrapment, aside from its important celebration of the general human capacity for survival, seemed to speak to another less existential, but more social condition that was becoming increasingly expressed in the public sphere in Australia at the time — a construction of social life as a 'trapped modality of being'.

Such a construction of social life has not been the preserve of any social group. It has also some very strong objective basis. Unemployment, especially in the form of chronic unemployment, is experienced as, and indeed is, a trap. Lack of job opportunities also makes the position of those who are employed, but are seeking a different job experience, a trap. Housewives looking for work experience their houses as a trap. Indeed, a recent national survey of Australian work-places has shown that more and more people see their work as a trap, something they are caught in and from which they cannot get out.[17]

Most importantly, being 'stuck' is only an experience for those who are or want to be 'on the move'. This is why social entrapment is a trauma primarily for those seeking or dreaming of social mobility, and this is why the poem above appears to be written by Hansonites. If it were to be politicised, it could have had the politics of White decline written all over it. The poem lucidly indicates that those who are structurally trapped know they can no longer rely on any ordinary event to pull them out. They await a miracle. In much the same way, the crisis of Whiteness in post-colonial Australia appears to be shaped by such strong, overdetermining and irreversible global currents that the politics capable of pulling the pro-ponents of White decline out of their trap can be nothing short of miraculous. It has to steer people's emotions and par-ticularly their 'envy', and in so doing operate a practical denial of reality. It has to activate a radical change to the very determining principles behind the 'order of things'. I am using 'emotion' and 'magic' and 'determinism' here in the way Sartre, in a very telling paragraph of his *The Emotions: Outline of a Theory*, understood them:

> At present we can conceive of what an emotion is. It is a transformation of the world. When the paths traced out become too difficult, or when we see no path, we can no longer live in so urgent and difficult a world. All the ways are barred. However, we must act. So we try to change the world, that is, to live as if the connection between things and their potentialities were not ruled by deterministic processes, but by magic. Let it be understood that this is not a game; we are driven against a wall, and we throw ourselves into this new attitude with all the strength we can muster.[18]

States of entrapment, by their very nature, produce an emotional magical politics. It is the politics of will, the politics of those who imagine themselves reaching out to the God of things to challenge the order of things. It is shamanic politics. Of course, it is also the politics of fascism. Hanson's pronouncements, peppered with 'All I want ...', indeed appear for those of us who are well tuned to the 'order of things' as something akin to shamanic incantations.

All I ask is that any Australian, regardless of their origin, should give Australia their full and undivided loyalty.[19]

I want a fair go for all Australians, no matter where they or their parents come from.[20]

All I want is an Australia for Australians.[21]

Hiding behind all those 'What I wants' is the enormity of 'wanting' and the fear of not being able to 'want' anything. As we have argued, national fantasies are enduring because they are well-grounded subjective realities. The anxiety that underlies the discourse of decline, however, is precisely rooted in its lack of groundedness. Because it hinges so much on portraying its subjects as the 'mainstream' demanding the assimilation of a non-assimilating 'minority', the discourse of decline is constantly haunted by a rude encounter with the multicultural reality of Australia. This encounter reveals the discourse to itself in the way it does not wish to be seen either by itself or by others — not only as a minority movement, but as a minority movement with redundant claims for governmental supremacy.

This is why what 'she wants' appears as so unrealistic — the very negation of the established order. As the history of fascism tells us, however, and as every anthropologist knows, the magic of both fascism and shamanism can actually work — and the deterministic processes behind the order of things can be wished away.

The Containment of the Multicultural Real: From the 'Immigration Debates' to White Neo-Fascism

Throughout this work, I have endeavoured to show that, despite their many differences, White multiculturalism and the White discourses of nationalist exclusion — recently represented by Pauline Hanson's One Nation — shared a similar fantasy structure. I argued that this fantasy structure is, ultimately, a fantasy of White supremacy: a well-grounded disposition to imagine Australia as a place where White Australians should reign supreme.

I examined how the 'White Australians' of this fantasy are not defined solely by either the colour of their skin or their ethnic background. Rather, I showed how Whiteness operates as a symbolic field of accumulation where many attributes such as looks, accent, 'cosmopolitanism' or 'Christianity' can be accumulated and converted into Whiteness. This also means, it should be stressed, that not all white-skinned people or English background people define themselves through this fantasy. The White Australian subjects of this fantasy are people who for various reasons related to their personal and social backgrounds end up finding within this fantasy a symbolic space for a viable definition of the meaning of their lives. This could be their lives 'in general' just as much as it could be their cultural or political lives.[1]

The White inhabitants of this fantasy are clearly divided over whether they should reign over an ethnically diverse population or not, or over how much of an ethnically diverse population they should reign. What they both share, however, is an undisputed belief in the reign of White Australians over Third World-looking migrants, who are constructed within this fantasy as a constant source of governmental problems.

Indeed, the White nation fantasy thrives on the perception of the migrant presence as one which poses problems. 'Let's have an immigration/multiculturalism debate!' has been, as we shall see, its chief organising principle for the past twenty years or so. Indeed, 'We *need* a debate' is how this desire is often expressed. It is immaterial whether the problematisation is aimed at extolling the virtues of multiculturalism and migration or at condemning them as divisive. What is important is the problematisation itself, for it is through it that the Third World-looking migrant is relegated to the position of a national object to be governed by the eternally worried White national subject. It could even be said that it is this 'right to worry' which differentiates White from non-White national subjects in Australia today. The White nation fantasy is a vision of a society divided into a class of White worriers and a class of Third World-looking problems.

Any honest journalist or researcher working in areas with high concentrations of 'Third World-looking' migrant populations cannot fail to encounter a reality which is hardly ever represented either in the discourse of White multiculturalism or in exclusionary discourses such as the discourse of Anglo decline. It is the reality of an unproblematic and pervasive multicultural interaction. It could be argued that this reality is absent in media representations of multiculturalism because of its ordinariness. There is nothing newsworthy about everyday events such as an Australian woman of British background giving her children breakfast in the morning, then picking up the children of her Indian neighbour to take them to school; Lebanese and Anglo parents chatting while their children are taking part in a sports event; a Vietnamese woman picking up her Italian friend and meeting up with an Anglo friend at the swimming pool for an exercise session; or elderly Australians of all backgrounds playing bingo together.

Such realities are never emphasised within the dominant discourses of White Australia. I want to argue that there is more to their suppression than their lack of newsworthiness. They are also suppressed because the dominant White fantasy that structures White Australian society cannot cope with such ordinariness.

Such social spaces do not have to be idealised as free of 'racist'-inspired interactions. However, such interactions neither define the nature of those spaces, nor are they experienced overdramatically by those concerned. They are often treated, as the woman in the conclusion to chapter 8 put it, as a 'family problem'. They are often stages in an ever evolving and developing set of social relations. It is this ordinariness and lack of overdramatisation — the fact that there is 'nothing to worry about' — that is anathema to the White Nation fantasy: no room here for a White nationalist to establish their career as a saviour of the victims of racism or of a lost national balance. People are too busy mixing even to notice such a thing as 'the mix' — which is inevitably produced by the field of vision of those who are not mixing.

The fact that the White nation fantasy has an interest in seeing as problematic Third World-looking Australians and the 'multicultural' social spaces they come to inhabit does not mean that these processes are necessarily problem areas. As I have argued throughout this book, the White nation fantasy, like all fantasies, actively reproduces the empirical ground on which it is based. This is why, part and parcel of the White fantasy are the 'technologies of problematisation' it puts into place to construct immigration, multiculturalism and migrant settlement into problems ready-made for the White national subject to worry about.

This is a process that complements the practices of regulating the modes in which Third World-looking people's inclusion is regulated in Australia — what I have called, in chapter 4, the dialectic of inclusion and exclusion. In this concluding chapter, I want to examine the more recent evolution of this dialectic of including/excluding migrants as problematic and governable entities. To do so, I want to begin by examining a few more aspects of the construction of the migrant as a 'problem' which are at the core of this dialectic.

Encountering the Real: Fantasies of the Migrant Presence as a White Problem

One of the greatest mystifications kept alive by the White nation fantasy is that of all the worrying things happening in Australia, nothing is more worrying than the lack of integration of Third World-looking migrants into Australian society. Every White multicultural debate has to go through the ritual of debating whether multiculturalism is 'dividing Australia' by fostering ghettoised subcultural groupings antagonistic to a unified national culture and, of course, 'Should we scrap multiculturalism?' or, even worse, lately, 'Should we utter the word?' and 'Should we "return" to assimilation?'

Regardless of how these questions are answered, their very nature as questions is based on the promotion of a kind of White policy fetishism — an exaggerated belief in the importance of the impact of a White 'choice' of policy, particularly the government's choice of policy, on the migrants' integration. It is part of a construction of multiculturalism that sees it as a reality almost entirely dependent on a White Australian decision. As we shall see, the whole construct is designed to inflate the importance of the relatively much less important White Australian decision-making as far as these issues are concerned. To come to terms with this lack of importance, however, we need to enter the domain of the White nation fantasy's multicultural Real: that part of social reality which, as I have argued, the inhabitants of the White fantasy cannot face without risking the undermining of the viability of their construction, including their construction of themselves.

To enter this domain of the Real we need to deconstruct a dominant White fairy tale that state multiculturalism (multiculturalism as state policy and official ideology) was a nice gift from White European Australians to the migrants institutionally referred to as 'NESB migrants'. This fairy tale is commonly used to infuse a sense of security among White Australians, for it views Australian settlement policies as a series of wilful choices made by increasingly enlightened, but totally in control, White Australian governments deciding to move away from the 'evil' and racist White Australia Policy to the 'good' and non-racist multicultural policy.

While this kind of 'from ethnophobia to ethnophilia' story does reflect an important element of truth, it is nevertheless a fairy tale because it abstracts from some very important, and less White-centred, processes that contributed to the rise of multicultural policy. Those processes have been well documented in many works on multiculturalism, so I am hardly breaking any new ground here.[2] These contain, however, precisely those undesirable histories that the White fantasy-based political polemics of recent times want to leave out of the popular 'debates' that are shaping the public space.

First, what the fairy tale abstracts from, of course, is the element of 'dull compulsion' that made the Australian government search for something with which to replace the policy of assimilation. If we are to inject a little dose of the Real and enhance the public debate on multiculturalism at the moment, we need to emphasise this. The move from assimilation to multiculturalism did not happen because some White Australian sat there, with their index on the lips, asking: 'Let's see now, what shall I chose? Assimilation or multiculturalism?' It happened because Australia's demographic and socio-cultural reality changed such that assimilation could no longer work. Despite the presence of an overwhelming policy of promoting assimilation, there were too many inevitable social and cultural processes happening outside the monocultural Australian mould that no assimilation program could prevent. These ranged from the reproductive usage of non-English languages in cross-generational communication, to the creation of ethnic media, to the emergence of strategic forms of ethnic communal solidarity designed to cushion and facilitate the process of settlement and integration. Policy makers knew that they needed to change the monocultural mould to keep Australia together in the face of these inevitable, and what were now Australian, culturally diverse aspects of social life.

Let us be clear about this, the spread of culturally diverse social forms and processes was happening regardless of assimilation and, if a new policy was not created to help encompass this spread, the latter would have had to remain outside the realm of policy, and as such ungovernable. That is, the recognition of diversity did not cause diversity to happen, it was precisely *because* diversity had already become an entrenched part of a social reality that no attempts to impose assimilation could change the fact that the government needed a policy that could recognise this diversity in order to govern it. Therefore, the recognition/governing of diversity was the way to secure the deeper structural cohesion of the nation that assimilation and integration had failed to secure.

The idea that multicultural policy is divisive is truly laughable from this perspective. One cannot resist emphasising this point today by pointing out that assimilation was dumped because it could no longer keep Australia 'one nation', while multiculturalism could. At a time when cultural diversity was nowhere near as widespread as it is now, policy makers were forced to recognise that assimilation was a policy of division and only a policy recognising diversity could secure the unity of the nation. How deep into the realm of the phantasmagoric one has to be to think that today the reverse can be true. It is an indication of the depth of the crisis of Whiteness manifested in the discourse of decline that it manages to convince itself of the possibility of such a 'solution'.

The second element that the fairy tale abstracts from is equally obvious, but also equally important to stress. It is the element of 'active compulsion'. That is, if the changes to Australia's demographic and cultural reality exerted an 'inert' pressure on the government and caused it to look for a change in policy, there were other, less inert elements of compulsion that forced the government to change direction. These were the struggles of the politicised elements within the migrant communities themselves.[3] Those political migrant elements actively aimed to open up the various institutions of Australian society so that they could participate more fully within them. They also struggled in factories, in welfare institutions, in hospitals, trade unions, schools and the like to secure conditions in which the migrant population could optimise the pursuit of their rights as citizens.

Multiculturalism was therefore a response to pressure by a section of the postwar migrants desirous of participating and being more politically and socially integrated in Australia's social life. As such, this kind of multiculturalism signalled the beginning of the integration of migrants into Australia's political life, even though this integration was largely restricted to 'NESB'-specific institutions designed to incorporate them.

Remembering these aspects of the history of multiculturalism should make clear the extent to which the 'Scrap multiculturalism' discourse is victim of its own fantasy construction of reality. Its proponents seem to think that scrapping multiculturalism is merely a 'White' governmental decision and, that if this decision is made, 'all will be well'. As Andrew Jakubowicz, however, has recently reminded those who would like to forget: 'the ethnic communities who came to this country were given nothing on a plate'.[4]

Consequently, 'scrapping multiculturalism' is a mystification by White social groups who still entertain images of themselves as the sole omnipotent shapers of the Australian landscape. At a time when the cultural diversity that constituted multiculturalism's emerging ground has become a far more salient and proportionally important part of Australian society, and when the migrant political forces that helped bring it about are even stronger than they were when multiculturalism was first introduced, neither would 'scrapping multicultural policy' be easy, nor will 'all be well' if a government decree somehow made it through a still overly White (and in this sense unrepresentative) Federal Parliament. There would still be an irremovable cultural diversity; there would still be the need to recognise and govern this cultural diversity; and there would still also be even more migrants eager to participate in the political game. This is why no assimilation policy can accommodate such a reality without a repression of fascistic proportions. Given the demographic, economic and socio-political strength of the migrant communities, even if such a repression were to take place it would be a quasi-impossibility.

This brings us to another aspect of the multicultural Real that the inhabitants of the White fantasy want to escape facing at any cost — the fact that the integration of migrants into Australian society is also minimally affected by White governmental decisions. The tendency for migrants to integrate into society is as inevitable as the change they bring into that very culture. The speed, the mode and the degree to which they become integrated is determined by social variables such as education, regional background, class, gender, religion and so on. Those factors, along with the migrant's length of stay, work to bring about an inevitable integration of the majority of migrants regardless of what the state's social policy orientation is.

European nation-states have very different settlement policies and citizenship rights vis-à-vis migrants. While not totally inconsequential, none of the national policies seems to have a drastically different effect on migrant integration, which is a matter-of-fact happening everywhere there are migrants settling and becoming citizens in a host society. This is one of the hardest aspects of the Real for White Australians to come to terms with: the idea that integration is not something one can usefully worry about, but is rather something that just happens and is happening all the time. Just as much as the maintenance of diverse cultural traditions, it is part of a natural social process of settlement. Governmental policy can, at best, facilitate or partially slow down this integration, but it can do very little to stop it happening. Integration — the attachment of migrants to Australia and their will to participate in its political, cultural and social life, each according to their capacity — occurred at the Whitest times of the White Australia Policy, and at the height of multicultural policy's promotion of diversity.

Why, then, do White nationalists need to express their worries concerning migrants who are 'not integrating enough'? I would like to propose that, paradoxically, this is because they subliminally fear Real integration. When White Australians express their desire for 'more integration', what they are really desiring is 'more supervised integration': the kind of 'I, the White Australian, would like you, the migrant, to pledge your loyalty to Australia *before me*' we have examined and shown to be present in both White multiculturalism and White neo-fascism.

It is a dependent integration. That is, rather than integration, it is more like an instrumental insertion which positions the White Australian subject, yet again, in the role of the great supervisor of integration. It is *solely* the preservation of this supervisory role that is behind the White Australian love of 'integration' and it is that very reason which makes them fear Real integration — the integration which constructs out of migrants Australian subjects who define their belonging to Australia independently of any supervisory White Australian will. Indeed, integration is the very thing that

White Australians try to *prevent* through the dialectic of inclusion and exclusion. What if, even if there were no White Australians involved in politics, Australia would still be governed by Aboriginal and other Third World-looking people who are fiercely patriotic Australians and fiercely committed to Australian democracy? What if Australia does not need White Australians to keep it together at all? Those operating from within the White fantasy would not want to acknowledge that such hypothetical questions are valid, let alone accept that the non-White reality they allude to is already in the making.

This is why the Real fear of those inhabiting this fantasy is directed towards the aggressively independent and political non-Whites: the Aboriginal people and the migrants who deploy an *Australian* will outside the supervisory tentacles of White governmentality. They are the ones to which the White technologies of containment and problematisation are constantly directed. This is why the White fantasy pathologises all attempts of non-Whites — ethnics and Aboriginals — to engage in independent political and managerial decision-making: from the 'branch stacking' of political parties, to lobbies and industries, to the 'mishandling of government funding' by non-White organisations. All of these aim at the reconstruction of some 'very worrying indeed' ethnic and Aboriginal objects in need of government, and are an open invitation for petty White managers to 'intervene' and re-establish the democratic–tolerant–freedom-of-speech national order to which they are so naturally attuned.[5] Indeed, the stronger the migrant drive towards integration appears to be, the stronger the need of White Australians has been for a mechanism that reproduced the belief in the primacy of the 'White governmental subject' to the preservation of Australian democracy, maintaining the mix and avoiding the disintegration of the nation. No mechanism has succeeded in doing this job as well as the 'immigration debate'.

Rituals of White Empowerment: The Rise of the 'Immigration Debate'

If White Australians love debating immigration and multiculturalism, as indeed they do, it is because — particularly in the 1980s and 1990s, and until the chance election of Pauline Hanson resuscitated the belief in the power of voting — those debates became a far more suitable alternative to parliamentary elections as a ritual which provided ordinary White people with an institutionalised form capable of reproducing their 'governmental belonging': a sense of control over their destiny and their nation. Throughout that period, the capacity of elections to do this diminished, as it became increasingly apparent that the political elite's overriding concern in politics was the desire for self-perpetuation. As electorates became more cynical, the election process became increasingly unable to provide them with the feeling that it is through voting that they can decide the kind of nation in which they want to live.

Immigration debates, on the other hand, still provided this kind of 'White governmental buzz'. This was not because immigration debates and polls actually decided anything. Indeed, it is one of the peculiarities of immigration policy in Australia that no other federal policy has been polled and debated more than it has, while, at the same time, no other policy has evolved more blatantly in disregard of public opinion.[6] This is why the explanation for the White media and the White government's clear commitment to a quasi-institutionalisation of immigration debates lies elsewhere.

I want to suggest that rather than being perceived as a meaningful tool for the formulation of policy, the immigration polls and debates should be seen, in a more anthropological spirit, as *rituals of White empowerment* — seasonal festivals where White Australians renew the belief in their possession of the power to talk and make decisions about Third World-looking Australians.

A quick look at the questions asked in the immigration polls gives us a clear indication of the kind of power White Australians are invited to think they have. Positioned in the role of masters of the earth's population movements, they are enabled to give opinions on whether the number of migrants that arrived the year before was to their liking or not, and even to venture an opinion about what would be just right for them.[7] Things about which even the most accomplished researchers find it hard to have a definite view — such as the effect of migration on the 'environment', or 'unemployment' or the 'national economy' — are suddenly transformed into objects of 'legitimate' popular debate about which people, regardless of their qualifications, can have definite views. Immigration debates and polls are the democratisation of the national manager's position so that 'everyone' (i.e. every White Australian) can become a 'cook' in control of the mix (see chapter 4) and 'have a go' at saying 'what they like'.

By their very nature, immigration debates and opinion polls are an invitation to judge those who have already immigrated, as well as those who are about to immigrate. Not only is this facilitated through the use of the word 'migrant', whose meaning slides freely between the two categories, but also, and inescapably, to pronounce a judgment on the value of future migration is to pronounce a judgment on the value of the contribution of existing Third World-looking Australians to the country's development. It is in the conditions created by all these discursive effects that a White immigration speak flourishes — a language operating in itself as a technology of problematisation and marginalisation: 'they should come' and 'they shouldn't', 'they have contributed' and 'they haven't', 'there are too many' and 'there aren't enough', 'they are' and 'they aren't', 'they will' and 'they won't'. It is on such fertile ground that the White nation fantasy seasonally rejuvenated itself and tried to keep the multicultural Real at bay. In this sense, the immigration debate became the main form in which the dialectic of inclusion and exclusion was ritualised and institutionalised in Australia.[8, 9]

It is the size and political power of the migrant population which has been the central variable which brought about change in Australia's settlement policy in the transition from assimilation to multiculturalism. Each stage of settlement policy had to open up a larger inclusionary space to accommodate a more numerous and a more political migrant population demanding more citizenship rights, more national recognition, more decision-making power and more political participation — that is, more integration. It has also, however, been in the very nature of the dialectic of inclusion and exclusion that, while forced to open up these new *inclusionary* spaces for the settling migrants, White politics has tried at the same time to deploy different *exclusionary* processes to contain them within those spaces. As we have seen, the ambivalence inherent in the White multiculturalism of tolerance and acceptance reflected the way this dialectic of inclusion and exclusion, and its mode of positioning the migrant in the liminal space of the 'not too excluded, but not too included either', was institutionalised by White multiculturalism .

The dialectic of inclusion and exclusion, however, can only be efficient in the short term. It cannot affect the long-term tendency of the political power and integration of the migrant population to go on increasing. This is why this dialectic has constantly to find new forms of operating. Consequently, if the spaces opened up for migrant participation by early multicultural policy correspond to a certain strength exhibited by the politicised migrants who fought for it in the 1970s, it should be hardly surprising to see multiculturalism entering a period of crisis in the 1980s, ten years after its inauguration. To expect a continuously stable state multiculturalism would be to expect unreasonably that, during that entire period, the number and the political power of the migrant population have somehow remained the same. This has hardly been the case.

From the early 1980s onwards, the electoral power of the 'migrant vote' has become a more pronounced factor in the calculations of all the political parties. Increasingly, non-White Australians are demanding more political participation in the mainstream political process still largely controlled by White and mainly Anglo and Celtic White Australians.[10] This demand for more participation is partly the result of the emergence of a younger generation more socially at ease in the power struggles of Australian intra- and inter-party politics, and unsatisfied with the marginal role of 'fund distributors' that the older generation of 'ethnic leaders' had used as the basis of their status and their social mobility.[11]

It is all of these tendencies that have put pressure on the capacity of White multiculturalism to regulate the dialectic of inclusion and exclusion of non-White Australians in the way it had done in its early history. It is in this context that the intensification of immigration polls and immigration debates in the 1980s has to be understood. The latter gradually became by far the most sacred of all the technologies of problematisation aimed at repositioning the White Australian in the role of the worried national manager and in relegating the 'migrant' to the role of national object.

The very frequency of these debates in the early 1990s was, however, an indication of what little effect they had on stopping the changes through which Australia was going. In fact, the 1990s has seen a marked increased in the capacity of Third World-looking Australians to advance their interests, even in the confines of White multiculturalism. These feelings were clearly exacerbated by the intensification of the processes of economic globalisation and international migration, leading to the 'White decline' backlash against Paul Keating's blend of internationalist economic rationalism and his cosmo-multiculturalism.

The election of John Howard's conservative government and, particularly, the election of Pauline Hanson have marked, as I have pointed out, the rediscovery by the disaffected White population of the power of voting and, more importantly, the taste of political power, as opposed to endlessly and fruitlessly raving on talkback radio. Hanson's election created an opening for the eternal self-serving White whingeing and worrying that marked immigration debates to be articulated once again with a new voting practice which takes the latter seriously as a mode of influencing governmental decision making. If nothing else, Hanson has succeeded in transforming White worrying, with all its denials of the Real and its flights from fantasy into the phantasmagoric, into an efficient political force which crystallised in the formation of the One Nation Party.

Conclusion

For anyone following the White media's fascination with Pauline Hanson, it does not take long to realise that this fascination is well beyond the ordinary. The amount of exposure Hanson personally received after her elections was well beyond any attention given to a newly emerging politician. Her political views were presented and represented at every possible opportunity — more so than any other member of parliament espousing similar views. The rise of the One Nation Party received more attention than the rise of the Democrats and the Greens ever received. What is the secret of this obsession?

I'd like to suggest that there is a good dose of infantile narcissistic fascination here. The White media is seduced by an infantile projection of itself. There is more than one psychoanalytic interpretation among many in this hypothesis. To develop my point, however, I'd like to begin by relating an incident from my youth in Beirut that has been lately resurfacing in my consciousness.

I was born in a middle-class, Maronite Catholic and culturally conservative environment. I often heard around me racist and derogatory remarks directed against Muslims. Like many families in Beirut, however, my parents and their friends had to deal, by necessity, with Muslim people.

I remember one day a Muslim merchant visiting a neighbour's house on some business. I and the neighbour's son were six or seven years old at the time, and we had already learned enough derogatory remarks about Muslims to last us a lifetime. Unfortunately, we had not learnt the art of recognising the appropriate time and place where such remarks can be made. When the guest picked up my friend and started teasing him in a common adult–child mode of play, my friend instinctively unleashed a number of venomous anti-Muslim remarks, telling him exactly what he has been taught to think of people like him. Needless to say, his remarks caused severe embarrassment in the *salon*. I particularly remember how we were unceremoniously dispatched from the lounge room, with his father sternly telling him, 'Shame on you.'

But this is not the end of the story, for I also distinctly remember what happened after the guest had left. I remember how everyone was laughing and saying how cute my friend has been and 'Ho ho ho! Did you see how the guy's face went red' and 'Good on you, Georges, you show them.'

When I look back at this event, I realise that my friend's unchecked and 'immature' abuse performed the 'Christian tribe' a function. Not having carried out the abuse themselves, the respectable Christian families continued to benefit from the relationship of proximity and 'business as usual' they maintained with the various Muslims with which they had dealings. Nevertheless, they also benefited from the many incidents of open abuse to which the Muslims were constantly subjected, for 'business as usual' also meant keeping the Muslim as the inferior partner — the marginalised and the not-too-comfortable party in this relationship of proximity. This was important for ensuring the Christian's position of dominance within this relation before the civil war — a position they have now lost.

I want to suggest that the respectable side of White Australia today relates to Hanson in the same way my friend's family related to his 'unchecked extremism'. Whether they are in the media, in politics, in academia or in any other workplace (they can be spotted as soon as they talk about having no problem with multiculturalism as long as migrants put the interest of Australia first), behind every White multiculturalist affecting a position of respectability — and a willingness to condemn 'Hansonite extremism' in the nation's lounge room — there is another White gleefully grinning and saying, 'Good on you, Pauline. You show them' or another saying, 'She's so naughty' as if saying it to one's own child after he or she has misbehaved.

This is not a mere sentimental issue. It is a self-interested politics of domination. In much the same way as the story above, those respectable White Australians have an interest in someone else perceived as 'irrational and/or immature' doing the exclusion for them. They benefit from both this marginalisation and from the relationship of proximity and dominance with the already marginalised that they are able to maintain thanks to, but also by distinguishing themselves from, the 'extremists'.

For White multiculturalists today, White neo-fascism represents the latest technology of containment and problematisation of Third World-looking migrants. Pauline Hanson has enabled White Australians to unleash a new phase in the dialectic of inclusion and exclusion, aiming to transform the increasingly demanding and 'arrogant' migrants into decent 'debatable problematised objects', safely positioned in the liminal spaces of inclusion/exclusion. The relation between the dominant White multiculturalism and White national exclusionism, which has always been a relation of affinity based on a shared fantasy structure, has evolved today into an active relationship of *complicity*. This is the fundamental basis for what has clearly become the more general Hansonisation of White culture.

In the face of this destructive White tendency, some questions need to be asked: Are Whites still good for Australia? Have they been living in ghettoes for too long? Are they dividing Australia? Do we need to have an assimilation program to help ease them into the multicultural mainstream? Clearly, it's time for Third World-looking Australians to do the 'worrying about the nation' number. And let's face it, there's plenty to worry about.

endnotes

Preface

1   Adolf Hitler, *Mein Kampf*, trans. by Ralph Manheim, Pimlico, London, 1993, p. 203.
2   See Paul Sheehan, *Among the Barbarians: The Dividing of Australia*, Random House, Sydney, 1998.
3   Earlier versions of various parts of the book have appeared in national and international journals: *Communal/Plural, UTS Review, Arena* and *New Formation*.

Introduction

1   See the excellent and still relevant works by Jean Martin, *The Migrant Presence: Australian Responses 1947–1977*, Allen & Unwin, Sydney, 1978; Andrew Jakubowicz, Michael Morrissey & Joanne Palser, 'Ethnicity, class and social policy in Australia', *SWRC Reports and Proceedings*, no. 46, 1984; and all the contributions to the seminal volume of essays edited by Gill Bottomley & Marie de Lepervanche, *Ethnicity, Class and Gender in Australia*, Allen & Unwin, Sydney, 1984. These works remain a must for anyone seriously interested in critically understanding Australian multicuturalism.
2   Ien Ang, 'The curse of the smile: Ambivalence and the "Asian" woman in Australian multiculturalism', *Feminist Review*, no. 52, Spring 1996, pp. 36–49.
3   See Ruth Frankenberg, *Displacing Whiteness: Essays in Social and Cultural Criticism*, Duke University Press, Durham, North Carolina, & London, 1997, for a brief review of the American literature.
4   See Ghassan Hage 1994, 'Anglo-Celtics today: Cosmo-multiculturalism and the phase of the fading phallus', in 'An inquiry into the state of Anglo-Saxonness within the nation', eds

Ghassan Hage, Justine Lloyd & Lesley Johnson, *Communal/Plural*, no. 4. This article is integrated into this book in a modified form.

5 Ghassan Hage, 'The Limits of "Anti-racist" Sociology, *UTS Review*, vol. 1, no. 1, 1995.

6 in Pierre Bourdieu (ed.), *La Misère du Monde*, Seuil, Paris, 1994, p. 7.

7 Historical literature on 'Australian racism' always included chapters which covered racism against Aboriginal people and racism against migrants (see, for instance, Ann Curthoys & Andrew Markus (eds), *Who Are Our Enemies?: Racism and the Working Class in Australia*, Hale & Iremonger, Sydney, 1978). This tendency has not developed towards a fusion of the interest in both and a creation of a wider, triangular field of inquiry, although there are exceptions: the postscript to the second edition of Stephen Castles et al., *Mistaken Identity: Multiculturalism and the Demise of Nationalism in Australia*, Pluto Press, Sydney, 1991, moves in this direction.

8 Although I have become recently aware of research being done on such an issue: Peter Read, 'Pain, yes; racism, no: The response of non-British Australians to indigenous land rights', in *The Resurgence of Racism*, eds Geoffrey Gray & Christine Winter, Monash Publications in History, Monash University, no. 24, 1997, pp. 87–96.

9 See my belated reflections on this issue in Ghassan Hage, op. cit. 1995; see also John Docker, 'Rethinking postcolonialism and multiculturalism in the fin de siècle', *Cultural Studies*, vol. 9, no. 3, 1995.

Chapter 1

1 National Inquiry into Racist Violence in Australia (NIRVA), *Racist Violence*, AGPS, Canberra, 1991, p. 146.

2 ibid., p. 516.

3 *Bulletin*, 15 Oct. 1990, in DIHR 1990, *Documentation of Incidents of Harassment of, and Racism towards, Australians of Arab Descent and Australian Muslims: August–October 1990*, Melbourne, p. 7.

4 The Melbourne-based Committee on Discrimination against Arab Australians and the Sydney-based Committee of Arab Australians have published two volumes documenting incidents of harassment towards Arab and Muslim Australians (op. cit. & DIHR, October 1992).

5 Michael Banton, 'The concept of racism', in *Race and Racialism*, ed. Sami Zubaida, Tavistock, London, 1970, p. 17.

6 This includes the belief in the existence of well-defined races,

of genetically transmitted behaviour and mental capacities specific to each race and of a hierarchy of the races based on these transmitted capacities.

7 This usually involves a declared rejection of a notion of hierarchy between cultures, but an insistence on the need for each cultural group to develop separately from others. This is usually backed by arguments about human nature. See Martin Barker, *The New Racism*, Junction Books, London, 1981, for the development of the 'new racism' theory and Miles's critique of it in Robert Miles, *Racism*, Routledge, London & New York, 1989.

8 Marvin Harris, *The Rise of Anthropological Theory: A History of Theories of Culture*, Routledge & Kegan Paul, London, 1969, usefully differentiates between 'scientific racism' and 'folk racism' (pp. 80–107).

9 Pierre-André Taguieff, *La Force du Préjugé: Essai sur le Racisme et ses Doubles*, Éditions La Découverte, Paris, 1987.

10 Robert Miles, *Racism and Migrant Labour*, Routledge & Kegan Paul, London, 1982, pp. 78–9.

11 Robert Miles, op. cit., 1989.

12 Pierre Bourdieu, *The Logic of Practice*, Polity Press, Cambridge, 1990, p. 36.

13 Gordon Allport, *The Nature of Prejudice*, Addison-Wesley Publishing Company, Inc., Cambridge, Massachussets, 1954.

14 The only exception to this is an existentially experienced racism where people are merely 'disgusted' to be near someone perceived to be of a different race. This does not, however, dictate a specific course of action, for this action can range from physical attack to strategies of avoidance.

15 A. Sivanandan, 'Challenging racism: Strategies for the '80s', *Race and Class*, vol. 25, no. 2, 1983, pp. 1–12.

16 in Michael Banton, *The Idea of Race*, Tavistock Publications, London, 1977, p. 157.

17 I managed to contact this person totally by chance after hearing someone talk about her during a family gathering. I will come back to her and reveal more of her 'sociological makeup' later when discussing the nature of the nationalist in chapter 3.

18 Interviewee B is a clerk living in Marrickville. This is how he expressed his desire: '... Muslims are a problem. I don't mind other people. But Muslims really annoy me. They're so immune to anything called civilisation ... And they look at you as if they are so proud that they lack civilisation. Especially the women ... if I see a Muslim woman wearing one of those ... veils ... you know ... I just want to rip it off her head and say, "Hey! Wake up damn it! You don't have to let yourself be treated like this. This is Australia."'

19 For example, scarves are considered an unacceptable form of subjugating women or, as interviewee B put it: 'It pains me to live in a society where such backward forms of subjugation are exhibited.' In a more complex manner, to European women, scarves can represent an intolerable, because too visible, mode of subjugation that only serves to render their own subjugation more visible. Because nationalists follow a 'one nation, one patriarchy' motto, the veil can also mean the subjugation of women to a non-national patriarchy. The desire to remove it is the desire to ensure that all women within the nation are subjugated to the dominant national patriarchal order. Finally, some non-Muslim migrant women, especially those who have a consciousness of themselves as Third World-looking, express a hatred of the scarf by fear of association. Here it is perceived as a migrant marker that some migrant women see as negatively affecting all migrant women by labelling them as backward.

20 This highlights the Bourdieu-ian point developed above, that practical racist classifications have to be understood in the same way as any other practical categories of thought, as 'classification(s) subordinate to a practical function' (Pierre Bourdieu, *Language and Symbolic Power*, Polity Press, Cambridge, 1991, p. 220).

21 Michael Billig, *Banal Nationalism*, Sage, London, 1995, p. 93. Billig quotes Norbert Elias who, in *The History of Manners*, argues that even contemporary sociologists take it for granted that 'society' refers to the nation-state (p. 53).

22 An interviewee in Marrickville formulated this in an exemplary way. Referring to what he sees as the existence of too many migrants in Marrickville, he said: 'When I walk the streets, I worry about what's going to happen to us in this country.' A Brisbane taxi driver informed me (uninvited) that there were so many Asians 'here' that he and other taxi drivers played a game they called 'Spot the Aussie'. Then he said, 'I tell you what, mate, one day we're gonna wake up and there'll be no Australia left.'

23 The reference to 'home' was often made in relation to the pulling down of Muslim scarfs. The *Racist Violence* report tells the story of 'an Anglo-Australian woman' who 'attacked an elderly Arab woman in Preston (Vic.), ripping off her *hijab* while yelling, "Go home, you fucking bitch."' (NIRVA, op. cit., p. 146).

24 I have treated this theme in relation to migrant conceptions of home in Ghassan Hage, 'At home in the entrails of the West', in *Home/World: Space, Communality and Marginality in Sydney's West*, Helen Grace, Ghassan Hage, Lesley Johnson, Julie Langsworth & Michael Symonds, Pluto Press, Sydney, 1997, pp. 99–153.

25 Alan Jones on radio station 2UE, 13 Aug. 1990.
26 John Laws on radio station 2UE, 15 Aug. 1990.
27 Radio 2KY, 27 Aug. 1990, in *Australian Society*, D. Bowman, December 1990, and DHIR 1990, op. cit.

Chapter 2

1 This does not mean, of course, that these migrants cannot be violent on other non-national grounds.
2 Jean Leca, 'Questions of citizenship', in *Dimensions of Radical Democracy: Pluralism, Citizenship, Community*, ed. Chantal Mouffe, Verso, London, 1992, p. 21.
3 *Australian*, 24 Oct. 1996, p. 11.
4 M. Dugan & J. Szwarc, *There Goes the Neighborhood!: Australia's Migrant Experience*, Macmillan & Australian Institute of Multicultural Affairs, Melbourne, 1984, p. 134
5 Barry Hindess, 'Citizens and people', *Australian Left Review*, June 1992, p. 22. For another critical perspective on migrants and citizenship see the excellent work by Alastair Davidson, *From Subject to Citizen: Australian Citizenship in the Twentieth Century*, Cambridge University Press, Melbourne, 1997.
6 See Pierre Bourdieu, 'The forms of capital', in *Handbook of Theory and Research for the Sociology of Education*, ed. J. G. Richardson, Greenwood Press, New York, 1986, pp. 241–58.
7 *Sydney Morning Herald*, 29 Nov. 1996.
8 Judith Butler, 'Imitation and gender insubordination', in *Inside/Out: Lesbian Theories/Gay Theories*, ed. Diana Fuss, Routledge, London, 1991, p. 24.
9 Jonathan Warren & France Twine, 'White Americans, the new minority?: Non-Blacks and the ever-expanding boundaries of Whiteness', *Journal of Black Studies*, vol. 28, no. 2, 1997, p. 201.
10 A. T. Yarwood, *Asian Migration to Australia: The Background to Exclusion, 1896–1923* (1964), quoted in J. McKay & T. Batrouney, 'Lebanese immigration until the 1970s', in *The Australian People*, ed. James Jupp, Angus & Robertson Publishers, Sydney, 1988, p. 667.
11 There are now a number of historical works detailing the construction of Whiteness in various contexts: Reginald Horsman, *Race and Manifest Destiny*, Harvard University Press, Cambridge, Massachussetts, 1981; David Roedigger, *The Wages of Whiteness*, Verso, New York, 1990; Theodore Allen, *The Invention of White Race*, Verso, New York, 1994.
12 Pierre Bourdieu, *Distinction: A Social Critique of the Judgement of Taste*, trans. Richard Nice, Routledge & Kegan Paul, London, 1984, pp. 23–4.

13 See Ghassan Hage, 'Racism, multiculturalism and the Gulf War', *Arena*, no. 96, Spring 1991, on how a dominant national group can put another national group in a position where they have to prove their national belonging.

14 Bourdieu, *Distinction*, pp. 23–4.

15 *ibid.*

16 See Stephen Castles et al., *Mistaken Identity*, op. cit.; Richard White, *Inventing Australia*, George Allen & Unwin, Sydney, 1981.

17 Pierre Bourdieu & Loïc J. D. Wacquant, *An Invitation to Reflexive Sociology*, Polity Press, Cambridge, 1992, p. 18.

18 I think there is a residue of a non-practical structuralism in Bourdieu's oft-stated definition of a field as a system of objective positions. This abstracts from the fact that those positions are the products of an ongoing struggle to position. That is, the relationship between positions can itself be part of the symbolic violence operating within the field, rather than being an external arena in which it is occurring.

19 See the excellent article by Norbert Elias, 'Violence and civilisation: The state monopoly of physical violence and its infringement', in *Civil Society and the State: New European Perspectives*, ed. John Keane, London and New York: Verso, London & New York, 1988.

20 E. Durkheim, *Le Suicide: Étude de Sociologie*, Presses Universitaires de France, Paris, 1960, p. 274. 'Quelque plaisir que l'homme éprouve à agir, à se mouvoir, à faire effort, encore faut-il qu'il sente que ses efforts ne sont pas vains et qu'en marchant il avance. Or, on n'avance pas quand on ne marche vers aucun butou, ce qui revient au même quelque chemin qu'on ait fait, tout sepasse comme si l'on s'était stérilement agité sur place. Même les regards jetés derrière soi et le sentiment de fierté que l'on peut éprouver en apercevant l'espace déja parcouru ne sauraient causer qu'une bien illusoire satisfaction, puisque l'espace à parcourir n'est pas diminué pour autant. Poursuivre une fin inaccessible par hypothèse, c'est donc se condamner à un perpétuel état de mécontentement.'

21 Slavoj Zizek, *Looking Awry: An Introduction to Jacques Lacan through Popular Culture*, MIT Press, Cambridge, Massachussetts, 1991; and Slavoj Zizek, *Tarrying with the Negative: Kant, Hegel and the Critique of Ideology*, Duke University Press, Durham, North Carolina, 1993.

22 Zizek, *Tarrying with the Negative*, p. 201.

23 ibid.

24 ibid., p. 202

25 Zizek, *Looking Awry*, ch. 1 passim.

26 Zizek, *Tarrying with the Negative*, p. 6.
27 ibid.
28 Zizek, *Looking Awry*, pp. 203–4.
29 NIRVA, op.cit, p. xvii.
30 ibid.

Chapter 3

1 *Sydney Morning Herald*, 12 Jan. 1991.
2 *Sydney Morning Herald*, 17 Oct. 1996, p. 17.
3 *Telegraph Mirror*, 13 May 1993.
4 *Sydney Morning Herald*, 26 July. 1993.
5 Tanya Koshechnika, *Political Tolerance and Ex-Soviet Society*, paper presented at BSA Conference, University of Canterbury, Kent, UK, 1992, p. 2.
6 M. Ashley, *England in the Seventeenth Century*, 8th edn, Hutchinson, London, 1978, pp. 133–4.
7 ibid., p. 188.
8 ibid., p. 40.
9 E. R. Norman, *Anti-Catholicism in Victorian England*, George Allen & Unwin, London, 1968, p. 131.
10 Maxime Rodinson, *Marxism and the Muslim World*, Monthly Review Press, London, 1981, p. 8.
11 It is important to remember that there are different ways of perceiving and experiencing multiculturalism. The state vision of it is only one, albeit a dominant one among the 'White' Australians of interest to us here. There are, however, modes of conceiving and living multiculturalism that are not grounded in the discourse of tolerance. Furthermore, it is important to stress that multiculturalism in Australia goes well beyond a cultural politics of recognition and aims at countering socioeconomic disadvantage and unequal access to the state. Different governments also differ in their emphasis. It is well known, for example, that the social-democratic Whitlam government of the early 1970s was far more orientated towards social equity than the conservative Fraser government that followed it, and which was more orientated towards 'cultural pluralism'.
12 *Sydney Morning Herald*, 3 Dec. 1996, p. 17.
13 *Australian*, 18 Oct. 1996, p. 15.
14 Non-English Speaking Background: This is the official mode of categorising those who are seen as the primary beneficiaries of the policy of multiculturalism.
15 See Jock Collins, *Migrant Hands in a Distant Land*, Pluto Press, Sydney, 1988.
16 Al Grassby, *The Tyranny of Prejudice*, A E Press, Melbourne, 1984, p. 64.

17 Jock Collins, *Cohesion with Diversity? Immigration and Multiculturalism in Canada and Australia*, Working Paper Series, School of Finance and Economics, no. 28, March 1993, University of Technology, Sydney, p. ii.

18 See Andrew Jakubowicz, 'Ethnic affairs policy in Australia: The failure of multiculturalism' in *Australia in Transition*, M. E. Poole et al., Harcourt Brace Jovanovich, Sydney, 1985, pp. 271–8.

19 *Australian*, 21 Nov. 1996.

20 Preston King, *Toleration*, George Allen & Unwin, London, 1976, p. 6.

21 ibid., p. 8.

22 Jean-François Lyotard, *Heidegger and 'the Jews'*, University of Minesota Press, Minneapolis, 1991, pp. 39–40.

23 Voltaire, 'Traité sur la Tolerance', in *L'Affaire Calas* (1763), Éditions Gallimard, Paris, 1975, p. 176.

24 John Locke, *Letters on Toleration* (1689), Education Society Press, Byculla, 1867, p. 1.

25 Voltaire, op. cit., pp. 135–6.

26 Locke, op. cit., p. 7.

27 See Pierre Bourdieu, *Outline of a Theory of Practice*, Cambridge University Press, Cambridge, UK, 1977.

28 Pierre Bourdieu, *In Other Words: Essays towards a Reflexive Sociology*, Polity Press, Cambridge, 1990, pp. 127–8.

29 *Sydney Morning Herald*, 13 Feb. 1995.

30 Among first generation migrants from Lebanon, it is common to refrain from making any comments as to what one wishes or does not wish to see happening in Australia. Often people say: 'We are guests here' or 'The guest should not criticise the host.'

31 King, op. cit., p. 21.

32 King, op. cit., p. 52.

33 It is important to stress, at this point, that this does not mean that such intolerance is not morally valuable or legitimate. Indeed, it may very well be so. The point remains, however, that someone has been given a legitimate power to be intolerant.

34 C. Lloyd & H. Waters, 'France: One culture, one people?', *Race & Class*, vol. 32, no. 3, 1991, pp. 60–1.

35 Here again, I am not questioning the moral worth of such a legitimate intolerance, but simply the fact that it mystifies itself as non-existent.

36 S. C. Maza, *Servants and Masters in Eighteenth Century France: The Uses of Loyalty*, Princeton University Press, Princeton, 1983, p. 206.

37 Michel Foucault, 'Governmentality', in *The Foucault Effect: Studies in Governmentality*, eds Graham Burchell et al., Harvester, Hemel Hempstead, 1991, p. 93.

38 King, op. cit., p. 9.

39 Slavoj Zizek 1991, *Looking Awry: An Introduction to Jacques Lacan through Popular Culture*, MIT Press, Cambridge, Massachussetts, p. 154.
40 King, op. cit., p. 15.
41 ibid., p. 32.
42 Locke, op. cit., p. 7.
43 See in this regard Joseph Lecler, *Toleration and the Reformation*, 2 vols, Longman, London, 1960.
44 King, op. cit., p. 82.
45 loc. cit.
46 See Ernest Renan, *Du Liberalisme Clerical*, *Oeuvres*, vol. 1, Calman-Levy, Paris, 1947.
47 Effy Alexakis & Leonard Janiszewski, *Images of Home*, Hale & Iremonger, Sydney, 1995, p. 157.

Chapter 4

1 *Sydney Morning Herald*, 23 Sep. 1991.
2 ibid.
3 *Sydney Morning Herald*, 13 Oct. 1995.
4 Michael & Rhonda Gray, *The Stew that Grew*, Walter McVitty Books, Glebe, 1990.
5 I have treated this phenomenon extensively in 'At home in the entrails of the West', in *Home/World: Space, Communality and Marginality in Sydney's West*, Helen Grace, Ghassan Hage, Lesley Johnson, Julie Langsworth & Michael Symonds, Pluto Press, Sydney, 1997, pp. 99–153.
6 Martin Heidegger, *Basic Writings*, Routledge & Kegan Paul, London, 1978, p. 226.
7 Paul Sheehan, 'The multicultural myth', *Sydney Morning Herald*, 25 May 1996, Spectrum section, p. 1.
8 Marshall Perron, 'Australia must develop and populate the North', in *BIPR Bulletin*, no. 10, November 1993, p. 6.
9 *Australian*, 4 Jul. 1996.
10 *Sydney Morning Herald*, 4 Dec. 193.
11 See Sneja Gunew's very suggestive analysis of the Department of Immigration film *No Strangers Here*. The film consciously associates assimilation with 'easy to mix' recipes; Sneja Gunew, *Framing Marginality*, Melbourne University Press, Melbourne, 1994, p. 61.
12 *Sydney Morning Herald*, 23 Jul. 1994, p. 10.
13 David Greason, 'Titans of power', in *I was a teenage fascist*, McPhee Gribble, Melbourne, 1994, pp. 191, 206–8.
14 Paul Keating, Opening speech to the Productive Diversity in Business Conference, Melbourne, 28 & 29 October 1992, p. 3.
15 Keating op. cit., pp. 1–2.
16 *Productive Diversity in Business: Profiting from Australia's Multicultural*

Advantage, Discussion paper for the Productive Diversity in Business Conference, Melbourne, 28 & 29 October 1992.

17 *Productive Diversity in Business,* Discussion paper.

18 Keating, op. cit., p. 7.

19 Perron, op. cit., p. 6.

20 Carmel Niland, *Towards Managing Diversity:* A Review of EEO in the South Australian Public Service, South Australian Government Publication, Adelaide, 1992, p.18.

21 The Real for Lacan is that which is produced, but cannot be symbolised within the symbolic order. I am modifying the concept to make it here a more sociologically specific and less of a general ontological category. Each symbolic domain produces a Real specific to it.

22 It can be said, for example, that most multicultural fantasies have the practical reality of Aboriginal Australia as their Real. Through the various discourses of multicultural settlement which see it solely in terms of a 'migrant'/'White Australian' problematic — and this book, as I indicated in the introduction, is partly complicit in this — there is an effacement of the Aboriginal question, and of the contribution of Australian post-World War II migration to what is, at least from one important perspective, a continuing invasion of Australia.

23 See Jock Collins, *Migrant Hands in a Distant Land,* Pluto Press, Sydney, 1988.

24 The same important point is made by Annette Hamilton in her study of the Aboriginal women's position within their own tribes (they are marginalised because they are useful and valuable, not because they are useless). Annette Hamilton, 'Aboriginal women: The means of production', *The Other Half: Women in Australian Society,* ed. J. Mercer, Penguin, Harmondsworth, 1975, pp. 167–79.

25 Isidore Geoffroy de Saint Hilaire, *Acclimatation et Domestication des Animaux Utiles* (1861), Flamarrion, Paris, 1986, p. 157.

26 Charles Taylor, 'The politics of recognition', in *Multiculturalism,* ed. Amy Gutmann, Princeton University Press, Princeton, New Jersey, 1994, p.64.

27 ibid, p. 81.

28 ibid, p. 82–3.

29 Emile Benveniste, *Problèmes de Linguistique Générale,* Gallimard, Paris, 1966, p. 198.

Chapter 5

1   See Malcolm Turnbull 1993, Foreword, in *The Republicanism Debate,* eds Wayne Hudson & David Carter, University of NSW Press, Sydney, p. xii.

2   See Ghassan Hage, 'Nation-building dwelling being', *Communal/Plural*, no. 1, 1993.

3   See Paul Keating, Foreword to Part Two, in Hudson & Carter, op. cit., p. 210.

4   Michael Kirby, in Hudson & Carter, op. cit, p. 75.

5   See Slavoj Zizek for a Lacanian analysis of the break as an *objet petit a*: 'From the point of view of wisdom, the break is not worth the trouble; ultimately, we always find ourselves in the same position from which we have tried to escape, which is why, instead of running after the impossible, we must learn to consent to our common lot and to find pleasure in the trivia of our everyday life. Where do we find the *objet petit a*? The *objet a* is precisely that surplus, that elusive make believe that drove the man to change his existence.' (Slavoj Zizek, *Looking Awry: An Introduction to Jacques Lacan through Popular Culture*, MIT Press, Cambridge, Massachussetts, 1991, p. 8.)

6   Olivier Burgelin 1979, 'Les outils de la toilette ou le contrôle des apparences', *Traverses*, No. 14–15, April 1979, p. 25.

7   ibid., p. 26.

8   ibid., p. 27.

9   loc. cit.

10   S. C. Maza, *Servants and Masters in Eighteenth Century France: The Uses of Loyalty*, Princeton University Press, Princeton, 1983, p. 206.

11   Raymond Corbey, 'Ethnographic showcases, 1870–1930', *Cultural Anthropology* vol. 8, no. 3, 1993, p. 340.

12   Erving Goffman, *The Presentation of Self in Everyday Life*. Penguin Books, London, 1959.

13   ibid., p. 85–6.

14   See Pierre Bourdieu, *Language and Symbolic Power*, Polity Press, Cambridge, 1991, ch. 10.

15   Erving Goffman, op. cit., p. 32–3.

16   ibid., p. 34.

17   ibid., p. 114.

18   ibid. p. 114.

19   A recent work by Michael Herzfeld examines the way this staging of the nation occurs on an everyday basis: Michael Herzfeld, *Cultural Intimacy: Social Poetics in the Nation-State*, Routledge, New York, 1997.

20   Benedict Burton, 'International exhibitions and national identity', *Anthropology Today*, vol. 7, no. 3, June 1991, p. 7.

21   Corbey, op. cit., p. 338.

22   loc. cit.

23   ibid., p. 342.

24   ibid., p. 345.

25   ibid., p. 339.

26 Carol Breckenridge, 'The aesthetics and politics of colonial collecting: India at world fairs', *Comparative Study of Society and History*, no. 31, 1989, p. 203.
27 Burton, op. cit., p. 8.
28 Susan Stewart, *On Longing, Narratives of the Miniature, the Gigantic, the Souvenir, the Collection*, Baltimore and London: John Hopkins University Press, Baltimore & London, 1993, p. 155.
29 ibid., p. 151.
30 ibid., p. 159
31 Mention should be made here of the increasingly crucial function of the accumulation of Aboriginality, from languages to other artefacts, in the process of exhibiting Australia as a distinct (see Bourdieu) national entity. Since 1901, the newly independent Australia began engaging in conscious strategies of exhibiting its Aborigines through the accumulation and collection of Aboriginal artefacts in its museums. Clearly, it was not the fact that Australia was Aboriginal that gave the nation its sense of identity, rather it was the fact that Anglo-Celtic Australia *had* Aborigines (and that no one else did) which was a source of distinction for the Anglo-Celtic nation. (See J. R. Specht, 'Anthropology' in *Rare and Curious Specimens: An Illustrated History of the Australian Museum 1827–1979*, Ronald Strahan et al., Australian Museum, Sydney, 1979, p. 143.)
32 Breckenridge, op. cit., p. 211.
33 *The Encyclopedia Americana*, International Edition, Encyclopedia Americana publishers, New York, 1979, p. 803.
34 Slavoj Zizek, op. cit., p. 154.
35 Marc Guillaume in *Figures de l'Altérité*, Jean Baudrillard & Marc Guillaume, Editions Descartes, Paris, 1992, p. 5.
36 ibid., p. 4.

Chapter 6

1 *Sydney Morning Herald*, 14 Apr. 1994.
2 In this sense, this is an attempt at uncovering a subjective structure that constitutes *one* of the conditions of possibility of ecologists thinking along White nationalist lines. There is neither a claim that this subjective structure is always empirically dominant within ecological thought, nor a claim that wherever it is empirically dominant it will necessarily lead to White nationalism.
3 E. U. Da Cal, 1992, 'The influence of animal breeding on political racism', *History of European Ideas*, vol. 15, nos 4–6, p. 717.
4 Keith Thomas, *Man and the Natural World: A History of the Modern Sensibility*, Pantheon Books, New York, 1983, pp. 17–18.
5 Ted Benton, *Natural Relations, Ecology, Animal Rights and Social Justice*, Verso, London, 1993, p. 182.

6   Luc Ferry, *Le Nouvel Ordre Écologique, L'Arbre, L'Animal et l'Homme*, Paris: Bernard Grasset, Paris, 1992, p. 20.
7   ibid., p. 193.
8   AESP (Australians for an Ecologically Sustainable Population), 'Curbing our population growth', *BIR Bulletin*, no. 5, 1991, p. 15.
9   ibid., p. 19.
10 J.-J. Rousseau, *Reveries of the Solitary Walker*, Penguin Books, Harmondsworth, 1979, p. 111.
11 G. Playret, 'Le rêve et la norme: L'idée de nature dans l'oeuvre de Rousseau', in *La Nature*, 2nd edn, ed. J.-C. Goddard, J. Vrin, Paris, 1991, p. 133.
12 ibid., p. 133. Even Rousseau's method here is 'psychoanalytic': 'Let us therefore begin by putting aside all the facts, for they have no bearing on the question' (p. 17).
13 Rousseau, op. cit., p. 111.
14 Lacan distinguishes within a fantasy between the goal which is the final point that the subject desires to reach and the aim which is the way the subject tries to reach that goal. He argues that it is the aim that the subject is really after since, as we have seen, the goal by definition cannot be reached and it is the constant repeated attempts at acquiring the Thing that gives life its affective consistency.
15 AESP, op. cit., p. 16.
16 Jacques Lacan, 'God and the jouissance of the woman', in *Feminine Sexuality: Jacques Lacan and the École Freudienne*, eds J. Mitchell & J. Rose, Macmillan Press, New York, 1982, p. 147.
17 M. O'Connor, *Selected Poems*, Hale & Iremonger, Sydney, 1986, p. 58.
18 ibid., p. 16.
19 Slavoj Zizek, *Looking Awry: An Introduction to Jacques Lacan through Popular Culture*, MIT Press, Cambridge, Massachussetts, 1991, p. 108.
20 Benton, op. cit., p. 88.
21 AESP, op. cit., p. 15.
22 AESP, ibid., p. 15.
23 Ferry, op. cit., p. 203.
24 Ferry, ibid., p. 203.
25 AESP, op. cit., p. 16.
26 AESP, ibid., p. 19.
27 O'Connor, op. cit., p. 171.

Chapter 7

1   These have been instigated by radio commentators (Ron Casey), Returned Services League Club officials (Bruce Ruxton), finance ministers (Peter Walsh) and ex-Treasury officials (John Stone).

2   *Sydney Morning Herald*, 17 Oct. 1994.

3   *Sydney Morning Herald*, 17 Oct. 1994.

4   *Sydney Morning Herald*, 17 Oct. 1994. The 'loss of English' theme was given an added respectability at the time through the media hype that surrounded a report written by the conservative academic Helen Hughes.

5   *Sydney Morning Herald*, 10 Oct. 1993.

6   *Sydney Morning Herald*, 20 Oct. 1993.

7   Geoffrey Blainey, *All for Australia*, Methuen Haynes, Sydney, 1984, p. 124.

8   Ron Casey, *Confessions of a Larrikin*, Lester-Townsend Publishing, Paddington, Sydney, 1989, p. 12.

9   *Pauline Hanson, The Truth*, Pauline Hanson's One Nation Party, Ipswich, Queensland, 1996, p. 1.

10 David Leser, 'Pauline Hanson's bitter harvest', *Good Weekend* magazine, *Sydney Morning Herald*, 30 Nov. 1996, p. 27.

11 Graeme Turner, *Making It National: Nationalism and Australian Popular Culture*, Allen & Unwin, Sydney, 1994, p. 3.

12 It would not be an exaggeration to say that since the emergence of Hansonism, hardly a day goes by without someone calling for 'tolerance'.

13 *Pauline Hanson, The Truth*, op. cit., p. 57.

14 ibid, p. 39.

15 See, for instance, John Docker's & Eva Cox's comments in the *Australian*, 17 May 1997 and 25 July 1997, respectively, and the general commentary of Padraic McGuinness.

16 As Meaghan Morris has shown through an excellent analysis of the famous 'Please explain' episode on '60 Minutes' (this is the episode of this television show where Pauline Hanson did not understand the meaning of the word 'xenophobia'), such attitudes hardly challenge Hansonite beliefs. In fact, they work very effectively at reinforcing and reproducing them. Meaghan Morris, 'Please Explain?': Gender, Class Conflict and Anti-Intellectualism in Australia's 'Asia' debates, or Poverty, Ignorance and the Past, Keynote Address presented to the Inter-Asia Cultural Studies Conference: Problematising Asia, 13–16 July 1998, Taipei, Taiwan.

17 Pierre Bourdieu (ed.), *La Misère du Monde*, Seuil, Paris, 1994, p. 7.

18 Pierre Bourdieu, *Sociology in Question*, Sage Publications, London, 1993, p. 42.

19 Blainey, op. cit., p. 24.

20 Charles Price in *Canberra Times*, 17 May 1984; also quoted by Blainey, op. cit., p. 55.

21 *Pauline Hanson, The Truth*, op. cit., p. 17.

22 Casey, op. cit., p. 187.

23 ibid., p. 187.
24 ibid., p. 187.
25 ibid., p. 39.
26 ibid., p. 39.
27 Leser, op. cit., p. 27.
28 *Pauline Hanson, The Truth*, op. cit., p. 119.
29 It should not be forgotten, however, that the same logic applies within the group. What the dominant ideals of the group are, have to also be seen as the product of the internal struggles for domination within it.
30 Richard White, *Inventing Australia*, Allen & Unwin, Sydney, 1981, p. 47.
31 White, ibid., p. 47.
32 Robert Hughes, *The Fatal Shore*, Pan Books, London, 1988, p. xii.
33 Unless explicitly stated, all national categories such as Britishness and Australianness are explicitly dominant male identities.
34 C. J. Koch, *Crossing the Gap: A Novelist's Essay*, Hogarth Press, London, 1987, p. 29.
35 Koch, ibid., p. 92.
36 Pierre Bourdieu, *Distinction: A Social Critique of the Judgement of Taste*, trans. Richard Nice, Routledge & Kegan Paul, London, 1984,, pp. 95–6.
37 Hughes, op. cit., p. xi.
38 Koch, op. cit., p. 113.
39 Hughes, op. cit., p. xii.
40 *ibid.*, p. 158.
41 See Bourdieu, *Distinction*, op. cit., passim.
42 Judith Wright, *Preoccupations in Australian Poetry*, Oxford University Press, Melbourne, 1965, pp. xiii–xiv.
43 ibid., p. xix.
44 ibid., p. xx.
45 Casey, op. cit., p. 75.
46 ibid., p. 64.
47 ibid., p. 66.
48 ibid., p. 75.
49 ibid., p. 50.
50 ibid., p. 37.
51 Grace et al., op. cit., p. 118.
52 Clifford Geertz, *Works and Lives: The Anthropologist as Author*, Polity Press, Cambridge, 1988, p. 79.
53 ibid., p. 127.
54 One could also find such a discourse in newspapers' letters to the editor (see, for example, *Sydney Morning Herald*, 12 Mar. 1995).
55 *Sydney Morning Herald*, 9 Mar. 1995.

56 Bourdieu, *Distinction*, op. cit., p. 7.
57 Although Keating's power lies further in his ability to articulate this eliteness to classical 'working-class turned politician' — type performances in parliament. See Meaghan Morris 1992, *Ecstasy and Economics*, Sydney: Empress, pp.17–83, for a fuller analysis of the significance of Keating's cultural persona.
58 *Sydney Morning Herald*, 20 Mar. 1995.
59 Bourdieu, *Distinction, op. cit.*, p. 2.
60 ibid., p. 5.
61 See Grace et al., op. cit., for the analysis of this phenomena.
62 Casey, op. cit., p. 187.
63 *Pauline Hanson, The Truth*, op. cit., p. 155.
64 Toril Moi, 'Appropriating Bourdieu', *New Literary History*, no. 22, 1991, p. 1023.
65 Blainey, op. cit., p. 124.
66 ibid., p. 14.
67 Moi, op. cit., p. 1022.
68 Turner, op. cit., p. 3.
69 Casey, op.cit., p. 158.

Chapter 8

1 Robert Hughes, *The Fatal Shore*, Pan Books, London, 1988, p. xii.
2 C. J. Koch, *Crossing the Gap: A Novelist's Essay*, Hogarth Press, London, 1987, p. xii.
3 Koch, ibid., p. 113.
4 Ron Casey, *Confessions of a Larrikin*, Lester-Townsend Publishing, Paddington, Sydney, 1989, pp. 42–3.
5 Geoffrey Blainey, *All for Australia*, Methuen Haynes, Sydney, 1984, p. 101.
6 Ron Casey, op.cit., p. 207.
7 Blainey, op.cit., pp. 3–4.
8 *Pauline Hanson, The Truth*, Pauline Hanson's One Nation Party, Ipswich, Queensland, 1996, p. 119.
9 Casey, op. cit., pp. 187–8.
10 *Pauline Hanson, The Truth*, op. cit, p.194.
11 This is why images of Pauline Hanson as Jeanne d'Arc as they featured in the media appeared as credible even after she had been elected as a member of Parliament and was able to make her views be heard on a regular basis.
12 See in this regard Murray Goot's important statistical critiques of the media's evaluation of Hanson's popularity in Murray Goot, 'The perils of polling and the popularity of Pauline', *Current Affairs Bulletin*, vol. 73, no. 4, December 1996/January 1997.
13 *Pauline Hanson, The Truth*, op. cit., p. 9.

14 *Sydney Morning Herald*, 28 Nov. 1996.

15 Jason Rupert McCall, 'Tribute to a Courageous Australian', in 'The miracle of Thredbo', *Australian Women's Weekly*, September 1997, p. 5.

16 In a truly heroic and invigorating human overcoming of the forces of 'the elements' Stuart Diver, survived a massive landslide which buried him alive in icy temperatures for three days.

17 Alison Moorehead et al., *Changes at Work: the 1995 Australian Workplace Industrial Relations Survey*, Longman, South Melbourne, 1997.

18 Jean-Paul Sartre, *The Emotions: Outline of a Theory*, Wisdom Library, New York, 1948, pp. 58–9. I want to thank Michael Jackson for pointing out this passage to me.

19 *Pauline Hanson, The Truth*, op. cit., 'A reply to my critics, House of Representatives, December 2, 1996', p. 25.

20 *Advertiser*, 11 Dec. 1996, p. 2.

21 ibid.

Chapter 9

1   Constructing oneself as 'worried about the nation' is not necessarily the path taken by those who have no other choice in life as far as constructing a viable sense of the self — although such affective nationalism is a common path for many who cannot derive a sense of viability from any other identity. But nationalism has many other usages. For instance, 'worrying about the nation' is a common strategy for converting academic capital into political capital for those academics who have political aspirations: 'I am the knowledgeable one and you'd better worry with me since I am worried.' One suspects that this has been the case with Geoffrey Blainey. There are also academics who, without aspiring for a political position, have devoted their career to a 'sociology of worrying'. Bob Birrel's work in the field of migration is a particularly striking example of this tendency. Here is an academic whose research over more than twenty years has been dedicated basically to producing 'research findings', the main conclusion of which has been unchanging ever since he has started researching: namely that whatever aspect of immigration or settlement one is examining there is always something about which to worry.

2   See Jean Martin's classic, *The Migrant Presence: Australian Responses 1947–1977*, George Allen & Unwin, Sydney, 1978, for a refresher.

3   See Stephen Castles et. al., *Mistaken Identity: Multiculturalism and the Demise of Nationalism in Australia*, Pluto Press, Sydney, 1992.

4   Geoffrey Gray and Christine Winter (eds), *The Resurgence of Racism*, Monash Publications in History, no. 24, Monash

University, 1997, p. 155.

5   See in this regard Paul Sheehan's admirable 'back from New York to save the nation' number mentioned in the introduction (page 9).

6   See Murray Goot, 'Public opinion and the public opinion polls', in *Surrender Australia?*, eds Marcus & Ricklefs (eds), George Allen & Unwin, Sydney, 1985, pp. 49–62.

7   Andrew Marcus, '1985, 1984 or 1901?: Immigration and some lessons of Australian history', in Marcus and Ricklefs (eds), ibid., p. 18.

8   One can imagine the serious structural and institutional changes that would affect talkback radio, for example, if it was not open to 'immigration debates'. See the hilarious book by Phillip Adams & Lee Burton, *Talkback: Emperors of Air*, Allen & Unwin, Sydney, 1997.

9   As it should be clear, debating Aboriginal affairs follows exactly the same logic. See the recent article by Steve Mickler, 'The 'Robespierre' of the air: Talkback radio, globalisation and indigenous issues', in Geoffrey Gray & Christine Winter (eds), op. cit., pp. 63–78.

10 See Gianni Zappalà, *Four Weddings, a Funeral and a Family Reunion: Ethnicity and Representation in Australian Federal Politics*, AGPS, Canberra, 1997. See in particular the author's de-fetishisation of 'branch stacking'.

11 This generational change is a very natural part of any immigration process. See, for comparative purposes, C. Withol de Wenden 1995, 'Generational change and political participation in French suburbs', *New Community*, vol. 21, no. 1, 1995, pp. 69–78.

bibliography

Adams, Philip & Burton, Lee 1997, *Talkback: Emperors of Air*, Allen & Unwin, Sydney.

Advertiser, 11 Dec. 1996.

AESP (Australians for an Ecologically Sustainable Population) 1991, 'Curbing our population growth', in *BIR Bulletin*, no. 5.

Alexakis, Effy & Janiszewski, Leonard 1995, *Images of Home*, Hale & Iremonger, Sydney.

Allen, Theodore 1994, *The Invention of White Race*, Verso, New York.

Allport, Gordon 1954, *The Nature of Prejudice*, Addison-Wesley Publishing Company, Inc., Cambridge, Massachussetts.

Ang, Ien 1996, 'The curse of the smile: Ambivalence and the 'Asian' woman in Australian multiculturalism', in *Feminist Review*, no. 52, Spring 1996.

Ashley, M. 1978, *England in the Seventeenth Century*, 8th edn, Hutchinson, London.

Banton, Michael 1970, 'The concept of racism' in *Race and Racialism*, ed. Sami Zubaida, Tavistock Publications Ltd., London.

Banton, Michael 1977, *The Idea of Race*, Tavistock Publications, London.

Barker, Martin 1981, *The New Racism*, Junction Books, London.

Baudrillard, Jean & Guillaume, Marc 1992, *Figures de l'Altérité*, Editions Descartes, Paris.

Benton, Ted 1993, *Natural Relations, Ecology, Animal Rights and Social Justice*, Verso, London.

Benveniste, Emile 1966, *Problèmes de linguistique générale*, Gallimard, Paris.

Billig, Michael 1995, *Banal Nationalism*, Sage, London.

Blainey, Geoffrey 1984, *All for Australia*, Methuen Haynes, Sydney.

Bottomley, Gill & Lepervanche, Marie de (eds) 1984, *Ethnicity, Class and Gender in Australia*, Allen & Unwin, Sydney.

Bourdieu, Pierre 1977, *Outline of a Theory of Practice*, Cambridge University Press, Cambridge, UK.

Bourdieu, Pierre 1984, *Distinction: A Social Critique of the Judgement of Taste*, trans. Richard Nice, Routledge & Kegan Paul, London.

Bourdieu, Pierre 1986, 'The forms of capital', in *Handbook of Theory and Research for the Sociology of Education*, ed. J. G. Richardson, Greenwood Press, New York.

Bourdieu, Pierre 1990, *In Other Words: Essays towards a Reflexive Sociology*, Polity Press, Cambridge.

Bourdieu, Pierre 1990, *The Logic of Practice*, Polity Press, Cambridge.

Bourdieu, Pierre 1991, *Language and Symbolic Power*, Polity Press, Cambridge.

Bourdieu, Pierre & Wacquant, Loïc J. D. 1992, *An Invitation to Reflexive Sociology*, Polity Press, Cambridge.

Bourdieu, Pierre 1993, *Sociology in Question*, Sage Publications, London.

Bourdieu Pierre (ed) 1994, *La Misère du Monde*, Paris: Seuil.

Breckenridge, Carol 1989, 'The aesthetics and politics of colonial collecting: India at world fairs', in *Comparative Study of Society and History*, no. 31.

Burgelin, Olivier 1979, 'Les outils de la toilette ou le contrôle des apparences', in *Traverses*, nos 14–15, April.

Burton, Benedict 1991, 'International exhibitions and national identity', in *Anthropology Today*, vol. 7, no. 3.

Butler, Judith 1991, 'Imitation and gender insubordination', in *Inside/Out: Lesbian Theories/Gay Theories*, ed. Diana Fuss, Routledge, London.

Casey, Ron 1989, *Confessions of a Larrikin*, Lester-Townsend Publishing, Paddington, Sydney.

Castles, Stephen, Kalantzis, Mary, Cope, Bill & Morrissey, Michael 1992, *Mistaken Identity: Multiculturalism and the Demise of Nationalism in Australia*, Pluto Press, Sydney.

Collins, Jock 1988, *Migrant Hands in a Distant Land*, Pluto Press, Sydney.

Collins, Jock 1993, *Cohesion with Diversity?: Immigration and Multiculturalism in Canada and Australia*, Working Paper Series: School of Finance and Economics, no. 28, March 1993, University of Technology, Sydney.

Corbey, Raymond 1993, 'Ethnographic showcases, 1870–1930', *Cultural Anthropology*, vol. 8, no. 3.

Curthoys, Ann & Markus, Andrew (eds) 1978, *Who Are Our Enemies? Racism and the Working Class in Australia*, Hale & Iremonger, Sydney.

Da Cal, E. U. 1992, 'The influence of animal breeding on political racism', *History of European Ideas*, vol. 15, nos 4–6.

Davidson Alastair 1997, *From Subjects to Citizens: Australian Citizenship in the Twentieth Century*, Cambridge University Press, Melbourne.

de Saint Hilaire, Isidore Geoffroy (1861) 1986, *Acclimatation et Domestications des Animaux Utiles*, Flamarrion, Paris.

de Wenden,. C. W. 1995, 'Generational change and political participation in French suburbs', *New Community*, vol. 21, no. 1, pp. 69–78.

DIHR 1990, *Documentation of Incidents of Harassment of, and Racism towards, Australians of Arab Descent and Australian Muslims: August–October 1990*, Melbourne.

DIHR 1992, *Documentation of Incidents of Harassment of, and Racism towards, Australians of Arab Descent and Australian Muslims: October 1992*, Melbourne.

Docker, John 1995, 'Rethinking postcolonialism and multiculturalism in the fin de siècle', *Cultural Studies*, vol. 9, no. 3.

Dugan, M. & Szwarc, J. 1984, *There Goes the Neighbourhood!: Australia's Migrant Experience*, Macmillan & Australian Institute of Multicultural Affairs, Melbourne.

Durkheim, Emile 1960, *Le Suicide: Etude de Sociologie*, Presses Universitaires de France, Paris.

Elias, Norbert 1988, 'Violence and civilisation: The state monopoly of physical violence and its infringement', in *Civil Society and the State: New European Perspectives*, ed. John Keane, Verso, London & New York.

Ferry, Luc 1992, *Le Nouvel Ordre Écologique, L'Arbre, L'Animal et l'Homme*, Bernard Grasset, Paris.

Foucault, Michel 1991, 'Governmentality', in *The Foucault Effect: Studies in Governmentality*, eds Graham Burchell et al., Harvester: Hemel Hempstead.

Frankenberg, Ruth 1997, *Displacing Whiteness: Essays in Social and Cultural Criticism*, Duke University Press, Durham, North Carolina, & London.

Geertz, Clifford 1988, *Works and Lives: The Anthropologist as Author*, Polity Press, Cambridge.

Goffman, Erving 1959, *The Presentation of Self in Everyday Life*. Penguin Books, London.

Goot, Murray 1985, 'Public opinion and the public opinion polls', in *Surrender Australia?*, eds Marcus and Ricklefs, George Allen & Unwin, Sydney.

Goot, Murray 1996, 'The perils of polling and the popularity of Pauline', *Current Affairs Bulletin*, vol. 73, no. 4, Dec. 1996/Jan. 1997.

Grace, Helen, Hage, Ghassan, Johnson, Lesley, Langsworth, Julie, & Symonds, Michael 1997, *Home/World: Space, Communality and Marginality in Sydney's West*, Pluto Press, Sydney.

Grassby, Al 1984, *The Tyranny of Prejudice*, A E Press, Melbourne.

Gray, Geoffrey & Winter, Christine (eds) 1997, *The Resurgence of Racism*, Monash Publications in History, no. 24, Monash University.

Gray, Michael & Rhonda 1990, *The Stew that Grew*, Walter McVitty Books, Glebe.

Greason, David 1994, *I Was a Teenage Fascist*, McPhee Gribble, Melbourne.

Gunew, Sneja 1994, *Framing Marginality*, Melbourne University Press, Melbourne.

Hage, Ghassan 1991, 'Racism, multiculturalism and the Gulf War', *Arena*, no. 96, Spring 1991.

Hage, Ghassan 1993, 'Nation-building dwelling being', *Communal/Plural*, no. 1.

Hage, Ghassan, Lloyd, Justine, & Johnson, Lesley (eds) 1994, 'An inquiry into the state of Anglo-Saxonness within the nation', *Communal/Plural*, no. 4

Hage, Ghassan 1995, 'The limits of "anti-racist" sociology', *UTS Review*, vol. 1, no. 1.

Hamilton, Annette 1975, 'Aboriginal women: The means of production', in *The Other Half: Women in Australian Society*, ed. J. Mercer, Penguin, Harmondsworth, pp. 167–79.

Harris, Marvin 1969, *The Rise of Anthropological Theory: A History of Theories of Culture*, Routledge & Kegan Paul, London.

Heidegger, Martin 1978, *Basic Writings*, Routledge & Kegan Paul, London.

Herzfeld, Michael 1997, *Cultural Intimacy: Social Poetics in the Nation-State*, Routledge, New York.

Hindess, Barry 1992, 'Citizens and people', *Australian Left Review*, June 1992.

Hitler, Adolf 1993, *Mein Kampf*, trans. by Ralph Manheim, Pimlico, London.

Horsman, Reginald 1981, *Race and Manifest Destiny*, Harvard University Press, Cambridge, Massachussetts.

Hudson, Wayne & Carter, David (eds), *The Republicanism Debate*, University of NSW Press, Sydney.

Hughes, Robert 1988, *The Fatal Shore*, Pan Books, London.

Jakubowicz, Andrew, Morrissey, Michael & Palser, Joanne 1984, 'Ethnicity, class and social policy in Australia', in *SWRC Reports and Proceedings*, no. 46.

Jakubowicz, Andrew 1985, 'Ethnic affairs policy in Australia: The failure of multiculturalism', in *Australia in Transition*, eds M. E. Poole et al., Harcourt Brace Jovanovich, Sydney.

Keating, Paul 1992, Opening speech to the Productive Diversity in Business Conference, 28–29 Oct. 1992, Melbourne.

King, Preston 1976, *Toleration*, George Allen & Unwin, London.

Koch, C. J. 1987, *Crossing the Gap: A Novelist's Essay*, Hogarth Press, London.

Koshechnika, Tanya 1992, *Political Tolerance and Ex-Soviet Society*, paper presented at BSA Conference, University of Canterbury, Kent, UK.

Lacan, Jacques 1982, 'God and the jouissance of the woman', *Feminine Sexuality: Jacques Lacan and the École Freudienne*, eds in J. Mitchell & J. Rose, Macmillan Press, New York.

Leca, Jean 1992, 'Questions of citizenship', in *Dimensions of Radical Democracy: Pluralism, Citizenship, Community*, ed. Chantal Mouffe, Verso, London.

Lecler, Joseph 1960, *Toleration and the Reformation* (2 vols), Longmans, London.

Leser, David 1996, 'Pauline Hanson's bitter harvest', Good Weekend, *Sydney Morning Herald*, 30 Nov. 1996.

Lloyd, C. & Waters, H. 1991, 'France: One culture, one people?', *Race & Class*, vol. 32, no. 3.

Locke, John 1689 (1867 edition), *Letters on Toleration*, Education Society Press, Byculla.

Lyotard, Jean-François 1991, *Heidegger and 'the Jews'*, University of Minesota Press, Minneapolis.

Marcus, Andrew 1985, '1984 or 1901?: Immigration and some lessons of Australian history', in *Surrender Australia?*, eds A. Marcus and M. Ricklefs, George Allen & Unwin, Sydney.

Martin, Jean 1978, *The Migrant Presence: Australian Responses 1947–1977*, George Allen & Unwin, Sydney.

Maza, S. C. 1983, *Servants and Masters in Eighteenth Century France: The Uses of Loyalty*, Princeton University Press, Princeton.

McCall, Jason Rupert 1997, 'Tribute to a courageous Australian', in 'The miracle of Thredbo', *The Australian Women's Weekly*, Sept. 1997.

McKay, J. & Batrouney, T. 1988, 'Lebanese immigration until the 1970s', *The Australian People*, ed. James Jupp, Angus & Robertson Publishers, Sydney.

Mickler, Steve 1997, 'The "Robespierre" of the air: Talkback radio, globalisation and indigenous issues', in *The Resurgence of Racism*, Monash Publications in History, no. 24, eds Geoffrey Gray & Christine Winter.

Miles, Robert 1982, *Racism and Migrant Labour*, Routledge & Kegan Paul, London.

Miles, Robert 1989, *Racism*, Routledge, London & New York.

Moi, Toril 1991, 'Appropriating Bourdieu', *New Literary History*, no. 22.

Moorehead, Alison et al, *Changes at Work:* the 1995 Australian Workplace Industrial Relations Survey, Longman, South Melbourne, 1997.

Morris, Meaghan 1992, *Ecstasy and Economics*, Empress, Sydney.

Morris, Meaghan 1998, ' "Please explain?" ': Gender, class conflict and anti-intellectualism in Australia's 'Asia' debates, or poverty, ignorance and the past, Keynote address presented to the Inter-Asia Cultural Studies Conference: Problematising Asia,

13–16 July 1998, Taipei, Taiwan.

National Inquiry into Racist Violence in Australia 1991, *Racist Violence*, AGPS, Canberra.

Niland, Carmel 1992, *Towards Managing Diversity: A Review of EEO in the South Australian Public Service*, South Australian Government Publication, Adelaide.

Norman. E. R. 1968, *Anti-Catholicism in Victorian England*, George Allen & Unwin, London.

O'Connor, Mark 1986, *Selected Poems*, Sydney: Hale and Iremonger.

Pauline Hanson, The Truth 1996, Pauline Hanson's One Nation Party, Ipswich, Queensland.

Perron, Marshall 1993, 'Australia must develop and populate the North', *BIPR Bulletin*, no. 10, Nov. 1993.

Playret, G. 1991, 'Le rêve et la norme: L'idée de nature dans l'oeuvre de Rousseau', in *La Nature*, 2nd edn, ed. J.-C. Goddard, J. Vrin, Paris.

Productive Diversity in Business: Profiting from Australia's Multicultural Advantage (1992), discussion paper for the Productive Diversity in Business Conference, 28–29 Oct. 1992, Melbourne.

Renan, Ernest 1947, *Du Liberalisme Clerical, Oeuvres*, vol. 1, Calman-Levy, Paris.

Rodinson, Maxine 1981, *Marxism and the Muslim World*, Monthly Review Press, London.

Roedigger, David 1990, *The Wages of Whiteness*, Verso, New York.

Rousseau, J.-J. 1979, *Reveries of the Solitary Walker*, Penguin Books, Harmondsworth.

Sartre, Jean-Paul 1948, *The Emotions: Outline of a Theory*, The Wisdom Library, New York.

Sheehan, Paul 1996, 'The multicultural myth', *Sydney Morning Herald*, 25 May 1996.

Sheehan, Paul 1998, *Among the Barbarians: The Dividing of Australia*, Random House, Sydney.

Sivanandan, A. 1983, 'Challenging racism: Strategies for the '80s', *Race and Class*, vol. 25, no. 2, pp. 1–12.

Specht, J. R. 1979, 'Anthropology', in *Rare and Curious Specimens: An Illustrated History of the Australian Museum 1827–1979*, eds Ronald Strahan et al., Australian Museum, Sydney.

Stewart, Susan 1993, *On Longing: Narratives of the Miniature, the Gigantic, the Souvenir, the Collection*, John Hopkins University Press, Baltimore & London.

Taguieff, Pierre-André 1987, *La Force du Préjugé, Essai sur le Racisme et ses Doubles*, Éditions La Découverte, Paris.

Taylor, Charles 1994, 'The politics of recognition', in *Multiculturalism*, ed. Amy Gutmann, Princeton University Press, Princeton.

Thomas, Keith 1983, *Man and the Natural World: A History of the*

Modern Sensibility, Pantheon Books, New York.

Graeme Turner 1994., *Making it National: Nationalism and Australian popular culture*, St Leonards: Allen and Unwin.

Voltaire 1763 (1975 edition), 'Traité sur la Tolerance' in *L'Affaire Calas*, Paris: Éditions Gallimard.

Warren, Jonathan & Twine, France 1997, 'White Americans, the new minority?: Non-Blacks and the ever-expanding boundaries of Whiteness', *Journal of Black Studies*, vol. 28, No. 2, 1997.

White, Richard 1981, *Inventing Australia*, George Allen & Unwin, Sydney.

Wright, Judith 1965, *Preoccupations in Australian Poetry*, Oxford University Press, Melbourne.

Zappalà, Gianni 1997, *Four Weddings, A Funeral and a Family Reunion: Ethnicity and Representation in Australian Federal Politics*, AGPS, Canberra. See in particular the author's de-fetishisation of 'branch stacking'.

Zizek, Slavoj 1991, *Looking Awry: An Introduction to Jacques Lacan through Popular Culture*, MIT Press, Cambridge, Massachusetts.

Zizek, Slavoj 1993, *Tarrying with the Negative: Kant, Hegel and the Critique of Ideology*, Duke University Press, Durham, North Carolina.

index